Social Networks with Rich Edge Semantics

Chapman & Hall/CRC
Data Mining and Knowledge Discovery Series

SERIES EDITOR
Vipin Kumar
University of Minnesota
Department of Computer Science and Engineering
Minneapolis, Minnesota, U.S.A.

AIMS AND SCOPE

This series aims to capture new developments and applications in data mining and knowledge discovery, while summarizing the computational tools and techniques useful in data analysis. This series encourages the integration of mathematical, statistical, and computational methods and techniques through the publication of a broad range of textbooks, reference works, and handbooks. The inclusion of concrete examples and applications is highly encouraged. The scope of the series includes, but is not limited to, titles in the areas of data mining and knowledge discovery methods and applications, modeling, algorithms, theory and foundations, data and knowledge visualization, data mining systems and tools, and privacy and security issues.

PUBLISHED TITLES

ACCELERATING DISCOVERY: MINING UNSTRUCTURED INFORMATION FOR
HYPOTHESIS GENERATION
Scott Spangler

ADVANCES IN MACHINE LEARNING AND DATA MINING FOR ASTRONOMY
Michael J. Way, Jeffrey D. Scargle, Kamal M. Ali, and Ashok N. Srivastava

BIOLOGICAL DATA MINING
Jake Y. Chen and Stefano Lonardi

COMPUTATIONAL BUSINESS ANALYTICS
Subrata Das

COMPUTATIONAL INTELLIGENT DATA ANALYSIS FOR SUSTAINABLE DEVELOPMENT
Ting Yu, Nitesh V. Chawla, and Simeon Simoff

COMPUTATIONAL METHODS OF FEATURE SELECTION
Huan Liu and Hiroshi Motoda

CONSTRAINED CLUSTERING: ADVANCES IN ALGORITHMS, THEORY, AND
APPLICATIONS
Sugato Basu, Ian Davidson, and Kiri L. Wagstaff

CONTRAST DATA MINING: CONCEPTS, ALGORITHMS, AND APPLICATIONS
Guozhu Dong and James Bailey

DATA CLASSIFICATION: ALGORITHMS AND APPLICATIONS
Charu C. Aggarawal

DATA CLUSTERING: ALGORITHMS AND APPLICATIONS
Charu C. Aggarawal and Chandan K. Reddy

DATA CLUSTERING IN C++: AN OBJECT-ORIENTED APPROACH
Guojun Gan

DATA MINING: A TUTORIAL-BASED PRIMER, SECOND EDITION
Richard J. Roiger

DATA MINING FOR DESIGN AND MARKETING
Yukio Ohsawa and Katsutoshi Yada

DATA MINING WITH R: LEARNING WITH CASE STUDIES, SECOND EDITION
Luís Torgo

DATA SCIENCE AND ANALYTICS WITH PYTHON
Jesus Rogel-Salazar

EVENT MINING: ALGORITHMS AND APPLICATIONS
Tao Li

FOUNDATIONS OF PREDICTIVE ANALYTICS
James Wu and Stephen Coggeshall

GEOGRAPHIC DATA MINING AND KNOWLEDGE DISCOVERY, SECOND EDITION
Harvey J. Miller and Jiawei Han

GRAPH-BASED SOCIAL MEDIA ANALYSIS
Ioannis Pitas

HANDBOOK OF EDUCATIONAL DATA MINING
Cristóbal Romero, Sebastian Ventura, Mykola Pechenizkiy, and Ryan S.J.d. Baker

HEALTHCARE DATA ANALYTICS
Chandan K. Reddy and Charu C. Aggarwal

INFORMATION DISCOVERY ON ELECTRONIC HEALTH RECORDS
Vagelis Hristidis

INTELLIGENT TECHNOLOGIES FOR WEB APPLICATIONS
Priti Srinivas Sajja and Rajendra Akerkar

INTRODUCTION TO PRIVACY-PRESERVING DATA PUBLISHING: CONCEPTS AND
TECHNIQUES
Benjamin C. M. Fung, Ke Wang, Ada Wai-Chee Fu, and Philip S. Yu

KNOWLEDGE DISCOVERY FOR COUNTERTERRORISM AND LAW ENFORCEMENT
David Skillicorn

KNOWLEDGE DISCOVERY FROM DATA STREAMS
João Gama

LARGE-SCALE MACHINE LEARNING IN THE EARTH SCIENCES
Ashok N. Srivastava, Ramakrishna Nemani, and Karsten Steinhaeuser

MACHINE LEARNING AND KNOWLEDGE DISCOVERY FOR ENGINEERING SYSTEMS
HEALTH MANAGEMENT
Ashok N. Srivastava and Jiawei Han

MINING SOFTWARE SPECIFICATIONS: METHODOLOGIES AND APPLICATIONS
David Lo, Siau-Cheng Khoo, Jiawei Han, and Chao Liu

MULTIMEDIA DATA MINING: A SYSTEMATIC INTRODUCTION TO CONCEPTS AND THEORY
Zhongfei Zhang and Ruofei Zhang

MUSIC DATA MINING
Tao Li, Mitsunori Ogihara, and George Tzanetakis

NEXT GENERATION OF DATA MINING
Hillol Kargupta, Jiawei Han, Philip S. Yu, Rajeev Motwani, and Vipin Kumar

RAPIDMINER: DATA MINING USE CASES AND BUSINESS ANALYTICS APPLICATIONS
Markus Hofmann and Ralf Klinkenberg

RELATIONAL DATA CLUSTERING: MODELS, ALGORITHMS, AND APPLICATIONS
Bo Long, Zhongfei Zhang, and Philip S. Yu

SERVICE-ORIENTED DISTRIBUTED KNOWLEDGE DISCOVERY
Domenico Talia and Paolo Trunfio

SOCIAL NETWORKS WITH RICH EDGE SEMANTICS
Quan Zheng and David Skillicorn

SPECTRAL FEATURE SELECTION FOR DATA MINING
Zheng Alan Zhao and Huan Liu

STATISTICAL DATA MINING USING SAS APPLICATIONS, SECOND EDITION
George Fernandez

SUPPORT VECTOR MACHINES: OPTIMIZATION BASED THEORY, ALGORITHMS, AND EXTENSIONS
Naiyang Deng, Yingjie Tian, and Chunhua Zhang

TEMPORAL DATA MINING
Theophano Mitsa

TEXT MINING: CLASSIFICATION, CLUSTERING, AND APPLICATIONS
Ashok N. Srivastava and Mehran Sahami

TEXT MINING AND VISUALIZATION: CASE STUDIES USING OPEN-SOURCE TOOLS
Markus Hofmann and Andrew Chisholm

THE TOP TEN ALGORITHMS IN DATA MINING
Xindong Wu and Vipin Kumar

UNDERSTANDING COMPLEX DATASETS: DATA MINING WITH MATRIX DECOMPOSITIONS
David Skillicorn

Social Networks with Rich Edge Semantics

Quan Zheng

Queen's University
Kingston, Ontario, Canada

David Skillicorn

Queen's University
Kingston, Ontario, Canada

CRC Press
Taylor & Francis Group
Boca Raton London New York

CRC Press is an imprint of the
Taylor & Francis Group, an **informa** business

A CHAPMAN & HALL BOOK

CRC Press
Taylor & Francis Group
6000 Broken Sound Parkway NW, Suite 300
Boca Raton, FL 33487-2742

First issued in paperback 2020

© 2017 by Taylor & Francis Group, LLC
CRC Press is an imprint of Taylor & Francis Group, an Informa business

No claim to original U.S. Government works

ISBN 13: 978-0-367-57325-6 (pbk)
ISBN 13: 978-1-138-03243-9 (hbk)

Version Date: 20170706

Visit the Taylor & Francis Web site at
http://www.taylorandfrancis.com

and the CRC Press Web site at
http://www.crcpress.com

Contents

Preface   xi

List of Figures   xiii

List of Tables   xvii

Glossary   xix

1 Introduction   1
   1.1 What is a social network?   1
   1.2 Multiple aspects of relationships   6
   1.3 Formally representing social networks   7

2 The core model   9
   2.1 Representing networks to understand their structures   9
   2.2 Building layered models 11
   2.3 Summary 16

3 Background   17
   3.1 Graph theory background 17
   3.2 Spectral graph theory 18
      3.2.1 The unnormalized graph Laplacian 21
      3.2.2 The normalized graph Laplacians 23
   3.3 Spectral pipeline 24
   3.4 Spectral approaches to clustering 24
      3.4.1 Undirected spectral clustering algorithms 26
      3.4.2 Which Laplacian clustering should be used? . . . 27
   3.5 Summary 28

4 Modelling relationships of different types   31
   4.1 Typed edge model approach 32
   4.2 Typed edge spectral embedding 32
   4.3 Applications of typed networks 34
   4.4 Summary 37

5   Modelling asymmetric relationships   **41**
  5.1   Conventional directed spectral graph embedding   41
  5.2   Directed edge layered approach   44
         5.2.1   Validation of the new directed embedding   46
         5.2.2   SVD computation for the directed edge model
                  approach   47
  5.3   Applications of directed networks   48
  5.4   Summary   67

6   Modelling asymmetric relationships with multiple types   **69**
  6.1   Combining directed and typed embeddings   69
  6.2   Layered approach and compositions   70
  6.3   Applying directed typed embeddings   72
         6.3.1   Florentine families   72
         6.3.2   Criminal groups   74
  6.4   Summary   78

7   Modelling relationships that change over time   **81**
  7.1   Temporal networks   81
  7.2   Applications of temporal networks   85
         7.2.1   The undirected network over time   85
         7.2.2   The directed network over time   89
  7.3   Summary   94

8   Modelling positive and negative relationships   **97**
  8.1   Signed Laplacian   97
  8.2   Unnormalized spectral Laplacians of signed graphs   98
         8.2.1   Rayleigh quotients of signed unnormalized
                  Laplacians   99
         8.2.2   Graph cuts of signed unnormalized Laplacians . .   100
  8.3   Normalized spectral Laplacians of signed graphs   102
         8.3.1   Rayleigh quotients of signed random-walk
                  Laplacians   102
         8.3.2   Graph cuts of signed random-walk Laplacians . .   104
  8.4   Applications of signed networks   105
  8.5   Summary   118

9   Signed graph-based semi-supervised learning   **121**
  9.1   Approach   122
  9.2   Problems of imbalance in graph data   127
  9.3   Summary   137

10   Combining directed and signed embeddings   **139**
  10.1   Composition of directed and signed layer models   139
  10.2   Application to signed directed networks   142
         10.2.1   North and West Africa conflict   143

10.3   Extensions to other compositions 152

10.4   Summary 155

11   Summary   **157**

Appendices   **161**

A   RatioCut consistency with two versions of each node   **163**

B   NCut consistency with multiple versions of each node   **167**

C   Signed unnormalized clustering   **175**

D   Signed normalized Laplacian L_{sns} clustering   **177**

E   Signed normalized Laplacian L_{bns} clustering   **181**

F   Example MATLAB functions   **183**

Bibliography   **199**

Index   **209**

Preface

As humans, we build relationships with one another. A fruitful line of research in the last 90 years has been to consider the structure that emerges from the aggregate of these relationships for a group of individuals, their *social network*. These networks are social because they are the result of human individual and social properties and so are quite different in structure from other kinds of networks (computer networks, electrical distribution networks, and so on).

The payoffs from analyzing social networks come because, although each relationship is formed based on the purely local choice of the individuals concerned, the resulting structure has properties that are not obvious from the individual relationships. These properties do not come from nowhere; rather they are consequences of deep human properties of the way that we, as humans, relate to one another. Thus *social network analysis* reveals much about the way that humans in groups arrange ourselves, mostly unconsciously. Understanding the macro-structure of a social network also provides a context to revisit each individual relationship, and understand it in a new way.

Much of the technical work on analyzing social networks has modelled the relationship between a pair of individuals as being of only a single kind. For example, Facebook considers all relationship as "friends" while LinkedIn considers all relationships as "colleagues". Even in a tribal society, the archetypal social network setting, relationships are of multiple kinds: hierarchical control relationships, relatives, friends, hunting partners, and so on. In today's world, we also have relationships with others of multiple kinds; all of those present in tribal societies, but also team members at work, telephone acquaintances, fellow enthusiasts about sports or hobbies, as well as variations of online connections. It is reasonable to consider an individual as participating in a collection of non-intersecting social networks, one at work, one in social life, one in family gatherings, but these networks often overlap — the same person can be both a friend and a colleague. To gather these separate social networks into a larger one requires a way to represent all of these different kinds of connections within a single framework.

We have already hinted that we need a way to model relationships of qualitatively different kinds (friends, family, colleagues). Relationships also naturally have an associated intensity; A's relationship to B may be much stronger or more important than A's relationship to C, and we need to be able to model this. Relationships can also be asymmetric: the intensity of A's relationship to B may be different from the intensity of B's relationship to A; indeed, A may have a relationship to B, while B has no relationship to A. Not all relationships are positive. A may be a friend or ally of B but an enemy of C. We need a way to model relationships of both kinds. Finally, the existence and intensity of relationships change with time, and a way to represent the changing structure of each social network is needed.

There has been research work investigating how to add these properties to social network analysis. The contribution of this book is to show that there is a single idea, which can be worked out in constructions, that solves all of these problems in essentially the same way. All of the properties described above are properties of the edges: edge types can be modelled as a property such as color, intensities as associated weights, asymmetries by directing the edges, and positivity and negativity by allowing weights to be both positive and negative. The key idea is that, instead of trying to model all of these possibilities at once, the nodes of the network are replicated into versions, each of which is associated with a property, and the original edges are connected to these versions in ways that capture and preserve their original semantics. The resulting graph is (notionally) much larger, but its edges are ordinary, and standard techniques can be used to analyze them. Of course, the analysis must take account of the multiple versions of the nodes, but this turns out be a win because the relationships among the versions themselves reveal aspects of the structure.

We show how this works out both mathematically, and with sets of examples that illustrate, sometimes forcefully, that the social network that represents these richer properties is very different from a representation in which they are ignored or conflated.

List of Figures

2.1   Illustration for within-layer connection and between-layer connection 13

2.2   The embedding of a simple graph with typed edges 13

3.1   The eigendecomposition of the cloud of points corresponding to graph nodes 20

4.1   The embedding of the Florentine families based on personal relationships 35

4.2   The embedding of the Florentine families based on financial relationships 36

4.3   The embedding of Florentine families ignoring edge types 37

4.4   Embedding of Florentine families with typed edges 38

4.5   Zooming in to the embedded Florentine families with typed edges 39

4.6   Zooming in even further 40

5.1   A circle graph Laplacian embedding 45

5.2   The difference between symmetric and asymmetric flow 50

5.3   Embeddings of synthetic datasets 51

5.4   Network embeddings of UK university faculties 52

5.5   Network embeddings of Florentine families 54

5.6   Network embeddings of Macaque monkey visuotactile brain . . . 56

5.7   The basic structure of tax avoidance using a shell company 58

5.8   The adjacency matrix of the largest connected component 58

5.9   Network embedding of the Panama Papers 6th component — directed 59

5.10   Network embedding of the Panama Papers 6th component — undirected 60

5.11   Network embedding of the Panama Papers 2nd component 61

5.12   Network embedding of the Panama Papers 41st component — directed 62

5.13   Network embedding of the Panama Papers 41st component — undirected 63

5.14   Network embedding of the Panama Papers 44th component — directed   64
5.15   Network embedding of the Panama Papers 44th component — undirected   65
5.16   Network embeddings of the Panama Papers 10th component, threshold 300   66
5.17   Edges between version, 10th component   67

6.1   Added edges between the multiple versions of a single node . . .   70
6.2   Chung directed embedding of the typed Florentine families   72
6.3   Our directed embedding of the typed Florentine families   73
6.4   Zoom-in of the Medici nodes   74
6.5   Our directed embedding of the Chalonero network (untyped edges)   76
6.6   Chung directed embedding of the typed Chalonero network . . .   77
6.7   Our directed embedding of the typed Chalonero network   78
6.8   Our directed embedding of the typed Stupor Mundi network . . .   80

7.1   The general embedding of the Caviar network   86
7.2   Zoom-in the general embedding of the Caviar network   87
7.3   The embedding of the Caviar network with the 11 time periods . .   88
7.4   The embedding of the 5 key participants over time   88
7.5   Growth of the embedded network over time   91
7.6   Average diameter of the undirected network over time   92
7.7   Trajectories — Chung's embedding   93
7.8   Trajectories — our embedding   93

8.1   Unnormalized signed graph embedding of a toy dataset   100
8.2   Graph cuts of a sample graph   101
8.3   Normalized signed graph embedding of a toy data   103
8.4   Embeddings of the enemy of my enemy   106
8.5   The embeddings of the tribes   108
8.6   The embeddings of the Sampson monastery network   110
8.7   The embeddings of the ACLED violent groups   112
8.8   The ratio values of the ACLED embedding   113
8.9   The ratio values of the Epinions embeddings (forest-fire sampling)   114
8.10   The ratio values of the Epinions embeddings (random-walk sampling)   115
8.11   The ratio values of the Slashdot embeddings (forest-fire sampling)   116
8.12   The Slashdot embeddings with 100 nodes (forest-fire sampling) .   117
8.13   The ratio values of the Slashdot embeddings (random-walk sampling)   118

9.1   Two ways to add negative edges   123
9.2   Applying GBE to two toy datasets   127
9.3   Plot of average error as a function of parameters   128

9.4   Comparing error rates, two classes, same size, same number of
       labels 130
9.5   Comparing error rates, four classes, same size, same number of
       labels 131
9.6   Comparing error rates for two classes, completely balanced   . . . 132
9.7   Comparing error rates, differing numbers of labelled records . . . 133
9.8   Boxplots of error rates 134
9.9   Comparing error rates, different class sizes 135
9.10   Comparing error rates, two classes, different sizes, same number
       of labelled nodes 136

10.1   Illustration of our typed directed connection model 140
10.2   Directed Sampson network with positive edges 142
10.3   Directed Sampson network with negative edges 143
10.4   Overall relationships among Algerian groups 145
10.5   Negative relationships among Algerian groups 146
10.6   Positive relationships among Algerian groups 147
10.7   Negative relationships among Libyan groups 148
10.8   Zoomed-in relationships among Libyan groups 148
10.9   Positive relationships among Libyan groups 149
10.10 Negative relationships among Nigerian groups 150
10.11 Positive relationships among Nigerian groups 151
10.12 Radical groups embedding with 173 groups 151
10.13 Positive relationships of radical groups embedding with 111 groups 152
10.14 Negative relationships of radical groups embedding with 111 groups154
10.15 Positive relationships of radical groups embedding with 16 groups 154
10.16 Negative relationships of radical groups embedding with 16 groups 155
10.17 Positive relationships of violent groups embedding with 65 groups 155
10.18 Negative relationships of violent groups embedding with 65 groups 156

A.1   A cut with two copies of a node in two different clusters 163

List of Tables

4.1	Alignment of Florentine families	34
5.1	Normalized edge lengths for Florentine families	53
5.2	Normalized edge lengths for Macaque monkey visuotactile brain .	57
5.3	Nodes remaining for choices of edge weight threshold	65
6.1	Normalized edge lengths for Florentine families	75
6.2	Normalized edge lengths for Chalonero	79
6.3	Normalized edge lengths for Stupor Mundi	79
7.1	Number of pairs in each time period	89
7.2	Individuals with the top 12 largest *in-out* edge lengths in each time period	94
8.1	Ratios for the embeddings of the tribes	109
8.2	Ratios for the Sampson monastery network embeddings	111
10.1	Edge lengths for the Sampson monastery network embedding . .	144
10.2	Normalized length of embedded edges for the 16 radical groups .	153
10.3	Normalized edge lengths for the 65-node violent subset	153

Glossary

SNA	Social Network Analysis.
G	a graph with vertices and edges.
V	vertex set in a graph.
E	edge set in a graph.
W	weighted adjacency matrix of a graph.
M	our layered model adjacency matrix of a graph.
$\mathbb{1}$	the constant one vector.
d_i	degree of ith vertex.
D	diagonal degree matrix of an adjacency matrix.
$\hat{D}$	modified diagonal total degree of signed graph.
L	unnormalized Laplacian matrix of a graph.
L_{sym}	symmetric normalized Laplacian matrix.
L_{rw}	random-walk normalized Laplacian matrix.
L_{dir}	Chung's directed combinatorial Laplacian matrix.
$\hat{L}_{dir}$	Chung's directed normalized Laplacian matrix.
L_{dsym}	our directed symmetric normalized Laplacian matrix.
L_{drw}	our directed random walk normalized Laplacian matrix.
$\bar{L}$	Kunegis's unnormalized signed Laplacian matrix.
$\bar{L}_{rw}$	Kunegis's random-walk normalized signed Laplacian matrix.
$\bar{L}_{sym}$	Kunegis's symmetric normalized signed Laplacian matrix.
L_{sign}	our unnormalized signed Laplacian matrix.
L_{sns}	our simple normalized signed Laplacian matrix.
L_{bns}	our balanced normalized signed Laplacian matrix.
$\overline{RatioCut}()$	Kunegis's signed ratio cut.
$SRcut()$	our defined signed ratio cut.
$\mathbb{1}$	constant one vector.
R_M	Rayleigh quotient of matrix M.
P	probability (random walk) matrix.
$cut()$	number of cut edges.
$RatioCut()$	ratio cut.
$Ncut()$	normalized cut.
$CheegerCut()$	Cheeger cut.

$|A_i|$	the number of the nodes in group A_i.
$vol(A_i)$	the sum of the degrees of the nodes in group A_i.
Π	the stationary distribution of a probability (random-walk) matrix.
AER	our defined average edge ratio.
ANR	our defined average node ratio.
MER	our defined median edge ratio.
SSL	semi-supervised learning.
$\hat{L}_{sns}$	our modified signed Laplacian for SSL.

Chapter 1

Introduction

1.1 What is a social network?

As humans, we form relationships with other humans. Although not all relationships are pairwise (for example, a newborn baby acquires relationships with both parents and siblings at the same time), it turns out to be useful to model most relationships as structures between two participants.

The creation of such pairwise relationships is usually intentional — the two participants decide to create a mutual relationship. When the creation process is not intentional, it is typically the result of biological, social, or legal forces. The adjective "social" in the phrase "social networks" reflects the property that pairwise relationships occur because of underlying properties of humans and human society. The networks that we build to connect computers, for example, have quite different structures and properties.

Although each individual connects to another individual as the result of a choice (or something like it) made locally, the aggregate of all of these choices is a network, a spider web of connections among many individuals. The overall structure of this network has many intriguing properties that do not obviously follow from the choices made by the individuals. The collection of local, individual choices create a structure that has global regularities. We say that a social network has *emergent properties*. Looking at these emergent properties enables us to understand something about the large-scale drivers that motivated (mostly unconsciously) the choice of each pair of individuals to create a relationship.

In other words, large-scale, mostly invisible, forces act to cause pairs of individuals to form relationships; the resulting structure can be analyzed to detect emergent properties; and these properties can, in turn, be used to understand the invisible forces, which might be difficult to see and interpret in any other way. Social networks, therefore, are a kind of lens that we can use to discover properties of society, of particular groups, and sometimes particular individuals.

Organizations can form relationships with other organizations too, and some of the forces that create relationships between individuals are in play in organizational networks as well. However, the relationship between organizations exists on two levels: the formal level which may be instantiated in a contract, or a memorandum of understanding, or a buying and selling process, or something less precise; but also on an informal level involving relationships between individuals inside each organization. The strength of the relationship between the organizations exists apart from the individuals in one sense (if one buyer resigns, another will be appointed to replace him or her), but relies on these individuals in another (if they get on, the two organizations may be able to interact more smoothly).

It is also difficult for one individual to have both a positive and negative relationship to another individual because it creates cognitive dissonance; but the relationship between two organizations can easily have both a positive and negative component, embodied by different sets of individuals within them. "Social networks" of organizations are therefore a useful construct, but they will not always behave in the same ways as social networks of individuals.

The analysis of social networks has revealed many properties about the way that humans, and human groups, operate and interact. Social networks exist at many different scales: within a single organization, in a town, or within a country; and they are of different sizes, from a few dozen individuals to several billion. It is also useful to distinguish between a social network whose relationships are created by face-to-face contact, versus one where the relationships are formed and built in an online environment, whether on a social media platform or by exchanging emails or text messages.

Broadly speaking, social network properties seem to apply regardless of scale, size, and modality, probably because they are driven by, or perhaps limited by, the cognitive and social properties that make us human. However, there are some special situations where the processes that drive social network formation may be qualitatively different. For example, a group of criminals may form an unusual social network because they explicitly consider how to make it difficult for law enforcement to find and track them. They may therefore decide to limit their connections to one another, for example by forming small subgroups that are only connected to one another by a few connections. Such exceptional social networks may have special properties.

Here are some examples of the properties of human social networks that emerge from the way that individual connections are made:

- The diameter (the distance between the furthest separated nodes) of a typical social network is logarithmic in the number of nodes it contains, rather than linear. When social networks were first considered, it seemed natural and intuitive that they should be mesh-like, as transportation networks are. After all, they exist on the surface of the earth. Milgram's famous experiments [60, 99], which led to the meme of "six degrees of separation", showed that this intuition is misleading: a surprisingly large number of individuals in social networks have relationships to those who are "far away" in the natural, planar view. There are enough of these "long" edges that the total distance between any two individuals, even at planetary scale, is a path of only length 6 or 7.

One easy way to reach someone far away in the world is to communicate to a local government official, who typically has a connection to someone higher in their government, and on to a country leader. Country leaders usually know other country leaders, and so could pass the communication down on the other side. Hierarchical structures are one way in which large networks can have small diameters.

Interestingly, most social networks are not like this: the long connections are not arranged in any careful way, but rather are present between many nodes, distributed throughout, and these long edges connect to other nodes at all distances. In other words, the edges in any part of a social network are not a careful mixture of mostly "short" edges and a few "long" edges, but instead a much less structured mixture of edges of many lengths. From the perspective of any single individual, most, perhaps all of her edges will be short; but some will be a bit longer, a few even longer than that, and perhaps one very long. This connection structure is one example of a "small world" property: the network looks qualitatively the same in a local neighborhood, in a region, in a country, and for the whole world.

Thus the way to reach someone far away in the world is to find a close neighbor with a long edge in the right direction. Milgram's subjects tended to use this strategy. If they had to send a package from, say, Denver to New York, they would send it to someone they knew in the New York area, on the assumption that the recipient would know someone in the right part of New York, and so on.

- The number of connections an individual has (the number of relationships in which s/he participates) is typically bounded above by a value between 125 and 150 that is known as Dunbar's Number [30, 31]. This limitation appears to be the result of cognitive limits on how many other individuals any one person can keep track of in a meaningful way. This number matches very well the number of individuals in traditional tribal groups, but seems to transfer well to the online domain too.

Especially, but not exclusively, in the online domain, there are social networks in which the relationships are weak, and it may be possible for an individual to maintain a larger set of connections in such networks. For example, if the relationships are such that they require almost no effort to maintain then an individual can have many relationships. Heads of state have "relationships" with most other heads of state in the sense that they could make a phone call to them, but these relationships do not necessarily require much attention or maintenance, which seems to be the constraint behind the Dunbar Number. Similarly, many social media platforms allow users to have many "friends" or followers who receive updates of their lives, but the amount of work to tell 5 people or 500 about some life event is the same, so again maintenance costs are low.

If the relationship is one with real activity, and real associated costs for maintaining it, then the Dunbar Number seems to be a quite hard limit.

- Many properties of social networks exhibit *power laws*. Histograms of how frequently some property is present, plotted in descending order of frequency, create curves that drop off extremely quickly. This drop-off is so steep that plotting both axes on logarithmic scales produces almost straight lines (whose slopes characterize global network properties).

  The first, and most important, implication of the presence of power laws is that average properties are almost always meaningless. For example, we expect the number of connections individuals have to vary widely, with relatively few having many connections and many having relatively few connections. The *average* number of relationships within a social network does not provide an accurate picture of how an arbitrary individual is connected because the distribution is so extremely skewed.

  For example, nodes such as national leaders may have very large degrees indeed. Individuals such as Queen Elizabeth or the Dalai Lama are plausibly within three steps of most of the world's population. Their neighborhood of diameter less than or equal to 3 is roughly 7 billion. A very outgoing person who has 125 immediate neighbors still will not have $(125)^2$ connections at distance two, or $(125)^3$ connections at distance three, because many of these neighbors, and neighbors of neighbors, will know one another. Hence their neighborhood of diameter less than or equal to 3 might only be a few thousands. A socially isolated person might only have a neighborhood of diameter less than or equal to 3 of size $5^3 = 125$. Thus neighborhood sizes can easily vary by a factor of 10^7.

- There is structure within the set of connections that each individual has. Typically, each individual has really close connections to k others, slightly less close connections to k^2 others, even less close connections to k^3 others, and perhaps tenuous connections to k^4 others. k typically has a value between 3 and 4, so the sum of the number of individuals in all of these layers agrees well with the total given by the Dunbar Number [122]. For example, the first layer for most people consists of family; the second layer of close friends; and so on. (It also seems plausible that there is a further layer of k^5 connections that reflects weaker forms of acquaintance — for example, many social media platform users have roughly 400 "friends".)

- The degree of an individual tends to be similar to the degrees of the others to whom that individual is connected. This property is called *assortativity*. In other words, if a person has many friends, then his or her friends will also tend to be people with many friends (and vice versa: if they have only a few friends, these friends will also tend to have only a few friends). This is very different from the networks connecting computers, where a node with high degree is likely to be connected to nodes of much lower degree. Many web clients connect to the web servers at both Microsoft and Google, but these are much less likely to connect to each other.

- While, from a human perspective, we conceive of ourselves as being members of multiple groups, such groupings are not, by and large, visible in the aggregate social network if all relationships are treated as the same. If the social network region around an individual is considered only as a network of relationships, there is no obvious signal that *this* subregion consists of relatives, this other subregion of work colleagues, and this third subregion of members of a club, team, or hobby group. In other words, clusters in a social network are a perceptual property rather than a structural property, so that finding clusters or communities in a social network requires some care. This is partly because there is often substantial overlap among such subregions (a family member shares an interest in a sport or hobby), and partly because of the presence of "long" edges.

- Properties that can be considered to flow along the edges of a social network (that is, properties that are influence-like) travel for surprisingly long distances. For example, there are some experiments that show that an individual is influenced by the happiness not only of immediate social-network neighbors, but also by neighbors of neighbors, and even neighbors of neighbors of neighbors [18, 19]. In general, someone three steps away may not even be known to the individual, so that these influence-like properties flow "over the horizon". Other properties that behave this way include sadness, tendency to smoke, and being overweight. Unsurprisingly, these effects are of great interest to those whose business is influence, for example, advertisers and many large-scale experiments have been enabled by access to internet-scale data [65].

These results show that the social networks in which we find ourselves are not much like we might expect them to be intuitively. We form relationships with a few other people based on local information and independent decision making, we build a mental picture of what the global social network that results is like, but this global network actually has many properties that are not obvious from the perspective of any single participant. Emergent structure is the payoff from social network analysis. Once it is understood, the resulting insights can be used to draw conclusions about individuals and society that have wide implications. For example, a node may be an outlier in a social network, that is connected to the network only at the periphery. This is not the same property as having low degree (although it may be related). Similarly, a node may be a key node, in some sense, located centrally in the network. Again, this is not necessarily the same property as having high degree. Emergent structure of the network as a whole acts as a background against which properties such as these can become visible.

1.2   Multiple aspects of relationships

A model of social interactions in which there is only a single type of connection — "relationship" — is extremely limited. In the real world, our connections are multifaceted in at least the following ways:

- Relationships are of different intensities. Some relationships are close, and some are not so close, and noticing the differences is important for understanding the global structures. For example, a property of influence might be expected to operate more forcefully in a strong relationship than in a weak one.

- Relationships are of qualitatively different kinds: family relationships, friendships, romantic relationships, work relationships, and acquaintance. This property is different from intensity: an intense family relationship and an intense work relationship are still inherently different.

   Noticing this shows that there is a new possibility: there can be more than one kind of relationship between the same two individuals — they might be colleagues but also friends — and there is clarity in regarding these as two relationships, not one.

- Relationships are not symmetric. Given any two individuals, A and B, it is likely that the intensity of the relationship as perceived by A is different from the intensity as perceived by B. It is natural to model the connection as two directed relationships, one from A to B and the other from B to A.

- Relationships are not always positive. Two individuals can be enemies rather than friends, and enemy relationships can also be of different intensities, and perhaps different kinds.

- Relationships change over time. Few relationships of any kind are actually static, and their intensities may change on a day-to-day basis, or over longer time frames.

Any social network analysis that lumps all of these multifaceted ways in which humans interact into a single generic category of "relationship" must surely miss important subtleties in the resulting structures. Models for social networks must allow all of these rich properties of the connections between one person and another to be represented if we are to fully understand social behavior and influence in their full complexity.

Furthermore, all or most of these properties must be modelled at once. It is entirely natural to consider a single relationship as being, simultaneously: directed, negative, associated with a particular qualitative experience, and changing over time. This book shows how to build and model such networks. Thus it enables unprecedented sophistication in representing and understanding social networks.

1.3   Formally representing social networks

Social networks are usually modelled as *graphs*. A graph consists of a set of *nodes* (or *vertices*) that represent the individuals, and a set of edges that connect nodes. These edges represent the relationship between the individuals associated with the nodes. Graphs are a natural way to represent networks, but they require awkward data structures, and so are difficult to work with computationally.

From the perspective of a drawing of a graph, it is easy to see how to model rich edge types. Each edge in the graph can be drawn with (say) a color that represents the qualitative kind of relationship (colleague vs. friend) it represents; an arrow to indicate the directionality of the relationship; and a positive or negative weight or label to indicate the positive or negative intensity of the relationship. However, temporal changes are already problematic unless the drawing becomes a video.

Direct renderings of a social network like this also do not scale as the number of nodes and edges increases. Even a small network, say 20 nodes, becomes a cluttered picture from which conclusions might be hard to draw visually. And there remains the challenging, and long-studied, problem of how to place the nodes for maximal effectiveness of the rendering (that is, for maximal interpretability by human eyes) [95].

For more mathematical analysis, it is conventional to represent a graph by an adjacency matrix. If the graph contains n nodes, its adjacency matrix is an $n \times n$ structure where the entries are zeros except at positions (i, j) whenever node i has a connection to node j.

For a simple social network, the ijth entry of the adjacency matrix is set to a 1 to indicate the existence of a connection between nodes i and j. If the edges are undirected, a connection from node i to node j necessitates a connection from node j to node i, so that the ijth and jith entries must always be the same. The adjacency matrix is then said to be symmetric.

It is easy to extend the adjacency matrix representation to allow edges to be positively or negatively weighted, by using the weight as the value in the corresponding entry of the adjacency matrix.

It is also easy to model directed edges (for then the ijth entry represents the edge from node i to node j and the jith entry the reverse edge). However, there is no convenient way to extend the adjacency matrix to represent different *kinds* of (weighted) relationships, nor relationships whose intensities change with time. Tensors (3-dimensional matrices) could be used, with one layer for the adjacency matrix of each kind or time, but this has not become a popular approach.

Adjacency matrices allow most kinds of social networks to be represented, and the machinery of linear algebra can be used to manipulate them, and to prove theorems about their properties. However, they do not provide an easy way for human-directed presentation of the graph's properties,

It is common to get the best of both the computational world and the drawing or rendering world by using *spectral embedding techniques*. This family of algorithms transform an adjacency matrix into one of a family of *Laplacian* matrices, compute an eigendecomposition of this Laplacian, and then use a subset of the eigenvectors as axes for a space in which each of nodes can be placed. Because of the properties of the eigendecomposition, it can be proven that the representation using, say, k eigenvectors is the most faithful possible in that dimensionality in the sense that the distances between nodes most accurately reflect the global similarity between them implied by the entire connection structure. In other words, this embedding is, in a strong sense, the best embedding from the point of view of representing the graph's *structure* (although it might not be the easiest to understand visually).

Using a spectral embedding, a social network is embedded in a geometry. The key property of the embedded network is that distances between nodes are meaningful — they reflect the similarities between every pair of nodes, as far as that is possible in a low-dimensional space — similar nodes are close, and dissimilar nodes are far apart. Properties that are based on similarity can be computed directly on the embedded graph, nodes that are placed centrally are in fact the most central nodes, and directions capture differences. The embedding can be rendered as a visualization which is accurate, even if it is not necessarily beautiful or easily comprehensible.

In particular, this distance measures the similarities between nodes that were not connected in the original graph, that is the social distance between two individuals who do not have an existing mutual relationship. Two individuals who are embedded close to one another can be thought of as being about to have a relationship, or having a relationship that failed to be noticed when the data for the network was collected. This approach is the basis of *edge prediction* or *link prediction* and is used for recommendation in several social media systems.

The magnitude of the distance between two nodes that are embedded close together could also be exploited to predict the *intensity* of the relationship that might come into existence. However, as we shall see, predicting intensity is much more difficult than predicting existence.

Many other useful properties of the social network can be read off from the visualization of the embedding. For example, nodes that are well connected tend to be placed centrally, so measures such as centrality are immediately apparent. Nodes that are mutually well connected are placed close together, so that clustering is also immediately visible.

The standard spectral embedding process requires that the adjacency matrix be symmetric. Thus the process can only be directly applied to social networks where the edges are undirected (although they can be weighted). As we have seen, this is extremely limiting. The remainder of this book is about a general construction that allows the full richness of edge types to be married to the power of spectral embedding techniques to enable general social networks to be modelled in their full detail.

Chapter 2

The core model

In this chapter, we introduce the key technique that we will develop and use to analyze social networks with rich semantics for the relationships between nodes. This will include all of the possibilities mentioned in the previous chapter: qualitatively different types of relationships, asymmetric relationship intensities, positive and negative relationships, and relationships that vary with time.

2.1 Representing networks to understand their structures

As we mentioned in Chapter 1, there are two main ways in which a social network, captured as a graph, can be understood. These methods can handle graphs whose edges are positively weighted and undirected — adding other features is already beyond their capabilities.

The first main way to understand a graph is *graph drawing*, collections of algorithmic ways to display, visualize, or render a graph in a way that humans can directly and easily understand. Graph drawing algorithms try to place the nodes so that any groupings that might be present are made obvious, so that nodes do not obscure one another, and so that edges are as uncluttered as possible. A simple intuition gives the flavor of these algorithms. Suppose that the nodes of the graph are connected by elastic bands whose pull is proportional to the weight of the corresponding edge (relationship) and that a gentle uniform outward pull is applied from all directions at once. The positions at which the outward pull on each node exactly balances the pulls from all of the other nodes are probably a good approximation to the structure of the graph. These positions can then be tweaked locally to remove occlusions and clutter. Of course, these algorithms work best for graphs that are close to planar, which many real-world graphs are, for example power grids and transportation networks. They perform less well when the graph is naturally high dimensional.

The problem with the graph-drawing approach is: in how many dimensions should this relaxation be done? A perfectly accurate representation of an n-node graph requires $n - 1$ dimensions, but a reasonable drawing can use at most 2, or perhaps 3, dimensions. If the relaxation is done in a high-dimensional space, then some kind of projection is still required to reduce it to 2 or 3 dimensions. If it is done in 2 or 3 dimensions from the start, the pulls from the other nodes are not quite in the right directions, so the stable configuration may not be what it "should" be.

The second main way to understand a graph is *spectral embedding*. First, the graph is created in its full $n - 1$-dimensional spatial complexity, with each node represented as a point in space with the distances between each connected pair of nodes exactly representing their similarity. (Euclidean distance corresponds to *dis*similarity, so well-connected nodes are close.) Second, this cloud of points is rotated in such a way that its maximal variation is aligned along an initial axis, its orthogonal next largest variation along a second axis, and so on — this corresponds to an eigendecomposition. Third, the cloud is projected into the space spanned by the most useful of these axes — those that reveal the maximal variation — and the values of the eigenvectors for each node are interpreted as coordinates in a lower-dimensional space.

The advantage of spectral approaches over graph drawing is that the construction comes with strong guarantees about the quality of the embedding. A projection to k dimensions is guaranteed to be the most faithful possible in that number of dimensions. Of course, this accuracy may come at the expense of direct intelligibility, since the visualization may not be as easy for a human viewer to understand as one produced by graph drawing. However, its inherent accuracy means that downstream analysis can be used to make sense of its properties, even if these properties cannot be captured in a nice picture. We will render spectral embeddings directly, but it is possible to tweak such embeddings to increase their human comprehensibility without sacrificing much of the geometric accuracy. For example, the Multinet package (**http://www.sfu.ca/personal/archives/richards/Multinet/Pages/multinet.htm**) [80] can render social networks in many different ways, based on underlying spectral embeddings.

It might seem natural to begin this eigendecomposition with the network's adjacency matrix, but this does not work. A well-connected graph node has a row in the adjacency matrix with many non-zero entries; when it is embedded in $n - 1$-dimensional space, it will be placed far from the origin. Conversely, a node with few connections will have many zeros in the corresponding row of the adjacency matrix, and so will be placed close to the origin. Hence the cloud will be "inside out". Worse still, the well-connected nodes will tend to be connected to one another in the network (assortativity) but, by being far from the origin, they are also embedded far from one another. So using the adjacency matrix as a starting point dooms the process to failure (which has not prevented the alarmingly large number of research papers that do it anyway).

Rather than starting from the adjacency matrix, a transformation is applied that is a kind of normalization. As we shall see, there are a number of ways of doing this, but the simplest one is to convert the adjacency matrix into a *combinatorial Laplacian* by summing the entries in each row (which corresponds to the weighted degree, d, of each node), placing this value on the diagonal, and replacing each non-zero off-diagonal weight w by $-w$. If W is the adjacency matrix and D the diagonal matrix of node degrees, the combinatorial Laplacian is given by:

$$L = D - W$$

The spectral embedding begins from the Laplacian matrix, computes an eigendecomposition, and uses k of the eigenvectors as the coordinates for the position of each point. Because of the normalization, the eigenvectors chosen are those with the smallest corresponding eigenvalues (rather than the largest, which is what happens in conventional, eigendecomposition-based dimensionality reduction techniques).

If the graph is connected, then the smallest eigenvalue is zero, and the corresponding eigenvector is ignored — it represents, in a sense which we will make rigorous later, a trivial embedding. In fact, the number of zero-valued eigenvalues reveals the number of connected components of the graph.

It is easy to see why this approach is limited in its modelling power for some kinds of edge properties. If some edge weights can be negative, then summing the entries in a row no longer corresponds to the total weighted degree. If there is more than one edge between the same pair of nodes, then there is nowhere to represent the information about the second, and subsequent, edges. And the eigendecomposition requires that the Laplacian matrix be symmetric, which prevents the immediate representation of edges with an orientation.

There are also some more subtle issues. The choice of this particular Laplacian implicitly assumes that the right model for similarity is the so-called electrical resistance model — the distance between two nodes depends not just on the shortest (weighted) path between them but on the number and weights of all paths between them, with weights interpreted as the reciprocals of resistance [45]. This choice also assumes that the degrees of nodes in different parts of the graph are roughly the same, and we have seen that this is not typical in social networks. We will therefore tend to prefer slightly different Laplacian normalizations that we will introduce in Chapter 3.

2.2   Building layered models

The difficulty with representing multiple kinds of edges at once is that adjacency matrices only have a single "slot" to capture all of the information about the relationship between a pair of individuals.

Our first key idea is to replicate the nodes of the social network so that each copy becomes the representative, and connection point, for edges with a particular property. When a social network has edges with many kinds of semantics, these edges can be connected to the appropriate copies of the nodes to record and preserve those semantics. In other words, an edge that has multiple associated semantics becomes a constellation of edges, each with a single semantics that is carried by how it is connected.

The second key idea is that we organize the different copies or versions of the nodes by placing them, conceptually, in different layers. In other words, if there

are, say, three different edge properties we replicate each node of the original social
network into three versions, and imagine that the versions of the same flavor are
arranged in a layer. The edges appropriate to that layer connect these versions of
the nodes. Thus the expanded graph has three layers, each containing the matching
versions of all of the nodes and a subset of the edges. Looking "down" on the graph
from above, the layers cannot be seen, and the graph can be seen in its original
form. To keep the versions of the "same node" aligned, we also add "vertical" edges
between them to maintain the integrity of the entire social network.

    We begin with the most intuitive case: the edges in the social network reflect
different kinds of relationships such as relatives, colleagues, and friends.

    Consider a social network with n nodes and two different edge types, repre-
senting roles or behaviors. There may, of course, be more than one edge between the
same pair of nodes if, for example, they are friends *and* colleagues.

    We begin by replicating the set of n nodes, arranging each of the versions of
the network in a layer. Each layer is assigned one of the possible connection types
or roles: friends and colleagues. The edges of the original social network are then
placed in the layer to which they naturally belong. For example, if A and B are
friends, then an edge joins the versions of A and B in the friends layer. As a result,
there is now at most a single edge between any two nodes in the expanded graph.
The semantics of an edge can be inferred from the layer in which it appears.

    We now connect each of the versions of the same node (for example, A in both
her versions) by a "vertical" edge, binding the new graph into a consistent whole.
These vertical edges both ensure that the graph is connected, and enforce a weak
global consistency among the versions of the same node.

    The resulting adjacency matrix is of size $2n \times 2n$. This is bigger than the
original $n \times n$ adjacency matrix, but the actual content has not increased by much.
The total number of within-layer connections in the $2n \times 2n$ graph is the same as
the total number of connections in the original graph, since that is where they came
from. The additional edges are the "vertical" edges; these cause the off-diagonal
submatrices to be themselves diagonal matrices. If the vertical edges are undirected,
then these two submatrices are the same; if the vertical edges are directed, they need
not be.

    Adjacency matrices representing social networks are typically sparse; the ap-
parently much bigger matrix produced by the layer construction does not actually
have many more non-zero entries than there were to begin with. The cost of the
computations required for spectral embedding can be made to depend only on the
number of non-zero entries in the matrices (using sparse matrix eigendecomposition
techniques), so that the cost for the larger matrix increases only linearly, rather than
quadratically.

    We can apply the spectral embedding technique to the new, larger graph and
embed it in a *single* geometric space. The distances between the positions of embedded nodes tell us how similar the corresponding nodes are in the context of the entire
social network, accounting fully for the different types of edges.

    If we consider one of the subgraphs to be red, and the other to be green, Fig-
ure 2.1 shows some possible connection patterns.

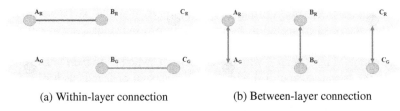

(a) Within-layer connection   (b) Between-layer connection

Figure 2.1: Illustration for within-layer connection and between-layer connection

If R is the adjacency matrix of the red layer, G is the adjacency matrix of the green layer, and T_{rg} and T_{gr} are the diagonal matrices representing the two vertical edges that connect different versions of the same nodes, then the adjacency matrix of the larger graph is

$$M = \begin{pmatrix} R & T_{rg} \\ T_{gr} & G \end{pmatrix}.$$

(If the vertical edges are undirected then, of course, T_{rg} and T_{gr} are identical.)

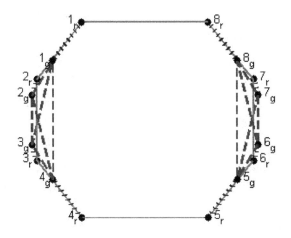

Figure 2.2: The embedding of a simple graph with typed edges

Figure 2.2 shows what happens when this idea is worked out. The original graph has 8 nodes. These nodes are connected by solid edges in a circle. They are connected by dashed edges into two 4-cliques. In the embedding (whose details we have not described yet) the solid layer distorts the 4-cliques of the dashed layer, pulling them into trapezoids; and the dashed layer distorts the solid-layer circle into an ellipse. There are two versions of each node, indicated by a subscript, The cross-hatched lines are the embeddings of the added vertical edges. The vertical edge joining the two versions of node 1, for example, is long, showing that the role of this node in the two networks is quite different.

There are three sets of distances that inform us about the social network. The lengths of the solid edges tell us how close any two individuals are as colleagues. The dashed edges tell us how close any two individuals are as friends. Suppose that individual A has friend B who has colleague C who has friend D. The distance between the friend version of A and the friend version of D tells us how similar A and D are likely to be as friends in the context of this entire social network. The key benefit of analyzing the social network in this combined way is that it takes into account the colleague similarity of B and C (as well as any friendship between them) in estimating the relationship between A and D. Analyzing the social network of friends and the social network of colleagues separately does not take into account the existence of these combined relationship chains.

We can also estimate how strong the relationship between A and D might be as colleagues by considering the distance between the colleague versions of their nodes in the embedding. The strength of a friend relationship and a colleague relationship between the same two individuals need not, of course, be similar.

When two nodes from the same layer are embedded close to one another, but there is no edge between them in the social network, this signals that, in some sense, there ought to be such an edge. The similarity of their positions in the embedding occurs because they see the rest of the social network in a similar way. This observation is the foundation for edge prediction, detecting pairs of nodes for which a relationship is (somehow) missing. In some contexts, this might indicate a problem with data collection; in others, it suggests that there is a potential relationship that can be suggested to both individuals. Social media platforms use this as the basis of suggesting "people you may know".

Using our typed-edge approach, such recommendations can be enriched because we are in a position to suggest what kind of relationship might or should exist. Thus the recommendation could be "this is someone who might be a potential colleague" or "this is someone who might be a potential friend". There are obvious commercial possibilities to this finer level of recommendation.

The lengths of the vertical edges also have two useful interpretations:

1. A long embedded edge indicates a dissonance between the roles played by the node in the different (sub)social networks that each layer represents. For example, if the red layer represents work colleagues, and the green layer friends, then the vertical edges represent the internal effort an individual requires to "change hats", for example, to remember to pass on some news or a joke heard at work to a friend. A long edge reveals the fact that there are significant differences between the role that the individual plays in the work-based social network, and the role played in the friend-based social network.

2. In settings where the edges represent properties that have flow associated with them, the length of embedded vertical edges more directly signals the amount of resistance to such flows. For example, the edges might represent *influence*. A short vertical edge signals little resistance, and so strong influence, internally from one role to the other. An individual with a short vertical edge in the embedding is someone who forms a good bridge for information or influence

flow between the two networks.

In the example so far, the edges connecting different versions have been vertical, but we will generalize the construction to allow "diagonal" edges for some settings as well.

We have not yet explained how weights are assigned to the edges between layers. This is obviously a critical choice, since it determines how closely each of the layers is aligned to the other. Choosing small weights means that the embedding of each layer will mostly depend on the structure in that layer; choosing large weights will force the versions of the same nodes to be embedded close together, so that the structures in one layer will distort the structures in the other layer more strongly.

There are principled ways to choose these new weights. We motivate them based on the idea of a random walk in the graph.

We can convert the adjacency matrix to a random-walk matrix by dividing the entries in each row by the sum of that row. The entries are all therefore values between 0 and 1, and the sum of each row is 1. Now imagine a random walker who moves around the graph in discrete steps, with the ijth entry of the random-walk matrix interpreted as the probability that the random walker who is currently at node i will move to node j in the next step. Because the outgoing edge weights sum to 1, a random walker is more likely to choose an edge with a higher weight than one with a lower weight.

This random-walk view of a graph is both intuitive and analytically helpful. For example, the fraction of time that a walker spends at a particular node, summed over a long sequence of probabilistic wandering steps, provides an estimate of how important that node is in the graph. Important nodes are visited often; less important nodes are visited less often.

This random-walk behavior is more stable if it is made *lazy*. The probabilities for each of the outgoing edges are divided by 2, so their sum is 0.5, and the other 0.5 probability is assigned to a self-loop at each node. In other words, at each step the random walker either stays put at the current node with probability 0.5, or takes one of the outgoing edges with probabilities proportional to their edge weights, which are all half what they were in the original random-walk scenario.

We use the idea of lazy random walks to motivate the choice of edge weights for the vertical edges. In particular, we allocate the "lazy" part of the probability to the vertical edges, giving them a total weight of 0.5. In the random-walk version of the larger adjacency matrix, therefore, the row sums of the submatrices on the main diagonal are 0.5, while the off-main-diagonal matrices are diagonal submatrices with 0.5 on the diameter. We model a random walker in the expanded graph as remaining within the current layer with probability 0.5, or moving to one of the other layers with total probability 0.5. If we ignore the typing of the edges, that is we take a monochrome view of the graph, then the random walker moves in the conventional lazy way, with the layer transitions appearing as self-loops.

So far, we have only considered two layers. If there are, say, c layers then the vertical edges between the c versions of the same node form a c-clique with total edge weight 0.5. In other words, if a random walker leaves the current layer, it has an equal chance of transitioning to any one of the other layers.

As we shall see, there are settings where it makes sense to adjust the relative weighting of within-layer and between-layer edges, but the motivation in terms of random walks provides a principled starting point from which to motivate deviations when they are needed.

2.3 Summary

The key construction that we will use to capture rich edge semantics is to replicate each node of the social network into multiple versions in the graph, connect edges to the appropriate version(s) to capture their semantics, and add edges between the multiple versions as necessary to keep them aligned. The resulting graph is notionally larger, but the additions are only linear in size so that the representation and computations also grow only linearly. The larger graph is embedded in a more or less standard way, but the resulting embedded graph has nodes and edges of different kinds, and so the downstream analysis changes because there are many more possible structures to understand and exploit.

Chapter 3

Background

Having provided some intuition for the kinds of constructions we will be using, we now introduce the mathematical notation and constructions more formally.

3.1 Graph theory background

A graph $G = (V, E)$ consists of a set of vertices $V = \{v_1, ..., v_n\}$ and edges $E = \{e_1, ..., e_k\}$, where $e_x = \{v_i, v_j\}$, that connect pairs of vertices. Vertices can also be called nodes, a more common usage in the social network literature.

There are various special kinds of graphs:

Undirected graph: A graph is undirected when the edges between vertices have no orientation, so that if $\{v_i, v_j\}$ exists, so does $\{v_j, v_i\}$. These are often called *undirected* edges.

Directed graph: A graph is directed when the existence of $\{v_i, v_j\}$ does not necessarily imply the existence of $\{v_j, v_i\}$. Such an edge is called a *directed* edge.

Unweighted graph: A graph is unweighted when the only property of an edge is its existence. The edge is typically modelled as having weight 1 if it exists and weight 0 if it does not.

Weighted graph: A graph is weighted when each edge has an associated positive numerical value representing, in some way, an intensity associated with that edge.

Signed graph: A weighted graph is signed when its edge weights can also be negative numerical values, representing an intensity associated with antipathy or opposition.

Simple graph: A graph is simple when it has no self-loops (edges that start and end at the same vertex) and no more than one edge between any two different vertices.

Multigraph: A graph is a multigraph when self-loops and multiple edges between the same pair of vertices are allowed. A directed graph is not normally considered a multigraph since multiple edges between the same pair of nodes go in different directions, but a signed graph must implicitly be a multigraph because it is possible for a pair of vertices to be connected by both a positively *and* negatively weighted edge.

Adjacency matrix: An adjacency matrix is one in which each row and column corresponds to a vertex of a graph, and the element a_{ij} of the matrix is the weight of the edge connecting node i to node j. For an undirected graph, the adjacency matrix is necessarily symmetric ($A = A'$); for a directed graph, it need not be. For a simple graph, the diagonal of the adjacency matrix is necessarily zero.

Degree: The degree of a node is the number of edges, or the sum of the weights of the edges, that connect to that node in an undirected graph.

In-degree: For directed graphs, the in-degree of a node is the number of edges, or sum of the weights of the edges, that end at the node.

Out-degree: For directed graphs, the out-degree of a node is the number of edges, or sum of weights of the edges, that start at the vertex.

Path: A path from node v_i to node v_j is a sequence of consecutive edges that start at v_i and end at v_j; the length of the path is the number of these edges, for an unweighted graph, or the total edge weight along these edges, for a weighted graph.

Geodesic distance: The geodesic distance between vertices v_i and v_j is the shortest (weighted) path between them.

Bipartite graph (or bigraph): A bipartite graph is one in which the nodes can be divided into two disjoint sets so that there is no edge between the nodes in each set. In other words, all edges connect nodes from different sets.

Clique: A clique is a subset of nodes of an undirected graph in which every pair of distinct nodes are connected.

Ego network: The ego network of a particular node is the subgraph of which it is the center. It consists of the node, all of its immediate neighbors, and all of the edges among them.

Connected graph: A graph is connected when there is a path between any pair of nodes. The graph representing a large social network may not necessarily be connected. The set of subgraphs, each of which is connected, are called the connected components of the graph. Often, the graph of a social network contains one connected component that contains almost all of the nodes, with a few other small components.

3.2   Spectral graph theory

Spectral graph algorithms are based on eigendecompositions of matrices derived from adjacency matrices. Conventionally, a matrix is regarded as an operator, but its eigendecomposition can also be understood as providing insight in the properties of the matrix as data, and this is the reason for the usefulness of eigendecompositions, principal component analysis, and matrix decompositions as tools in knowledge discovery [85].

For example, one way to understand an eigendecomposition of a matrix is that it determines a basis with respect to which the matrix can be expressed in diagonal form (where the diagonal entries are the eigenvalues).

From another perspective, an eigendecomposition represents a transformation of an initial space, where the matrix entries are coordinates with respect to the standard basis, to a new space, spanned by the eigenvectors, and coordinates in this space that are better behaved. For example, if the space is not of full rank, such a transformation can reveal that the data lie on a lower-dimensional manifold.

From yet another perspective, an eigenvector–eigenvalue pair represent the amplitude and frequency of vibration if the structure associated with the matrix were to be struck parallel to one of the original axes.

All three of these perspectives on eigendecompositions arise from regarding the original matrix as defining a cloud of points, each one at a position described by a row of the matrix. The eigendecomposition finds a view of this cloud that emphasizes the aspects of its structure with the greatest variation.

An eigendecomposition of an adjacency matrix can reveal the importance of each node in the graph, an idea exploited by Google in their PageRank algorithm. The rows of the adjacency matrix can be regarded as points in n-dimensional space, in fact in the positive hyperquadrant of n-dimensional space since edge weights are positive. The principal eigenvector of this matrix points through the center of this cloud of points, and the projection of each of the n nodes onto it determines a ranking from most- to least-important node. For an undirected graph this corresponds to the edge weight sum of each node, but for a directed graph, such as the random-walk version of the adjacency matrix, this is no longer the case.

Unfortunately, further eigenvectors of the adjacency matrix do not provide similar insights since the second, and subsequent, eigenvectors are constrained to be orthogonal to the first — but the direction of the principal eigenvector is determined by the overall weights of the graph edges. In other words, the vector connecting the origin to the cloud of points in the positive hyperquadrant depends on the total structure of the graph, but not its internal structure, and so the requirement for orthogonality to this eigenvector is not revealing.

This can be seen in Figure 3.1. The graph edge weights are all non-negative, so that the representation of each node as a point in n-dimensional space is a cloud in the positive hyperquadrant. Since the eigendecomposition is a purely numerical algorithm, it finds the principal eigenvector, v_1, pointing along the direction of greatest numerical variation, so from the origin to the center of the cloud. The second eigenvector, v_2, is constrained to be orthogonal to it, but this direction is not meaningful as a property of the cloud of points.

As we described earlier, the adjacency matrix needs to be converted to a Laplacian matrix before eigendecomposition to create a structure in which *all* of the eigenvectors reflect the structure of the graph. Because of this normalization, the eigenvectors that are most useful for embedding are those associated with the smaller eigenvalues, rather than those associated with the largest eigenvalues used for conventional eigendecompositions. These eigenvectors are the columns at the right-hand end of the decomposed matrix when the eigenvalues are sorted into descending order.

In such an eigendecomposition, the eigenvalue associated with the last column is 0, and the corresponding eigenvector is conventionally ignored. (It plays no role in the corresponding matrix product, although several of the algorithms that compute eigendecompositions do actually place meaningful values in this last column.)

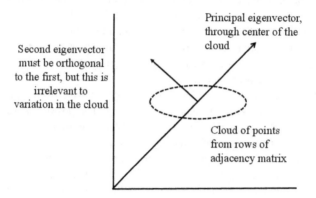

Figure 3.1: The eigendecomposition of the cloud of points corresponding to graph nodes. Only the first eigenvector reveals anything about the graph's structure.

It is possible that other eigenvalues at the right-hand end of the spectrum are zero as well — the number of such zero-valued eigenvalues corresponds to the number of connected components in the graph. We will assume, for simplicity, that the social networks we consider contain only a single component, and the constructions we use tend to make the constructed graphs connected anyway.

The rightmost eigenvector corresponding to a non-zero eigenvalue is known as the Fiedler vector of the graph [34] and represents the best 1-dimensional embedding of the graph, that is an embedding in which the nodes are placed on a line. This embedding is best in the sense that the distances between the embedded nodes corresponds as closely as possible to the similarities between them (Euclidean distance is small when nodes are similar).

A k-dimensional embedding can be constructed using the eigenvectors associated with the $n-1$ to $n-k$ smallest eigenvalues as coordinates. As before, distances in this k-dimensional space reflect (dis)similarity. Euclidean distances can be computed between pairs of nodes, whether connected or not, and geometric clustering algorithms such as K-means, Expectation-Maximization, hierarchical clustering, and others can be applied to the embedded nodes.

If $k = 2$ or 3, then direct visualization of the graph can also be carried out. This will be more accurate, but typically less immediately intelligible, than a graph-drawing algorithm would produce.

3.2.1 The unnormalized graph Laplacian

We now outline more carefully the process for embedding a graph using a spectral approach.

Given an adjacency matrix, what would be considered a good embedding? We shall see that there are multiple answers to that question, but we will start with the simplest case. Suppose we want to embed the nodes of the graph in a single dimension (that is, along a line) in a way that best reflects their mutually connected structure. A plausible objective function is:

$$\frac{1}{2} \sum_{i,j=1}^{n} w_{ij}(f_i - f_j)^2$$

where f is a non-zero vector of the positions on the line of the graph's nodes, and w_{ij} is the ijth entry of the adjacency matrix, W. This function preferentially places nodes that are strongly connected close together, and penalizes separation by an amount proportional to Euclidean distance. The division by 2 is required because every term appear twice in the sum.

There is no special scale for the vector f describing positions on the line. To remove the effect of the magnitude of f, we can refine the objective function to:

$$\frac{\frac{1}{2} \sum_{i,j=1}^{n} w_{ij}(f_i - f_j)^2}{\sum_{i=1}^{n} f_i^2}$$

This function is called the *Rayleigh quotient*.

If f corresponds to the position of each node of the graph in a 1-dimensional embedding, then a small value for the Rayleigh quotient corresponds to a "good" embedding. One particular good, but rather uninteresting, embedding would be to place every node at the same location.

Note also that a vector of locations could be altered by adding or subtracting a constant from all of its values, but this does not change the embedding in any useful way. Thus there is still a normalization issue to consider.

A choice for the trivial embedding would be $\mathbb{1}$, placing every node at location 1, for which the Rayleigh quotient is, of course, equal to zero. This is a very uninteresting embedding, but it is useful to impose the property that every other embedding must have the property that $f \perp \mathbb{1}$, that is they must be centered at the origin, and so have mean 0. This orthogonality constraint acts to normalize all of the other potential solutions for the vector f.

A little algebra reveals the matrix equation:

$$R_L(f) = \frac{f'Lf}{f'f} = \frac{\frac{1}{2} \sum_{i,j=1}^{n} w_{ij}(f_i - f_j)^2}{\sum_{i=1}^{n} f_i^2}$$

for a matrix, L, which is

$$L = D - W$$

where D is the diagonal degree matrix of W. We have seen this matrix before. This matrix, L, is called the unnormalized, or combinatorial, Laplacian of the graph, and

R_L is its Rayleigh quotient [61, 62]. The diagonal of L consists of the degrees of each of the corresponding nodes, and the off-diagonal entries are the negations of the weights in the corresponding positions of W. The row sums are all zero, so the Laplacian can be viewed as a kind of normalization of the cloud of points corresponding to the nodes, since they are now (in a curious way) centered around the origin.

Any vector can be viewed as a linear combination of the eigenvectors U of the Laplacian matrix L. Since all eigenvectors are orthogonal, the equation $Ux = f$ is always solvable, where x is the combination coefficient vector. If f is an eigenvector, the Rayleigh quotient is equal to the corresponding eigenvalue λ. If f is an arbitrary vector, the Rayleigh quotient value of $f = Ux$ can be calculated as:

$$R_L(f) = \frac{f'Lf}{f'f} = \frac{(Ux)'L(Ux)}{(Ux)'(Ux)} = \frac{x'U'LUx}{x'U'Ux} = \frac{x'\Lambda x}{x'x} = \sum_{i=1}^{n} \frac{x_i^2}{\sum_{i=1}^{n} x_i^2} \lambda_i$$

Thus, the Rayleigh quotient value of an arbitrary vector is the sum of the eigenvalues multiplied by a percentage that is calculated by the square of the combination coefficient. Therefore, the range of the Rayleigh quotient value lies between the minimum and maximum eigenvalues.

Because the Laplacian matrix is symmetric, we can always find a set of real-valued orthogonal eigenvectors for L. Furthermore, if a network is connected, only one eigenvalue of L can be 0, Because the eigenvectors are orthogonal to each other, any other eigenvector or linear combination of other eigenvectors will automatically eliminate this trivial solution.

The Rayleigh quotient can be expanded for a set of vectors as coordinates in multiple dimensions. Thus, the eigenvectors corresponding to the first few smallest eigenvalues can be viewed as the optimum graph embedding in low dimension. In the embedded graph, the central node of a group will be placed in the center of the group, nodes in the same group will be placed close together, and groups that are different will tend to separate.

The Rayleigh quotient as defined above models embeddings where distance reflects dissimilarity (since similar nodes are embedded close to one another). However, if some nodes have degrees much higher than the rest, those nodes with high degrees contribute more to the numerator of the Rayleigh quotient since they have more non-zero entries in the corresponding rows of the adjacency matrix. The effect is to place such high-degree nodes slightly closer to their neighbors than they "should be". In other words, the embedding space is distorted to become slightly denser in the region(s) around high-degree nodes. Since the degrees of nodes in social networks tend to follow a power law distribution, this distortion can become significant. The distorting effect that arises from highly imbalanced node degrees has motivated the definition of other Rayleigh quotients, and so other Laplacians, to compensate.

3.2.2 The normalized graph Laplacians

The next Rayleigh quotient we shall consider is:

$$R_{L_{sym}}(f) = \frac{f'L_{sym}f}{f'f} = \frac{\frac{1}{2}\sum_{i,j=1}^n w_{ij}(\frac{f_i}{\sqrt{d_i}} - \frac{f_j}{\sqrt{d_j}})^2}{\sum_{i=1}^n f_i^2}$$

which adjusts the distances between embedded positions based on the degrees of the corresponding nodes. As before, there is a corresponding Laplacian matrix, L_{sym}, which is called the symmetric (normalized) Laplacian, and can be expressed as:

$$L_{sym} = D^{-1/2}LD^{-1/2} = I - D^{-1/2}WD^{-1/2}$$

where D, as before is the diagonal degree matrix of the adjacency matrix, W. The diagonal entries of L_{sym} are all 1s, and the value of the ijth entry is

$$-\frac{w_{ij}}{\sqrt{d(v_i)d(v_j)}}$$

when the ijth entry of W is non-zero.

The minimum value of the Rayleigh quotient of the symmetric normalized Laplacian is still 0, but the corresponding vector is the square roots of the degrees, rather than the constant one vector $\mathbb{1}$. The symmetric normalized Laplacian L_{sym} is still positive semi-definite, and its smallest eigenvalue is 0.

The second variant of the Rayleigh quotient is defined as:

$$R_{L_{rw}}(f) = \frac{f'Lf}{f'Df} = \frac{\frac{1}{2}\sum_{i,j=1}^n w_{ij}(f_i - f_j)^2}{\sum_{i=1}^n d_i f_i^2}$$

with the corresponding random-walk Laplacian given by:

$$L_{rw} = D^{-1}L = I - D^{-1}W$$

The minimum value of the Rayleigh quotient of the random-walk normalized Laplacian is 0, and the corresponding eigenvector is the constant one vector $\mathbb{1}$. Thus, the random-walk normalized Laplacian L_{rw} is positive semi-definite, and its smallest eigenvalue is 0, but its eigenvectors are no longer orthogonal. It is easy to see why from Figure 3.1. The points corresponding to each row of the random-walk matrix are all in the positive hyperquadrant in the obvious direct embedding. Eigenvectors that capture the variation in the cloud of such points cannot be guaranteed to be orthogonal. They are, however, orthogonal to $D^{1/2}$ and $f_i D f_j = 0$.

The two normalized Laplacians are closely related:

$$L_{rw} = D^{-1/2}(I - L_{sym})D^{1/2}$$

Both normalized matrices have the same eigenvalues. The vector f is an eigenvector of L_{rw} if and only if $g = D^{1/2}f$ is an eigenvector of L_{sym}; λ and f are an eigenvalue and eigenvector of L_{rw} if and only if λ and f solve the generalized eigenproblem $Lf = \lambda Df$.

3.3   Spectral pipeline

The overall approach to spectral embedding follows these steps:

- Construct an adjacency matrix based on the node–node relationship intensities.

- Choose a Rayleigh quotient objective function that captures the desired properties of a "good" embedding.

- Find the Laplacian matrix corresponding to this Rayleigh quotient (the choice of objective function is constrained by the necessity to find such a matrix). Once this step has been done, adjacency matrices can be directly converted to Laplacians without explicit attention to the Rayleigh quotient.

- Compute an eigendecomposition of the Laplacian matrix.

- Perform a projective embedding of the nodes and edges into the space spanned by some number of the eigenvectors of the eigendecomposition, ignoring the last eigenvector (with corresponding 0 eigenvalue).

- In this geometric representation of the graph, positioning of the point corresponding to each node corresponds to its global importance (more central = more important), distances reflect similarity as it was expressed by the structure of the Rayleigh quotient, and standard operations on geometric spaces, such as clustering, can be applied. If the dimensionality is low enough, the graph can be visualized.

We will almost always be interested in networks that are connected. However, the number of zero-valued eigenvalues equals the number of connected components of the graph, so it is easy to tell when the network is not fully connected.

3.4   Spectral approaches to clustering

So far, we have concentrated on embedding a graph using spectral techniques. However, a substantial amount of work has focused on the role of spectral embedding in graph clustering. This is both an application of spectral embedding, and a means of justifying certain choices of spectral embedding techniques.

Large social networks tend not to have well-defined clusters because of the number of different kinds of connections among individuals. But there are other settings where the number of nodes is smaller, or only particular kinds of relationships are being considered, where it makes sense to ask whether a social network contains clusters. The concept of a cluster is hard to make rigorous, but the intuition is that clusters are subgroups of nodes that belong together and are therefore, somehow, well connected internally but sparsely connected to other parts of the graph. Laplacian clustering techniques can be divided into graph cut, random-walk, or commute distance approaches.

Graph cut approaches to clustering

For social network data, the graph cut approach is as follows: find a partition of the network into clusters such that the number of edges between different clusters is low, and each cluster has a higher density of edges than the network as a whole. When this is the case, the nodes within a cluster are similar to another, and the nodes in different clusters are dissimilar to one another. Finding an optimum partition is done by solving the min-cut problem, defined as minimizing:

$$cut(A_1,...,A_k) := \frac{1}{2} \sum_{i=1}^{k} W(A_i, \overline{A}_i),$$

where k is the number of groups, $\overline{A}_i$ is the complement of A_i, and $1/2$ accounts for the fact that we count each edge twice.

However, in practice, this does not lead to satisfactory partitions because simply separating the node with the lowest degree from the rest of the graph may give the minimum cut value [101]. To avoid this problem, two more sophisticated graph cuts, *RatioCut* and *NCut*, were introduced by Hagen and Kahng [38], and Shi and Malik [84], respectively. The definitions are:

$$RatioCut(A_1,...,A_k) := \sum_{i=1}^{k} \frac{W(A_i, \overline{A}_i)}{|A_i|} = \sum_{i=1}^{k} \frac{cut(A_i, \overline{A}_i)}{|A_i|},$$

and

$$NCut(A_1,...,A_k) := \sum_{i=1}^{k} \frac{W(A_i, \overline{A}_i)}{vol(A_i)} = \sum_{i=1}^{k} \frac{cut(A_i, \overline{A}_i)}{vol(A_i)},$$

where $|A_i|$ is the number of the nodes in group A_i, and $vol(A_i)$ is the sum of the degrees of the nodes in group A_i. Both approaches try to find an optimal partition that not only achieves a small cut value, but also keeps the groups in "balance".

Solving min-cut problems with balance conditions is NP-hard and so is intractable for large datasets [105]. Fortunately, spectral clustering can be viewed as an approximate way to solve these problems. Relaxing NCut leads to normalized spectral clustering, and relaxing RatioCut leads to unnormalized spectral clustering. The details of proof and discussion can be found in the tutorial written by von Luxburg [101]. However, the quality of the solution to the relaxed problem is not guaranteed, so they should be interpreted with some caution. Spielman and Teng [91] and Kannan et al. [43] have explored some of the relationships between graph properties and clustering solution quality.

Random walk approaches to clustering

Another way to explain spectral clustering is based on a random walk in the network. We want to find an embedding in which it is easy for a random walker to travel among the nodes of one cluster but hard to travel to nodes in a different cluster. The effect of placing all nodes at the same spot, and the effect of the size of the graph, have to be eliminated, and the degree of nodes needs to be considered. The non-trivial eigenvectors associated with the smallest eigenvalues of the random-walk normalized Laplacian matrix, L_{rw} is a good approximate solution, since the random-walk matrix and random-walk normalized Laplacian matrix L_{rw} have the same eigenvectors with corresponding eigenvalues λ and $1 - \lambda$, respectively.

Meila and Shi [58] proved that NCut and transition probabilities of the random walk are formally equal. In other words, finding the minimum value of NCut is actually looking for a partition where a random walk seldom transitions from one group to another.

Commute distance approach

In a graph, the commute distance between two nodes is the expected distance of a random walk from one node to another and back again. Because of the randomness, this commute distance takes into account all possible paths between the two nodes. Even the presence of a long path between two nodes may reduce the commute distance between them. Based on electrical network theory, Klein and Randić [45] proved that the general commute distance c_{ij} between node i and j could be computed with the help of the graph Laplacian

$$c_{ij} = \text{vol}(V) \sum_{k=1}^{n} \frac{1}{\lambda_k} (f_i^{(k)} - f_j^{(k)})^2$$

where λ_k and $f^{(k)}$ are the k-th eigenvalue and eigenvector of L. The equation tells us that the commute distance between two nodes is the sum of the differences in all eigenvectors divided by the corresponding eigenvalues. Therefore, the smaller eigenvalues (except 0) and the corresponding eigenvectors play the most important roles in the commute distance. This commute distance can also be viewed as the average first-passage time based on a Markov-chain model of random walk [35]. Even though the commute distance seems to be helpful to explain the spectral embedding, there is only a rather loose relation between spectral embedding and the commute distance [101].

3.4.1   Undirected spectral clustering algorithms

Here three clustering algorithms for undirected graphs are introduced based on these different approaches. All the algorithms begin with an adjacency matrix, W, and a number, k, of clusters into which the graph is to be partitioned.

Unnormalized Laplacian clustering

After the Laplacian matrix L is constructed, the k smallest eigenvalues and the corresponding eigenvectors of L are computed. The ith entries of the k eigenvectors are viewed as the position coordinates of the node i. Thus, we can directly cluster the nodes by comparing their positions based on Euclidean distance. The clustering algorithm can be K-means or any other geometric method.

Random walk normalized Laplacian clustering

In random-walk normalized Laplacian clustering [58], the k smallest eigenvalues and the corresponding eigenvectors of L_{rw} are first computed, and then the eigenvectors are used to cluster the graph in the same way as the unnormalized Laplacian clustering. It should be noted that the (generalized) eigenvectors are not orthogonal to each other. (Eigenvectors may not be real in some computational environments. For example, eigenvectors in MATLAB are always orthogonal. If the real part cannot be orthogonal, it adds an imaginary part to make the eigenvectors orthogonal. We only need the real part, which is the same as the generalized eigenvectors of the generalized eigenproblem $Lf = \lambda Df$. Alternatively, we can compute the k smallest eigenvectors of L_{sym} first, and then convert them to the eigenvectors for L_{rw} by multiplying by $D^{-1/2}$.)

Symmetric normalized Laplacian clustering

In symmetric normalized Laplacian clustering [71], the k smallest eigenvectors are first computed, each row considered as coordinates of the corresponding node, and then the coordinate value of each node is renormalized to norm 1. This corresponds to projecting the nodes onto the surface of a unit hypersphere with the origin as the center. The nodes can then be clustered based on the new positions.

3.4.2 Which Laplacian clustering should be used?

When the network is connected, and the degrees of all nodes are approximately the same, the eigenvectors of the three Laplacian matrices are similar, and the eigenvalues of the unnormalized Laplacian matrix are just the degree times the eigenvalues of the normalized Laplacian matrices. The clustering result will be similar regardless of which technique is used.

However, if the degrees of nodes in a network are quite different, the three different techniques will produce different clusterings. As before, there is some evidence that using a normalized Laplacian will lead to better results than using the unnormalized Laplacian.

One of the arguments is based on the graph cut point of view. As mentioned earlier, unnormalized Laplacian clustering is an approximation of RatioCut, and normalized Laplacian clustering is an approximation of NCut. The differences between RatioCut and NCut are the denominators — one uses the number of nodes in a cluster, and the other uses the volume of edges in a cluster. Both cuts minimize the edges between groups and also maximize the edges within groups. From the definition of RatioCut and NCut, we can infer that the definitions of within-group RatioCut and NCut are:

$$WRatioCut(A_1,...,A_k) := \sum_{i=1}^{k} \frac{W(A_i,A_i)}{|A_i|} = \sum_{i=1}^{k} \left(\frac{vol(A_i)}{|A_i|} - \frac{W(A_i,\overline{A_i})}{|A_i|} \right)$$

$$WNCut(A_1,...,A_k) := \sum_{i=1}^{k} \frac{W(A_i,A_i)}{vol(A_i)} = \sum_{i=1}^{k} \left(1 - \frac{W(A_i,\overline{A}_i)}{vol(A_i)} \right)$$

It is easy to prove that $WNCut(A_1,...,A_k) = k - 2 * NCut(A_1,...,A_k)$, but RatioCut and WRatioCut do not have such a simple relationship, which means that RatioCut and WRatioCut may not be in one-to-one correspondence. Therefore, NCut is more natural than RatioCut, and normalized Laplacian clustering is preferable.

In addition, von Luxburg et al. [102–104] presented another argument for the superiority of normalized Laplacian clustering based on statistical analysis. They draw data from an underlying probability distributions with different sample sizes. They showed that the normalized Laplacian clustering converged under some very general conditions, while the unnormalized Laplacian clustering was only consistent under strong additional assumptions. Furthermore, they also demonstrated that the unnormalized Laplacian clustering could fail to converge or converge to trivial solutions in real data. Therefore, the normalized Laplacian clustering is better than the unnormalized one from both the theoretical and practical points of view.

There are two normalized Laplacian algorithms, and they are closely related. The question is which normalized Laplacian clustering should be used. Ng et al. [71] claimed that the random walk Laplacian might be susceptible to bad clustering compared with symmetric Laplacian clustering when the total degree of the different groups varies substantially across clusters. However, the claim is weak without any explanation or proof. Furthermore, the random-walk Laplacian has a more direct meaning. Thus, it is preferable to use the random-walk Laplacian [101].

3.5 Summary

The general strategy for spectral embedding of a graph requires a transformation of the adjacency matrix into a Laplacian matrix. This can be thought of as a kind of normalization, turning the graph inside out so that high-degree nodes are no longer naturally on the outside of the embedding; or as a result of choosing an objective function — the Rayleigh quotient — that defines what a "good" embedding should be.

The eigendecomposition of this Laplacian matrix is then computed. This eigendecomposition corresponds to a change of basis in which new axes — the eigenvectors — are arranged in mutually orthogonal directions in which the cloud of points corresponding to the nodes has large variation.

The final stage is to project the nodes into a subspace of appropriate dimensionality, where geometric calculations can be used to assess similarity, centrality, clustering, outliers, and so on.

Notes

Donath and Hoffman [25, 26] were the first to suggest partitioning of graphs based on eigenvectors of connection matrices. At the same time, Fiedler [34] discovered that the graph partition was closely connected with the second smallest eigenvector of a Laplacian [91]. Since then, spectral clustering has been investigated and extended by many researchers. Applications of the spectral approach were made popular by the studies of Shi, Malik [84] and Ng et al. [71]. They developed two versions of normalized spectral clustering algorithms. They also interpreted the idea of clustering in two different ways, minimum cut and random walk. The non-linear counterpart, p-Laplacian clustering algorithm was developed by Bühler and Hein [10]. Subsequently, many extended spectral clustering approaches have been presented, including spectral co-clustering [23], image segmentation based on spectral clustering [33], detecting the community structures in networks [69] and improved spectral clustering algorithms [54, 55]. An overview over the properties and interpretation of Laplacian clustering can be found in von Luxburg [101] and an overview focused more directly on social networks in Seary and Richards [81].

Chapter 4

Modelling relationships of different types

Our first use of the layer approach is to model relationships that are of qualitatively different kinds, such as the examples of friends and colleagues that we have already mentioned. There are, of course, many different possible relationships: not only friends and colleagues, but close family members, more distant family members, school and university friends, fellow members of interest groups, and professional contacts. These different kinds of relationships have different properties. As the simplest example, not all of the facts about an individual's life would necessarily be appropriate to share with everyone that individual has a relationship with. As a result, the property of influence would operate differently along some edges than others because of the kind of information that could/should traverse them.

As we have indicated, our approach will be to use a layer for each kind of relationship. So there might be a friends layer, a family layer, a colleagues layer, and so on. There is no difficulty allowing any edge to have an associated weight, reflecting the intensity of that relationship. Note, however, that these weights have to be on the same scale, no matter what kind of relationship they are associated with. For example, it might be natural that family edges have weights that are, on average, larger than those of colleague edges. To simplify the exposition, we will think of the different edge types as being labelled with different colors. These colors can be mapped to any set of relationship types.

The payoff from modelling a social network with typed edges is that we can determine the structure of the complete ecosystem of individuals with all of their multiple relationship types. We can also measure the social distance between any pair of individuals, taking into account *all* of the ways in which they are connected, directly and indirectly.

Ignoring the different kinds associated with the relationships — taking the monochrome view of the social network — loses information about the ways in which humans relate to one another. In particular, the social network will seem smaller than it should be; individuals will seem more similar than they "should".

31

4.1   Typed edge model approach

Formally, we model a graph with n nodes and c different edge types by extracting c subgraphs, each one consisting of copies of *all* of the nodes, but just the edges of one particular type. We then connect the subgraphs (layers) together by adding edges connecting the c versions of each node together in a c-clique. We cannot use a path to connect the c versions of each node because (a) there is no obvious order for the different colors, and (b) the embedding of a path is a curved structure which makes the top and bottom layers special, aggravating (a).

This new, enhanced graph will then be embedded, using a standard spectral embedding since it is just a conventional graph with cn nodes. Information associated with the types of edges has been coded in their connection pattern, that is which nodes they are connected to.

The weights on the edges in each subgraph are just the weights from the original graph. The embedding of each subgraph, therefore, reflects the intensity of the connections of that particular type — a popular social individual may be richly connected in the social subgraph and so will tend to be embedded centrally within the embedding of that layer.

However, new edges have been created between the versions of the same node in different subgraphs. What weights should be allocated to these edges that connect the c copies of each of the original nodes into a c-clique? These edges serve to align the embeddings of each subgraph because they force the copies of nodes that represent the same individual to be close to one another. The greater the weights on these edges, the more the global embedding aligns the subgraphs. It is therefore a critical choice.

4.2   Typed edge spectral embedding

We have hinted at a principled way to allocate weights to the new vertical edges that connect the versions of the same node: compute the total degree incident at a node in a layer, divide the weights of all of the incident edges in that layer by two, and allocate the remaining half evenly among the $c - 1$ edges that connect the node to its versions in the other $c - 1$ layers. The motivation for this choice is that, from the perspective of each individual subgraph (layer), it behaves like a lazy random walk — the transitions to other layers are similar to the transitions around a self-loop.

Implicit in our layered model is that each individual plays a different role in the specialized social networks of each layer. An individual's role in the friendship social network is not necessarily the same as in a work-related social network. In particular, the same individual might be quite central in a friendship social network, but quite peripheral in a work-related social network. Thus we expect that the (weighted) degree of versions of the same node might be quite different in different subgraphs.

It is possible that a node might have versions with no connections in a particular subgraph — they have no relationships of a particular kind. However, the addition of the vertical edges ensures that they are connected in the larger graph.

The vertical edges model a kind of resistance associated with the differences between roles. How this works out is easiest to see from an influence or information flow perspective. For example, an individual might hear a joke at work. If the joke is to reach that individual's social domain, they have to remember and repeat it in a social context, and there is a certain resistance or cost associated with making that happen.

Our association of the weight of the vertical edge to the total weight of the individual in a subgraph also reflects the assumption that an individual who is central or powerful in one subgraph plausibly is in a better position to be central or powerful in other subgraphs. If they hear more jokes at work (so to speak), they are more likely to disseminate jokes into their social domain.

We have constructed a $cn \times cn$ network in which all of the edges are now of the same type, so we can embed it in the standard way using spectral embedding, and project it into an appropriate number of dimensions.

In the embedding, distances represent dissimilarity (equivalently, geometric closeness represents relationship closeness), but there are now multiple nodes corresponding to each individual. For nodes of the same color, distance represents similarity within the subgraph of that color — for example, the distance between two individuals in a layer representing friendship represents how close they are, or could be, as friends, *but* in the context of all of the other relationships of other types in which they, and their entire group, participate. It is not meaningful to consider the distance between the embedded point representing the friend role of one individual and the embedded point representing the colleague role of another.

The length, in the embedding, of each vertical edge reveals the magnitude of the difference between the role an individual plays in one social network and the role they play in another. For example, someone who is a key person in both a friend- and work-related network will be placed centrally in both, and so the vertical edge connecting those roles will be short. On the other hand, someone who is key in a friend network but peripheral in the work-related network is being pulled towards the center of the friend layer, but towards the outside of the work-related layer, and so his or her vertical edge will tend to be long. The information revealed by the vertical nodes is only available because of the layered approach to representing typed edges.

Edge prediction uses proximity of two unconnected nodes as the basis for suggesting that the two individuals "should" or "might" have a relationship. Having multiple versions of nodes corresponding to each individual in the embedding makes it possible to do *typed edge prediction*.

If the friend layer versions of two nodes are close but they are not connected, then we could predict for each of them that "this might be a potential friend" while if the work-related layer versions are close, we could predict "this might be a potential colleague". Such predictions are both more accurate and richer than those that could be generated from an untyped version of the same social network.

The layer approach imposes costs for creating and embedding a larger matrix, and the analyses of the embedded network are complicated by the multiple copies of each node, but there are benefits as well that arise from access to these embedded multiple versions and, in particular, the similarities and differences between them.

Medici bloc	Oligarch bloc	Oligarch bloc
Medici	Bischeri	Guadagni
Fioravanti	Ardinghelli	Da Uzzano
Dietsalvi	Altoviti	Solosmei
Davanzati	Rondinelli	Guasconi
Orlandini	Pepi	Castellani
Cocco-Donati	Peruzzi	Scambrilla
Valori	Benizzi	Strozzi
Guicciardini	Panciatichi	Aldobrandini
Ginori	Rucellai	Lamberteschi
Tornabuoni	Baroncelli	
Dall'Antella, Albizzi, Della Casa, Velluti with divided loyalties.		

Table 4.1: Alignment of Florentine families

4.3   Applications of typed networks

To illustrate the power of the typed-edge representation, we build the combined social network of Florentine families in the 15th Century. This period has been extensively studied because of the Medici family, who rose from humble beginnings to dominate Tuscany and the Papacy over the ensuing two centuries. Padgett constructed, by hand, a social network [74] of these families in which the edges captured a variety of relationships. We will use this dataset as a running example. Here we divide the edges into two general categories: those associated with financial relationships, and those associated with social relationships (mostly marriages). Although these edges are directed, we ignore this for now by adding the directed adjacency matrix to its transpose, so that the initial adjacency matrices are undirected.

These Florentine families are divided, by historians, into two blocs: those associated strongly with the (upstart) Medicis, and a group of longer-established, oligarch families. The families and their alignment are shown in Table 4.1.

One popular theory explaining the growth in Medici power at the beginning of the 15th Century is that they developed two separate social networks. On one hand, they built financial relationships with *nouveau riche* families; on the other, they built marriage ties with the "old money" *oligarch* families [74]. By keeping these two kinds of ties distinct, they were able to act as gatekeepers between two communities, a role they parleyed into power broking.

For the major families of Florence during this period, Figure 4.1 is the graph of personal ties and Figure 4.2 is the graph of financial ties. There are some families who have only one type of relationship and so they are placed at the origin in the embedding in which they are not connected. Figure 4.3 shows the embedding when both types of edges are used, but their types are not differentiated. We can already

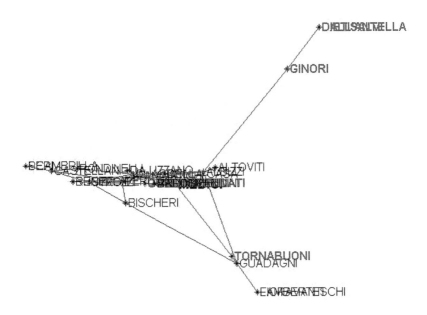

Figure 4.1: The embedding of the Florentine families based on personal relationships and undirected edges. Color versions of all of the figures are available at the Github repository **https://github.com/PHDZheng/Social-Networks-with-Rich-Edge-Semantics**, which also has MATLAB code and dataset so that you can look at the embedding results live.

see that the historical hypothesis, that the Medici family acted as middlemen between two groups of other families, is reasonably well supported.

Figure 4.4 is the embedding when the two types of relationships are modelled as separate layers. Nodes from the financial layer are labelled in upper case, and the edges from this layer are represented by solid lines. Nodes from the personal layer are labelled in lower case, and the edges are represented by dashed lines. The "vertical" edges between versions of the same nodes are represented by dotted lines.

Figures 4.5 and 4.6 show the cluster of oligarch families in greater detail, but with the same orientation. The "vertical" edges can be seen, at least for some of the families.

The differences between the roles of each family are small. There are obvious differences for the peripherally placed families (Davanzati and Valori), but these are the *least* important families because they are placed peripherally, and the length of their edges is also mostly a side effect of how unusual they are. The placement of the personal Medici node is closer to the oligarch families, while the placement of the financial node is closer to the Medici-aligned families, providing some evidence to support the hypothesis that the Medici family acted as a middleman in Florentine society, as suggested by Padgett and Ansell [74].

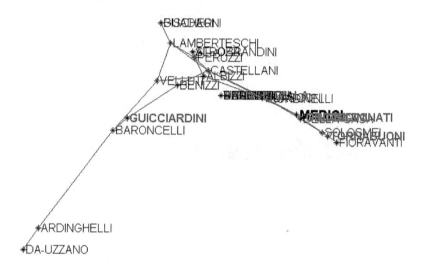

Figure 4.2: The embedding of the Florentine families based on financial relationships and undirected edges

Edge prediction

Edge prediction uses the structure of the embedding and, in particular, the existence of Euclidean distance as an encoding of similarity, to predict pairs of nodes that are not already connected but for which an edge is plausible.

Edge prediction is a nice illustration of how social networks integrate local information into a global whole which then has local implications. The two nodes for which a joining edge is recommended are detected as similar because of all of the other nodes and edges in the entire social network, and their mutual similarities.

Although the embedding is quite cluttered, we can get insights by computing the pairwise distances. One of the shortest distances is between the Pepi and Scambrilla families. Castellani is the only family that has a relationship (marriage) with them. Since the Pepi and Scambrilla families have the same connections, they are embedded in the same place, suggesting that they play effectively equivalent roles in the social system of Florence and so should have an edge between them.

The Strozzi and Medici families are quite remote from one another in this social network, but the embedding suggests that, if they make a connection, it is significantly more likely to be a marriage connection rather than a financial connection — the distances between them in the embedding are 0.124 (personal) and 0.145 (financial). That is indeed what happened: the Strozzis married into the Medicis, but not until years later.

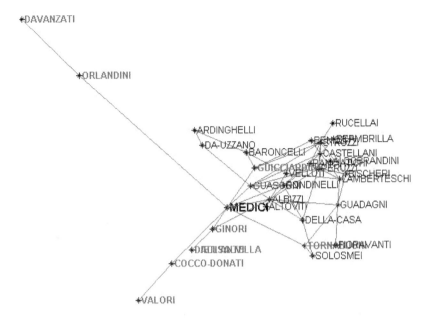

Figure 4.3: Undirected embedding of Florentine families ignoring edge types

4.4 Summary

Our first use of the layered-subgraph embedding approach has been used to embed and analyze graphs with multiple edge types, where the edges are weighted but undirected. The construction requires allocating weights to the new edges that connect different versions of the same node. We have motivated this by appealing to the intuition of lazy random walks as a formal justification, and to the reality that individuals who are influential in one domain are often influential in others as a pragmatic justification.

We have illustrated how this approach works with a practical example, which we will revisit throughout the book, the power structure around the Medici family in 15th Century Florence. The embedding provides a more nuanced representation of the social network of the city than those based on either the financial or personal networks alone, and more than the social network obtained by simply combining them. We have also illustrated how edge prediction can be generalized to predict not only the potential existence of an edge, but also its probable type.

Notes

There have been two different ways to frame the problem of typed edges based on different assumptions. One way to consider the problem is to assume that the underlying graph structures of the different edge types in a dataset are somehow consistent with one another. Another way to consider this problem is to assume that each edge

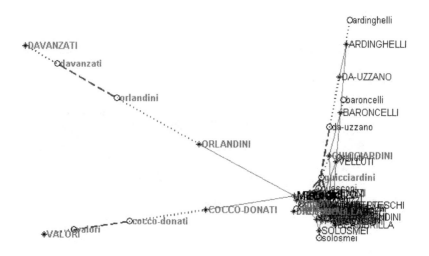

Figure 4.4: Embedding of Florentine families with typed but undirected edges; there are now two versions of each node. Financial layer: solid lines; personal layer: dashed lines; vertical edges: dotted lines. Little can be seen of the central structure in this view, but zoomed-in versions are shown in subsequent figures.

type graph has its own underlying structure, but is influenced by others.

Most attempts to represent graphs with different edge types are based on the first assumption, and two common strategies can be applied. One strategy is to combine all the subgraphs of each edge type into a consistent whole, and then do further analysis based on the new graph. Directly adding all subgraphs together is the easiest way. However, when the density of each edge type is quite different, the final embedding of the whole graph tends to be based mostly on the structure of the edge type with the greatest density. Thus, some kind of normalization is usually the first step. For example, Zhou and Burges [119] combined random walk normalized Laplacian matrices of different views with user-determined weights for the views. Xia et al. [107] used iterative techniques to optimize the weights of different views, and then combined symmetric normalized Laplacian matrices into a whole. Cheng and Zhao [16] combined the distances in each separate Laplacian embedding to create a completely new similarity matrix and then repeated the spectral clustering of this matrix to produce the final embedding. Muthukrishnan et al. [66] fused all subgraphs together using a regularization framework over edges in multiple graphs, and then applied the Laplacian approach. Dong et al. [28] and Tao et al. [97] used a similar way to merge the Laplacian matrices of each subgraph into a general Laplacian matrix for embedding. The problem with this strategy is deciding how the individual representations should be combined, and there is usually not enough information to

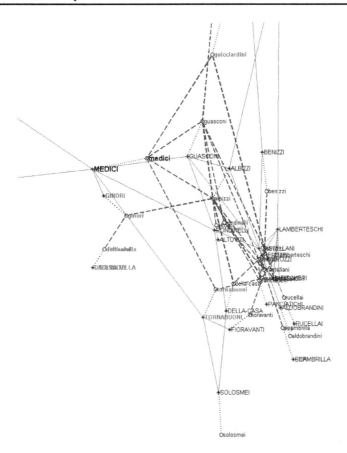

Figure 4.5: Zooming in to the embedded Florentine families. Financial layer: solid lines; personal layer: dashed lines; vertical edges: dotted lines.

decide this in a principled way.

The other strategy is to find an optimum embedding that somehow represents all the subgraphs, whose values are determined using a regularization framework. For example, Tang et al. [96] used an approach that they called Linked Matrix Factorization to decompose each graph and then found the common factor for all graphs as a low-dimensional embedding of entities characterized by multiple graphs. Dong et al. [27] used an approach to find a set of vectors that are close to all the random walk Laplacian eigenvectors of all subgraphs, and then used the first k vectors as a common representation. Kumar et al. [46, 47] used iterative techniques to find low-dimensional embeddings of each subgraph which were highly similar to each other. Regularization is problematic because it is not clear whether we should build a global regularizer that applies equally to edges of each type and to the edges that connect different subgraphs, or whether each subgraph should have its own regularizer and

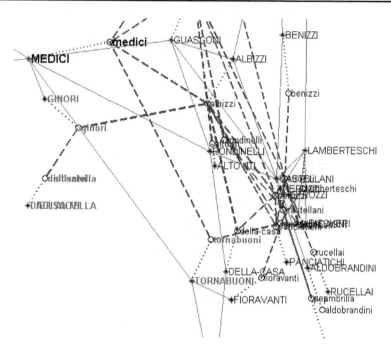

Figure 4.6: Zooming in even further. Financial layer: solid lines; personal layer: dashed lines; vertical edges: dotted lines.

there should also be another regularizer for connecting different edge types. There do not seem to be compelling arguments for any of the above possibilities, let alone a way to relate them to one another.

The approach in this chapter was first described in Skillicorn and Zheng [87].

Chapter 5

Modelling asymmetric relationships

We have seen that there are advantages to modelling connections between nodes in a social network as edges of qualitatively different types. We now turn to settings in which it is appropriate to represent edges as having a direction, *from* one node *to* another node. Arguably this is actually the normal case. Experiments with social groups have shown that relationships are rarely symmetric; A believes that B is a close friend, while B believes that A is an acquaintance. There are also many settings where direction is obvious: a hierarchical organization such as some businesses and militaries, where relationship has an element of command; and networks where relationships reflect influence or information flow from one participant to the other.

As a practical matter, edges with a direction can be represented straightforwardly in an adjacency matrix, by allowing different weights on the ijth and jith edges. However, the adjacency matrix is now no longer symmetric. The spectral embedding technique we have used so far requires that the adjacency matrix, and so the Laplacian derived from it, are symmetric, so we must develop a new method that deals with this issue. We will develop a layer approach that handles directed graphs, but first we will review the state-of-the-art approach to spectral embedding of directed graphs.

5.1 Conventional directed spectral graph embedding

The conventional way to embed directed graphs is due to Chung [20]. Let W be the asymmetric adjacency matrix of the directed graph, and P the random-walk matrix obtained, as usual, by dividing each row by the corresponding row sum.

The following Rayleigh quotient provides some insight into what a good embedding should be like. We want to find embeddings, f, for which this function is small:

$$R(f) = \frac{\sum_{i,j=1}^{n} \pi_i P_{ij}(f_i - f_j)^2}{2\sum_{i=1}^{n} \pi_i f_i^2}$$

where P is the random-walk matrix and π is a measure of the importance of the ith node. In other words, this function tries to place well-connected important nodes close together.

P is defined by $P_{ij} = W_{ij}/d_i$ or, if D is the diagonal degree matrix, by $P = D^{-1}W$ This implies $d'P = \mathbf{1}'DP = \mathbf{1}'W = d'$ for the undirected case. π is computed as the principal left eigenvector of the transition matrix P with the corresponding eigenvalue 1, that is $\pi'P = \pi'$. Thus $\pi = d/\sum_{i=1}^{n} d_i$ for undirected graphs. In other words, for an undirected graph, the degree of a node is directly interpretable as its importance. The importance of a node is proportional to its accessibility to a random walker, which is equivalent to the proportion of time a random walker spends at that node.

In a directed graph, the relationship between degree and importance is more subtle. From a random-walk perspective, the fraction of time that a random walker spends at a particular node does not just depend on the total weight of its incoming edges. It also depends on how accessible its upstream nodes are, which in turn depends on the weight of the incoming edges to those upstream nodes, and so on. Thus importance is a property that depends on the global structure of the network, rather than being a mostly local property as it is for an undirected graph.

The π_i in this Rayleigh quotient plays the role of degree in earlier Laplacians. It captures the property of global importance, and therefore requires that the embeddings of important nodes count for more in the objective function that the Rayleigh quotient describes. Computing these π_is requires a global computation; they are the elements of the principal left eigenvector of the transition matrix, P. Call this eigenvector Π. (Note the similarity to the PageRank calculation used for ranking by Google.)

Based on this Rayleigh quotient, we define the *symmetric* Laplacian as:

$$\hat{L}_{dir} = I - \frac{\Pi^{1/2}P\Pi^{-1/2} + \Pi^{-1/2}P'\Pi^{1/2}}{2}$$

and the combinatorial Laplacian as:

$$L_{dir} = \Pi - \frac{\Pi P + P'\Pi}{2}$$

Both of these Laplacians are more sophisticated versions of symmetrizing a matrix by adding its transpose; in this case adjusting the entries based on the global importance of each node.

It can be proved that

$$R(f) = \frac{< fL_{dir}, f >}{< f\Pi, f >} = \frac{< g\hat{L}_{dir}, g >}{< g, g >}$$

where $g = \Pi^{1/2}f$.

Furthermore, it is easy to prove that both Laplacians have the same eigenvalues and eigenvectors as the conventional Laplacian when the adjacency matrix is undirected.

Since Chung's approach is conceptually rigorous and has provable properties, it is widely used for analyzing directed networks, for example Zhou et al. [120, 121], Zhou and Burges [119], Huang et al. [40], Chen et al. [15], and Skillicorn and Zheng [88].

An extra technical step is required for most directed graphs. A random walker in a directed graph can become trapped at a sink node, one that has only incoming edges. However, this is easy to detect because the row corresponding to that node has no non-zero entries. The same problem, however, can happen for an entire region of the graph — there are no outgoing edges from the region — and this is expensive to detect in practice. The conventional solution is known as the "Google trick". It consists of adding a constant ε matrix to the transition matrix, allowing a random walker to escape from any node of the graph to any other node, with some low probability, ε.

In its use by Google, this constant matrix models the behavior of web users who visit one page and then change to another by some process other than following links (perhaps typing in a URL directly, or using a bookmark). For social networks with directed relationships, the semantics of this constant matrix is more problematic. For example, if the edges are directed because they are modelling influence, then a constant matrix models the ability of every node to influence, weakly, every other node. It is not obvious what this might represent; perhaps something like mass media. If edges are directed because they are modelling positive affect, then a constant matrix models a global positive feeling. These are strong assumptions which may not be appropriate in social network applications.

The use of the Google trick also has two substantial computational drawbacks. First, the adjacency matrix is now dense which prevents the use of sparse matrix techniques for the eigendecompositions, and so increases the computational time and storage required. Second, outlying nodes tend to be placed in positions folded back towards the center of the embedding. This is because, although the added edges are individually weak, there are many of them. This tends to make such nodes seem to be, misleadingly, more important than they actually are.

After these refinements, Chung's spectral embedding uses these steps [20]:

1. Convert the non-symmetric adjacency matrix of the (directed) social network to a random walk matrix, R, by dividing each row by the row sum.

2. Add a constant matrix, ε to R, and compute its Laplacian.

3. Compute the principal left eigenvector of this Laplacian matrix and create a diagonal matrix, Π, with these values on the diagonal.

4. Form the symmetric matrix:

$$L = I - \frac{\Pi^{1/2} L_{rw} \Pi^{-1/2} + \Pi^{-1/2} L'_{rw} \Pi^{1/2}}{2}$$

and use an eigendecomposition to embed L in the standard way.

The drawbacks of the Chung approach are not trivial. Computational times are long, even for networks of moderate size, and the resulting embedding, as we shall show, has significant distortions.

5.2 Directed edge layered approach

We now develop a new way to embed directed networks, using our layer intuition, but in a different way than the way it was used for typed networks. The common theme is that we transform information about the properties of edges into patterns of connection of those edges, which can then be simplified to undirected, untyped, although still weighted, edges.

The key idea, as before, is to split each node v into two versions, v_{in} and v_{out}. The *in* versions are placed in one layer, and the *out* versions in another.

If we have a directed edge from, say, node p to node q, then it becomes an *undirected* edge from p_{out} to q_{in}. The *out* versions of each node are the connection points for the outgoing edges of directed edges, and the *in* versions are the connection points for the incoming edges. The connection pattern encodes the direction of the edges, allowing them to be undirected in the expanded graph. The original directed edges become connections *between* a layer containing the outgoing versions of each node, and a layer containing the incoming versions of each layer.

As before, we add edges ("between the layers" but vertically) to connect v_{in} and v_{out}. The weight associated with these edges is the sum of the in-degree and out-degree of the nodes v_{in} and v_{out}, because this weight provably ensures that both v_{in} and v_{out} will be placed in the same cluster by any reasonable clustering of the larger graph, and also ensures that the result of the directed embedding agrees with the embedding of the graph if edge directions are ignored.

Unlike the previous embedding of typed edges, *all* of the edges connect from one layer to the other; those from the original graph as "diagonal" edges, and the added edges as "vertical" edges. As a result, the graph is bipartite (there are no connections within each layer).

The resulting $2n$-node graph is symmetric, and so standard spectral embedding techniques can be used to embed it. Formally, let W be the (non-symmetric) adjacency matrix of the directed graph, and D_{in} and D_{out} be the diagonal matrices of the in-degrees and out-degrees, respectively: $din_1, ...din_n$ and $dout_1, ...dout_n$. Let M be the adjacency matrix of the larger graph in which nodes have been split into *in* and *out* copies. M is a $2n \times 2n$ matrix defined as

$$M = \begin{pmatrix} 0 & W + D_{in} + D_{out} \\ W' + D_{in} + D_{out} & 0 \end{pmatrix}.$$

Let T be the diagonal degree matrix of M with the degrees $t_{1out}, ...t_{nout}, t_{1in}, ...t_{nin}$, where $t_{iout} = din_i + 2*dout_i$ and $t_{iin} = 2*din_i + dout_i$. The corresponding Laplacian matrices are:

$$L_d = T - M,$$

$$L_{drw} = I - T^{-1}M.$$

An eigendecomposition is used to embed L_d or L_{drw} in the standard way.

Computationally, the matrix is now $2n \times 2n$ but, as before, the only new non-zero entries are the diagonal submatrices representing the "vertical" edges. Thus the matrix is sparse, only one eigendecomposition is required, and so execution times are much smaller than for the Chung technique.

There are two points corresponding to each node, one corresponding to its *in* version and one corresponding to its *out* version. This has two new, substantial benefits:

1. The distance between the two versions of a node captures how much *asymmetric flow* there is through that node. If the flow primarily originates and terminates in the same subset of other nodes, then this flow will be small. However, if it originates in one subset of nodes and terminates in another, this flow will be large (and the distance between versions will also be large). Thus, this distance in the embedding defines a new, and useful, form of *flow betweenness*.

2. Directed edge prediction now becomes possible. For example, if an *in* version of one node is embedded close to an *out* version of another node and they are not connected in the original graph, then a *directed* edge from the node associated with the out-node to the node associated with the in-node can be predicted.

Both of these properties are shown in the embedding of a directed cycle, shown in Figure 5.1.

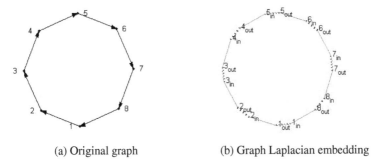

| (a) Original graph | (b) Graph Laplacian embedding |

Figure 5.1: A circle graph Laplacian embedding in two dimensions. The solid edges are the original edges of the directed graph and the dashed edges are the edges connecting the versions of each node.

As expected, there is net flow through each node, shown by the length of the dashed edges connecting the two versions of each node. Also, for example, 1_{out} and 3_{in} are closer than 1_{in} and 3_{out}. So if we were to predict an edge between nodes 1 and 3, we would predict that it would be directed from 1 to 3, rather than the converse, which is clearly correct.

5.2.1   Validation of the new directed embedding

The above example shows how our approach works. To justify this approach, we demonstrate that the following two properties hold:

- The connection between the *in* and *out* versions of each node is strong enough to keep them in the same cluster if the graph is partitioned or clustered.

- When applied to an undirected graph, the result is the same as for the conventional Laplacian embedding.

The proofs of these properties are as follows:

Property 1: Consistency in clustering

The proofs can be found in Appendices A and B.

Property 2: Consistency with the undirected Laplacian

For an undirected graph, if λ is an eigenvalue of L with eigenvector f, λ is an eigenvalue of L_d with eigenvector $\left[\begin{smallmatrix} f \\ f \end{smallmatrix}\right]$.

Since matrix W is symmetric for an undirected graph, $W = W'$ and $din_i = dout_i = d_i$. Thus, $T = \left[\begin{smallmatrix} 3D & 0 \\ 0 & 3D \end{smallmatrix}\right]$, and

$$
\begin{aligned}
L_d \begin{bmatrix} f \\ f \end{bmatrix} &= \left(T - \begin{bmatrix} 0 & W + D_{in} + D_{out} \\ W' + D_{in} + D_{out} & 0 \end{bmatrix} \right) \begin{bmatrix} f \\ f \end{bmatrix} \\
&= \begin{bmatrix} 3D & -W - 2D \\ -W - 2D & 3D \end{bmatrix} \begin{bmatrix} f \\ f \end{bmatrix} \\
&= \begin{bmatrix} (3D - W - 2D)f \\ (-W - 2D + 3D)f \end{bmatrix} \\
&= \begin{bmatrix} (D - W)f \\ (D - W)f \end{bmatrix} \\
&= \lambda \begin{bmatrix} f \\ f \end{bmatrix}
\end{aligned}
$$

Furthermore, the eigenvalues of the other "half" of L_d are β with eigenvectors $\left[\begin{smallmatrix} g \\ -g \end{smallmatrix}\right]$ if β is an eigenvalue of $5D + W$ with eigenvector g. Based on the graph cut point of view, the eigenvector $\left[\begin{smallmatrix} g \\ -g \end{smallmatrix}\right]$ will separate the *in* and *out* copies into two different groups. The corresponding cut value is so big that we would not consider it as a good partition. It is the same with the eigenvalue β. Therefore, a good embedding of the Laplacian matrix L_d for an undirected graph is the same as the Laplacian matrix L.

For an undirected graph, if λ is an eigenvalue of L_{rw} with eigenvector f, $\lambda/3$ is an eigenvalue of L_{drw} with eigenvector $\left[\begin{smallmatrix} f \\ f \end{smallmatrix}\right]$.

Since $L_{rw} = I - D^{-1}W$,

$$L_{drw} \begin{bmatrix} f \\ f \end{bmatrix}$$

$$= \begin{bmatrix} I & -\frac{D^{-1}}{3}(W+Din+Dout) \\ -\frac{D^{-1}}{3}(W'+Din+Dout) & I \end{bmatrix} \begin{bmatrix} f \\ f \end{bmatrix}$$

$$= \begin{bmatrix} I & \frac{-D^{-1}W-2I}{3} \\ \frac{-D^{-1}W-2I}{3} & I \end{bmatrix} \begin{bmatrix} f \\ f \end{bmatrix}$$

$$= \begin{bmatrix} \frac{I-D^{-1}W}{3}f \\ \frac{I-D^{-1}W}{3}f \end{bmatrix}$$

$$= \frac{\lambda}{3} \begin{bmatrix} f \\ f \end{bmatrix}$$

The eigenvalues of the other "half" of L_{drw} are $2 - \frac{\lambda}{3}$ with eigenvectors $\begin{bmatrix} f \\ -f \end{bmatrix}$. Since $0 \le \lambda \le 2$, the eigenvalues $\lambda/3$ are always smaller than the eigenvalues $2 - \frac{\lambda}{3}$. Therefore, a good embedding of the Laplacian matrix L_{drw} for an undirected graph is the same as the Laplacian matrix L_{rw}.

5.2.2 SVD computation for the directed edge model approach

The larger matrix constructed by replicating each node into in and out versions has edges only between the layers, and so represents a bipartite graph. The eigenvalues and eigenvectors of L_{drw} (the generalized eigenproblem of $L_d u = \lambda T u$) can be solved using singular value decomposition (SVD). The proof is similar to the normalized spectral technique for bipartite graphs [23]. The size of the matrices for SVD is the same as the size of the original adjacency matrix, and the computational time is also the same as conventional Laplacian approaches.

The directed spectral embedding algorithm for connected graphs can be computed in these four steps.

Algorithm: Given a directed adjacency matrix W, and a choice of $k - 1$ dimensions for embedding.

---

1. Compute the diagonal matrices of outgoing and incoming degrees from W: D_{out} and D_{in}.

2. Add directed edges to connect the *in* and *out* versions of each node, and normalize as:

$$A = (2D_{out} + D_{in})^{-1/2} * (W + D_{out} + D_{in}) * (2D_{in} + D_{out})^{-1/2}.$$

3. Compute the first k singular values α_i and the corresponding singular vectors u_i and v_i of A.

4. Modify and combine the embedding vectors as:

$$f_i = \begin{bmatrix} (2D_{out} + D_{in})^{-1/2} u_i \\ (2D_{in} + D_{out})^{-1/2} v_i \end{bmatrix}.$$

and embed the graph into $k-1$ dimensions by using the $k-1$ vectors f_i (omitting the trivial vector $\mathbb{1}$ with singular value 1).

The range of eigenvalues λ of the directed Laplacian matrix L_{drw} is from 0 and 2. However, the range of singular values α of matrix A is between 0 and 1. The eigenvalues of the other "half" of L_{drw} are $\lambda_{2n-i} = 2 - \alpha_i$ with eigenvectors

$$f_{2n-i} = \begin{bmatrix} (2D_{out} + D_{in})^{-1/2} u_i \\ -(2D_{in} + D_{out})^{-1/2} v_i \end{bmatrix}$$

In contrast to previous approaches, our directed graph embedding has the following advantages:

1. The directional information about each original edge is now encoded by the structure of the (undirected) connections between the new versions of the original nodes; that is, the graph to be embedded is now undirected. This avoids the need to use the Google trick to address reducibility, and therefore keeps the graph sparse. This is a great performance advantage.

2. Because the (expanded) graph is undirected, there is no need to compute a left eigenvector to determine each node's importance. Degree in the undirected graph, a local property, suffices.

These two advantages are obtained at the cost of making the graph nominally twice as big, but the additional cost remains linear in the original size of the network; we can use sparse matrix decomposition techniques, and so this adds only a small constant factor.

5.3 Applications of directed networks

We have shown that our methods are mathematically well behaved and motivated. As applications of our methods for embedding and clustering, we use a synthetic dataset and four real-world directed networks to demonstrate the effectiveness of the directed graph spectral embedding. By comparing our results with Chung's directed embeddings we show how our approach is an improvement.

In the embedding of directed networks, there are two versions of each node, one corresponding to incoming edges and the other to outgoing edges. The position of each member of a pair is important, but so is their distance from one another —

the greater this distance, the more different their upstream and downstream sets of neighbors.

For larger networks, where visualizations of the graph become cluttered and hard to understand, tabulating edge lengths can indicate regions of the graphs whose nodes are unusual in some way. For example, connected nodes that are placed far from one another are anomalous, since connection and closeness are naturally associated. However, edges on the periphery of the graph tend to be long simply because of their poor connectivity to the rest of the graph. We therefore need a measure that differentiates *expected* long edges from *unexpected* long edges. An unexpected long edge is one that is being "pulled" because different subsets of its neighbors all want it to be close to them.

The embedding of a graph can be considered as the fixed point of a relaxation in which edge weight is proportional to internode pull. Therefore, globally, the distance between two nodes reflects their global dissimilarity. In other words, *length* $\propto 1/\textit{edgeweight}$. We call the product of *length* and *edgeweight* the *normalized edge length* of an edge. Normalized edge lengths should be roughly constant for all "normal" edges of the graph. Edges for which this value is far from average, especially much larger than average, are those whose local environment is distorted. Such edges are likely to connect nodes of special interest. For example, a node that acts as a "broker" between two disparate subgroups will tend to have the relevant edges pulled towards the subgroups; these edges will tend to be longer in the embedding than their edge weight and local neighborhood would suggest.

We can now see why edge weight prediction is much harder than edge (existence) prediction. For the ordinary or typical regions of the network, the closeness of two unconnected nodes may indeed reflect the strength of the potential relationship between them, and a weight prediction might be quite accurate. However, in less typical regions of the network, those for which the normalized edge lengths are far from average, the embedded distance is no longer an estimate of intensity. The problem is that it is difficult to tell these regions apart since a deviation in normalized edge length is a property of an edge and not of a region. In other words, a network region may be typical (embedded edge lengths match edge weights), distorted (most embedded lengths deviate from edge weights), or a hybrid (embedded lengths mostly match edge weights, but some edge lengths deviate from their expected lengths).

The difference between a node that brokers symmetric flow and one that brokers asymmetric flow is shown in Figure 5.2. The graph consists of two directed cliques connected to one another in two ways. One connection (via node 12) is bidirectional; the other (via node 11) is one-directional. The embedding shows, by the length of the dotted line, the strength of the asymmetric flow through node 11, in comparison to the flow through node 12.

Our second example is a more complex synthetic dataset. It consists of two circles in two dimensions, with small random variations for each node, and a joining bridge, shown in Figure 5.3(a), with the subgraphs given different shadings. Each node is connected to its five nearest neighbors by outgoing directed edges. Hence the nodes in the bridge are better connected to the adjacent circle nodes than those circle nodes are connected to nodes in the bridge. Figure 5.3(b) shows the new

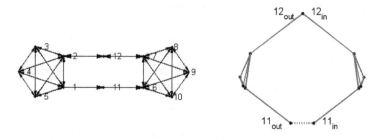

(a) Graph with two clusters   (b) Embedding of the two broker nodes

Figure 5.2: The difference between symmetric and asymmetric flow

directed embedding, and Figure 5.3(c) shows Chung's directed embedding of this graph with the bridge nodes highlighted. Visually, our approach separates the three groups, but the Chung embedding is not as revealing, especially for the bridge nodes. Figures 5.3(d) and 5.3(e) show the nodes shaded by average normalized embedded lengths of incident edges, and length of *in-out* edges. Figure 5.3(d) shows that the nodes that have longer average lengths usually occur in gaps in the two-dimensional map. Figure 5.3(e) shows that the node at the bottom of bridge has the longest *in-out* length in the embedding and therefore is the most important node for net flow. This node is not only one of the bridge nodes, but it also connects to the inner circle nodes, while the inner circle nodes tend not to connect to it.

U.K. university dataset

To further compare the quality of the different directed Laplacian embeddings, we use four real-world datasets. First, we use the social network of the academic staff of a Faculty in a U.K. university, consisting of three separate schools. This data was used by Nepusz et al. [68]. Figure 5.4 shows the embeddings of the network, shaded by schools, in two dimensions. From the visualization, it can be seen that our directed embedding is better than Chung's, even though both detect the difference in school affiliation.

Florentine families with edges directed by power

Second, we return to the social network of Florentine families in the 15th Century. For financial interactions between families, we direct the edges to represent power — a family that lends money to another is surely the more powerful of the two. Similarly, we direct the edges representing marriages between families. Here it is less clear how to direct the edges to capture information about which family is more powerful. We direct them from the family providing the son to the family providing the daughter. The families and their alignment are shown in Table 4.1.

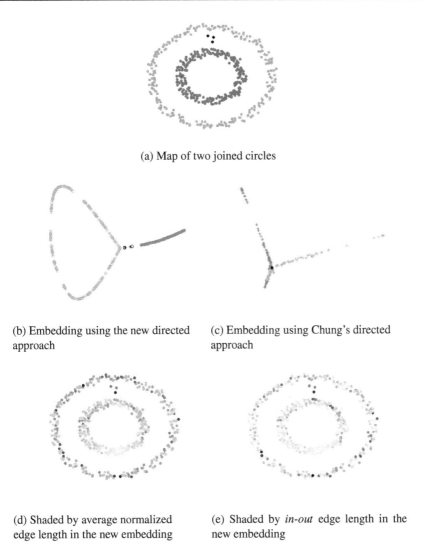

(a) Map of two joined circles

(b) Embedding using the new directed approach

(c) Embedding using Chung's directed approach

(d) Shaded by average normalized edge length in the new embedding

(e) Shaded by *in-out* edge length in the new embedding

Figure 5.3: Embeddings of synthetic datasets

Figure 5.5(a) shows the directed graph embedding using Chung's directed approach in three dimensions. There is a clear separation between the Medici group and oligarch families, except for Guicciardini and Tornabuoni. Medici is located in the center and is the key family that connects the two blocs. The Medici group forms three long arms in the embedding.

This embedding shows that the oligarch families are well connected, since they are all placed close to one another; but the Medici group is only weakly connected. This embedding is consistent with historians' views.

(a) New directed embedding

(b) Chung directed embedding

Figure 5.4: Network embeddings of UK university faculties

Names	in-out	average	Din	Dout
BISCHERI	19	45	5	4
GUADAGNI	50	75	6	6
FIORAVANTI	30	46	1	1
DALL'ANTELLA	13	36	0	1
DIETSALVI	13	38	1	0
DAVANZATI	55	**155**	0	1
ORLANDINI	78	**264**	2	0
COCCO-DONATI	49	134	3	0
VALORI	23	65	0	1
GUICCIARDINI	28	89	4	5
GINORI	36	64	6	3
TORNABUONI	**111**	70	4	3
MEDICI	**136**	147	6	19
ARDINGHELLI	42	67	1	2
DA-UZZANO	6	98	2	2
ALTOVITI	4	12	1	0
SOLOSMEI	7	40	2	2
RONDINELLI	18	70	5	4
GUASCONI	76	98	9	8
ALBIZZI	26	68	12	7
DELLA-CASA	26	64	3	3
PEPI	9	25	1	0
CASTELLANI	42	43	7	8
PERUZZI	**93**	52	6	9
SCAMBRILLA	9	25	1	0
BENIZZI	31	31	2	2
STROZZI	43	51	6	8
PANCIATICHI	43	33	2	1
ALDOBRANDINI	5	15	1	0
RUCELLAI	9	45	2	1
LAMBERTESCHI	8	52	5	6
BARONCELLI	55	77	3	2
VELLUTI	4	67	3	3
Means	36.3	68.6	3.4	3.4
Std	32.2	48.9	2.8	3.9

Table 5.1: Normalized edge lengths for Florentine families ($\times 1000$) and degrees

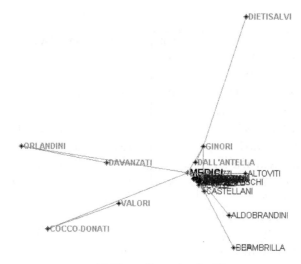

(a) Chung directed embedding

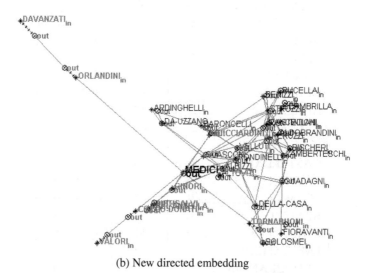

(b) New directed embedding

Figure 5.5: Network embeddings of Florentine families

One of the problems caused by the use of the "Google trick" is the folding back of the arms on the left of the embedding which makes, for example, Valori seem more important (central) than Cocco-Donati, when the opposite is the case.

Figure 5.5(b) shows the three-dimensional embedding using our new directed approach. Edges between the *in* and *out* versions of each individual node are drawn with hatched lines. More detail is evident within the oligarch cluster, and the spurious placement of poorly connected nodes (for example, Valori) does not occur. The embedding indicates that Medici tends to be the channel for net flow from oligarch families to the Medici group since the Medici *in* node is close to the oligarch families and the Medici *out* node is close to the Medici group.

We can use this data for edge prediction by computing and comparing the distances between the *out* version of a node and the *in* version of the other and the converse. For example, the Strozzi family were one of the most powerful of the oligarchs. The distance from Medici to Strozzi is 0.0458 and from Strozzi to Medici is 0.0413 so we would (weakly) predict that such an edge, if created, would point from Strozzi to Medici. At the time of this dataset, Medici was still relatively weak, so this seems plausible. A more asymmetric example is the relationship between the Tornabuoni family and the Guasconi family. The distance from Tornabuoni to Guasconi is 0.2186 while the converse distance is 0.2412, so we would predict the direction of such an edge to be from Tornabuoni to Guasconi.

While the figures could provide more detailed useful information if they could be rotated and zoomed into in real time, there is also useful information to be gleaned from measures computed about the embedding. The *in-out* normalized edge length and the average neighborhood edge length are given in Table 5.1. Recall that the *in-out* lengths reveal the amount of asymmetric flow through each (original) node, while the normalized edge length reveals the amount of local distortion associated with each (original) edge.

The Medici-aligned families tend to have long normalized edges since they are weakly connected. However, the fact that Medici has long normalized edges but high degrees makes it special. The average neighborhood edge length indicates that Medici is the key broker between the two blocs in the embedding. The *in-out* edge associated with Medici has the highest normalized value of all normalized added edges, indicating their importance to flow of influence, and the direction indicates that the oligarch families can influence the Medici-aligned families via the Medici family, but influence does not flow strongly in the reverse direction. Again, this is consistent with historians' views of this period.

Macaque brain connections

The third real-world dataset we use is the visuotactile brain areas and connection network model of the macaque monkey. The model was defined by Felleman & Van Essen [32] as well as Hilgetag et al. [39] and used by Négyessy et al. [67]. The model consists of 45 areas and 463 directed connections.

Figure 5.6 shows the embeddings of the network of the main cortical areas in two dimensions. Both embeddings reveal similar structure for this network, and there is a clear separation between visual and sensorimotor areas in both embeddings. The area VIP occupies a central position in both embeddings, and areas LIP, 7a, and 46 of the visual cortex are also close to the center. This is similar to the findings of Négyessy et al. [67]. However, in Figure 5.6(a) (Chung's embedding), the perirhinal cortex areas, 35 and 36, are far from the visual cortical areas, even though they have connections to both groups. In Figure 5.6(b) (our new embedding), areas 35 and 36 are not only closer to the visual cortical areas, but it becomes obvious that they tend to transmit information from visual cortical areas to sensorimotor areas.

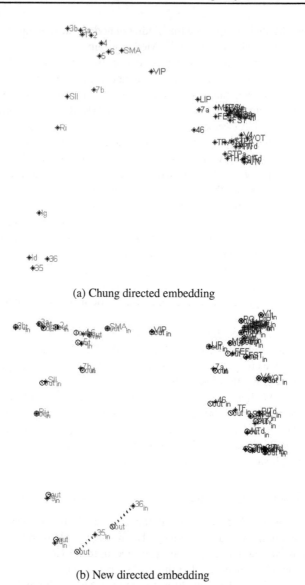

(a) Chung directed embedding

(b) New directed embedding

Figure 5.6: Network embeddings of Macaque monkey visuotactile brain

Table 5.2 shows that the average neighborhood edge lengths of areas VIP, LIP, 7a and 46 are also all well above average among the visual cortical areas. Area VIP has a small *in-out* normalized edge length, while area 46 has a large *in-out* length. The perirhinal cortex areas 35 and 36 have the longest *in-out* length in the sensori-motor areas. This means that they play roles not only in the connection between the two groups, but also in net flow from one group to the other.

Names	in-out	av	Din	Dout	Names	in-out	av	Din	Dout
V1	2	77	8	8	V2	92	80	13	15
V3	13	97	14	14	V3A	14	72	12	13
V4	17	189	20	20	V4t	32	77	8	9
VOT	4	139	5	5	VP	15	104	13	14
MT	13	88	16	16	MSTd/p	61	126	16	17
MSTl	17	101	11	8	PO	26	86	15	13
LIP	82	168	18	20	PIP	83	78	8	8
VIP	69	225	20	20	DP	24	95	10	10
7a	179	190	14	10	FST	111	142	18	17
PITd	28	152	5	8	PITv	181	162	11	9
CITd	26	121	3	6	CITv	7	118	8	8
AITd	91	141	9	5	AITv	38	119	7	5
STPp	17	178	10	10	STPa	25	115	4	5
TF	493	212	12	17	TH	128	150	9	12
FEF	432	158	18	20	**46**	566	225	16	20
3a	13	123	6	6	3b	6	114	4	4
1	71	123	7	8	2	126	130	10	10
5	192	158	10	10	Ri	5	237	4	4
SII	245	271	13	10	7b	206	223	12	10
4	319	132	9	8	6	21	148	10	10
SMA	13	149	8	8	Ig	170	321	6	5
Id	108	280	3	4	**35**	480	292	4	2
36	**773**	**336**	6	2					
Means	125.2	156.0	10.3	10.3	Std	173.0	67.4	4.7	5.2

Table 5.2: Normalized edge lengths for Macaque monkey visuotactile brain ($\times 10000$) and degrees

Panama papers

The Panama Papers are a set of documents leaked from a Panamanian law firm, Mossack Fonseca, detailing the setting up of a large number of shell companies for the purpose of tax avoidance (but also conceivably tax evasion, money laundering, and terrorist financing).

The files can be downloaded from: **cloudfront-files-1.publicintegrity.org/off shoreleaks/data-csv.zip**.

Figure 5.7 shows the basic structure of tax avoidance using a shell company. An individual with assets arranges with an intermediary to set up a shell company, and to give it assets. The apparent owners of the shell company now own these assets on behalf of the individual. Often these owners are simply "bearer" so that anyone who can authenticate himself or herself can remove assets from the shell company.

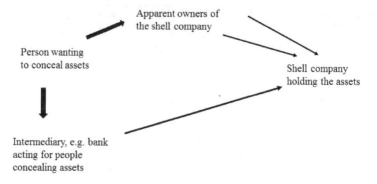

Figure 5.7: The basic structure of tax avoidance using a shell company

The 2016 version of the Panama Papers contains 1,040,331 nodes of three kinds: intermediaries, businesses like banks that set up shell companies; entities, the shell companies themselves; and officers, the apparent owners of these businesses. There are 4,505,738 directed edges. Edges are directed from intermediaries to the entities they create, and from the officers to the entities that they apparently own.

A social network this size is too large to examine exhaustively to try and understand it. We can, however, look at some of its connected components that are small enough to be intelligible. In particular, we will show that a directed network embedding is essential; without it, most of the structure disappears.

There are 10,425 connected components, but they shrink in size quite quickly — the 500th in rank connects only 30 nodes. The largest connected component connects 942,176 nodes. Its adjacency matrix is shown in Figure 5.8. Notice that it is asymmetric as expected.

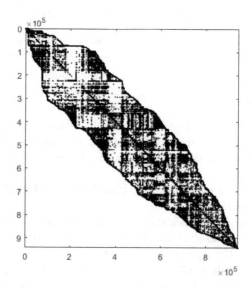

Figure 5.8: The adjacency matrix of the largest connected component

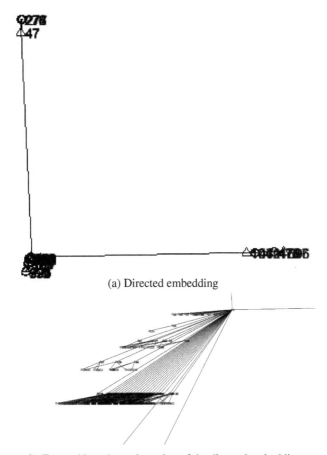

(a) Directed embedding

(b) Zoomed into the main region of the directed embedding

Figure 5.9: Network embeddings for the 6th component of the Panama Papers social network with directed edges. The out versions of each node are indicated by circles, the in versions by triangles, and layer nodes that are not connected in the graph are omitted.

The 2nd-largest connected component connects 1599 nodes, the next 1295, and so on. All of these components show one of a small set of connection patterns: a directed star with an intermediary at the center, or patterns connecting an intermediary and a set of officers in a few slightly different ways.

We begin with the 6th component, which exhibits the structure indicated in Figure 5.7. A single intermediary, Sociata Europenne de Banque in Luxemburg, sets up 139 shell companies in the British Virgin Islands (for example, Jeddi Industries). These shell companies are owned by 449 different owners, most being owned by 2 officers, almost all of whom are "bearer".

Figures 5.9 and 5.10 show the embeddings based on the social network with directed edges (using our new embedding), and the corresponding embeddings with

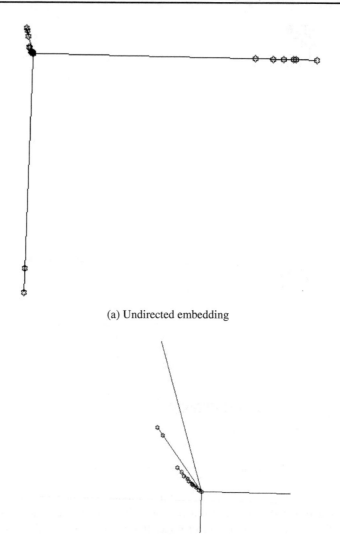

(a) Undirected embedding

(b) Zoomed into the main region of the undirected embedding

Figure 5.10: Network embeddings for the 6th component of the Panama Papers social network treating edges as undirected

the edges treated as undirected. The zoomed-in versions show what happens in the main region of the network. The intermediary node is the central one. From it, directed edges go to a cluster of entity nodes that are quite similar to one another. Officials are placed further from the center, and directed edges go from these officials to the entities they own. In contrast to the detailed structure in the directed embed-

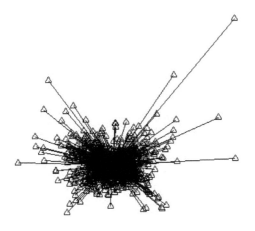

(a) Directed embedding

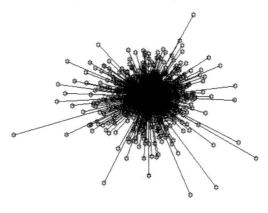

(b) Undirected embedding

Figure 5.11: Network embeddings for the 2nd component of the Panama Papers social network. The out versions of each node are indicated by circles, the in versions by triangles, and layer nodes that are not connected in the graph are omitted.

ding, the undirected version places entity and officer nodes in the same region, and there is no straightforward way to understand their structure.

The 2nd component is a pure star, with an intermediary at the center and 1598 entities, each connected to it by a single edge. The embeddings can be seen in Figure 5.11. The embeddings for the directed and undirected cases are quite similar, but the directed embedding makes it possible to see immediately that the structure is a star with outgoing directed edges.

The 41st component connects 201 nodes by 208 edges. The embeddings are shown in Figures 5.12 and 5.13. Although the directed and undirected versions are roughly the same, the directed version makes it possible to understand the structure

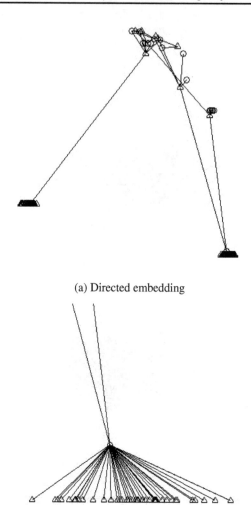

(a) Directed embedding

(b) Zoomed into the lower-right region of the directed embedding

Figure 5.12: Network embeddings for the 41st component of the Panama Papers social network with directed edges. The out versions of each node are indicated by circles, the in versions by triangles, and layer nodes that are not connected in the graph are omitted.

more clearly. The zoomed-in figure is for the lower-right structure in the directed embedding, and lets us see that this is another star-like structure with a single intermediary and a large number of quite similar branches from it.

The 44th component resembles the 6th component (Figures 5.14 and 5.15) with similarities between the outlier structure of the directed and undirected versions, but

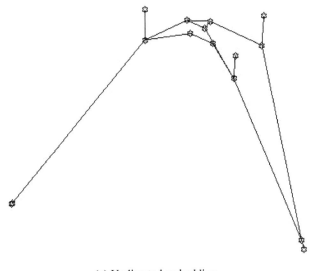

(a) Undirected embedding

Figure 5.13: Network embeddings for the 41st component of the Panama Papers social network treating the edges as undirected.

large differences in the fine-grained structure of the embeddings.

We can also get some understanding of the structure within the largest connected component by beginning from the subgraph of well-connected nodes, that is the subgraph all of whose edge weights exceed a given threshold. Table 5.3 shows how the number of nodes that remains decreases as the threshold on edge weights changes. Unsurprisingly, a threshold as small as 3 removes almost 90% of the nodes, so that there are many nodes (mostly individuals) who only have one or two connections to the network. However, there is clearly also a core set of nodes that interact with one another often, since increasing thresholds reduce the size of the graph only a little. For example, increasing the required threshold from 11 to 20 reduces the number of nodes in the subgraph by only about a third.

Using a threshold selects only the strong relationships in the social network, and there is no guarantee that these form a connected subset. For example, when the threshold of 300 is used, there are only 12 connected components that contain more than a single pair.

These 12 connected components all have similar structures. The example of the 10th component is shown in Figure 5.16. The embeddings of the undirected and directed networks are quite different. This particular component connects all of the different roles played by Circle Corporate Services as an officer. The structure is a complex chain where the nodes at one end of the boat-like shape have primarily outgoing edges, while those at the other end have primarily incoming edges. The plot of the edges between the two versions of each node, shown in Figure 5.17, show

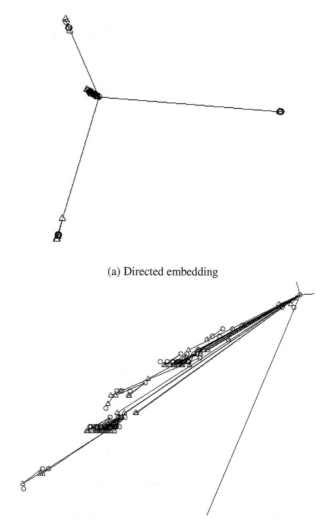

(a) Directed embedding

(b) Zoomed into the main region of the directed embedding

Figure 5.14: Network embeddings for the 44th component of the Panama Papers
social network. The out versions of each node are indicated by circles, the in versions
by triangles, and layer nodes that are not connected in the graph are omitted.

that the net flow is greatest for the two extremal nodes and smallest for those in the
(lower) center.

In contrast, the undirected embedding shows simply that there are a collection
of high degree nodes.

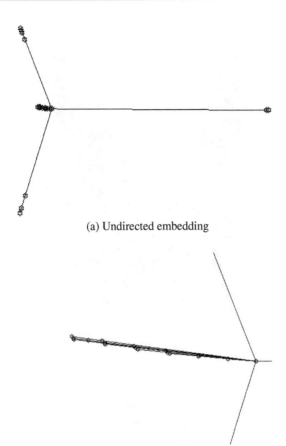

(a) Undirected embedding

(b) Zoomed into the main region of the undirected embedding

Figure 5.15: Network embedding for the 44th component of the Panama Papers social network treating edges as undirected

Threshold	Number of nodes
3	156,626
5	70,696
9	32,256
11	26,888
20	19,000
30	16,258
40	14,802
60	12,896
300	5542
600	3284

Table 5.3: Nodes remaining for choices of edge weight threshold

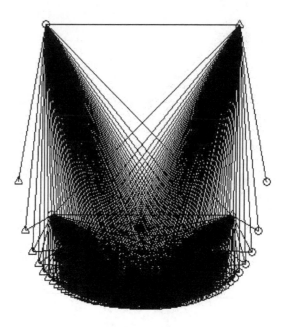

(a) Directed embedding

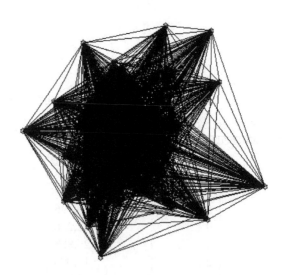

(b) Undirected embedding

Figure 5.16: Network embeddings for the 10th component of the subgraph of Panama Papers social network when an edge weight threshold of 300 is used. The out versions of each node are indicated by circles, the in versions by triangles, and layer nodes that are not connected in the graph are omitted.

Figure 5.17: Edges between the in and out versions of each node from the 10th component

5.4 Summary

A second way in which edges can have rich properties is by being directed — representing relationships that are of different intensities between the same two individuals. Such asymmetries are common in the real world. They cause difficulties for the spectral embedding approach, however, because the natural representation as an adjacency matrix is asymmetric, but spectral embeddings require symmetric matrices.

Chung's approach represents a well-motivated way to compute a symmetric Laplacian from an asymmetric adjacency matrix. However, it has two weaknesses: for most matrices, the "Google trick" has to be used to address reducibility, which in turn makes the matrices dense, with substantial performance costs; and as a result it tends to fold peripheral nodes inwards in the embedding, creating a misleading impression of their importance.

We have shown that a variation of the layer approach can avoid all of these problems. By creating a bipartite layered graph of undirected edges, the computations can remain sparse, the eigendecomposition can be done using SVD, and we get new information about net flow from the lengths of the edges between in and out versions of the same node.

Notes

The simplest way to convert a directed matrix into an undirected matrix is to ignore the directionality of edges via the transformation $\overline{W} = W + W'$, where W is the directed matrix and $\overline{W}$ is the resulting symmetric matrix. This ignores the useful information of edge direction.

By counting the common connections we can get a symmetric matrix; $\overline{W} = WW'$, $\overline{W} = W'W$ or $\overline{W} = WW' + W'W$. However, these methods only work well when it is true that the number of the nodes connected in common is a meaningful value of local similarity. If this assumption holds true, the degree-discounted symmetrization method [79] is suitable when the degree of nodes in a network varies.

Chung [20] was the first to present a formal model and proof for use of the Laplacian approach for directed graphs. This algorithm is based on random walk strategy in which a transition probability matrix P and its associated stationary distribution Π are used to reconstruct the symmetric matrix.

The weighted cut algorithm is a generalized version of the Laplacian approach for directed graphs and was developed by Meila and Pentney [57]. Instead of using the stationary distribution Π as the weight (importance) of each node, the weighted cut offers a more flexible way to define the node's weight used to symmetrize the adjacency matrix of a directed graph. It is always a problem to decide what node weights should be used to normalize and transform the adjacent matrix to a symmetric Laplacian matrix.

There are some modularity based community structure detection techniques for directed networks [13, 14, 49]. There is also an earlier version of a non-symmetric matrix decomposition spectral approach [110]. An overview of approaches for directed networks can be found in Malliaros and Vazirgiannis [56].

However, in the embedding of the above approaches, the directionality between nodes is lost. Thus in the embedding we know the distance between two nodes A and B, but cannot tell the direction of the original edge that joined them. This limits the analysis possible within the embedding.

The material in this chapter was first presented in Zheng and Skillicorn [111] and [114].

Chapter 6

Modelling asymmetric relationships with multiple types

We now turn to constructions that compose the layered models we have built so far. For example, we have seen that the Florentine families data captures different kinds of relationships (especially financial and social); but also directed relationships, representing family power or political leverage. Can we combine our approaches that have modelled each of these aspects separately, to model both at once?

Our basic strategy is to separate the edge properties into layers, as before, but to combine different sets of layers orthogonally. For example, if we create two versions of each node to connect two different edge types, and two versions to connect the in and out ends of directed edges, then we have *four* versions of each node. However, if we keep in mind the property that each version represents, then it is straightforward to connect the edges of the original social network to the right versions of each node.

In our example of the Florentine families, we would have four versions of each node, whose meanings are social-out, social-in, financial-out, and financial-in, and so a directed social edge would connect from a social-out node to a social-in node.

Of course, the "vertical" edges still need to be added. Here there are some choices, depending on the details of exactly how we compose the constructions. For example, we could imagine a clique connection between all four versions, or some subset connecting only versions from the same subconstruction. We also need to decide on principled ways to assign weights to these new edges.

6.1 Combining directed and typed embeddings

For simplicity, we continue to assume that there are two types of edges, which we will think of as colors (say, red and green). Adding more types complicates the explanation, but does not complicate the construction.

Each node of the original network is now replaced by four versions: red in, red out, green in, and green out. The resulting graph contains two layers representing the typed subgraphs, and two (orthogonal) layers representing the in and out layers.

Replacing each node of the original graph is a four-node nexus. The key to the construction is the additional edges that are present in this nexus.

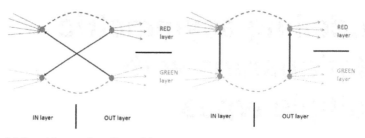

(a) Typed layers, then directed layers   (b) Directed layers, then typed layers

Figure 6.1: Added edges between the multiple versions of a single node

The construction could be done in two ways:

1. Split the data into typed subgraphs, and then apply a second split to represent the directed edges (shown in Figure 6.1(a));

2. Split the nodes into *in* and *out* versions, and then split them by type (shown in Figure 6.1(b)).

The different orders lead to different constructions and result in different embeddings. The question is which is the more reasonable? Separating the data by typed subgraphs, and then encoding the directed edges seems more plausible, because it embeds the *in* and *out* versions close to each other and therefore tends to keep the community structures in each layer.

6.2   Layered approach and compositions

Each node of the original graph is first replicated into red and green versions. We will assume that all of the edges in the red and green subgraphs are directed. If an edge is undirected, we can easily model it as a pair of directed edges with the same weight in opposite directions.

Now we add "vertical" directed edges between the versions of the same original node with different colors. (When there are more than two colors, this becomes a directed clique connecting the c versions of each node.) This generalizes the previous typed graph construction, where the vertical edges were undirected.

Each red node has incoming and outgoing red edges; each green node has incoming and outgoing green edges; and both have incoming and outgoing vertical (say, blue) edges.

We now have a directed graph that represents the typed structure of the graph, so we can temporarily forget the color coding, and treat it as an ordinary directed graph, for which we already know a construction.

In the second part, each of the nodes of this $2n \times 2n$ graph is replicated into an *in* version and an *out* version, using the construction in Section 4.4. The newly added blue edges, since they are directed, are also included in this next step. The new configuration of node versions and added edges that result is shown in Figure 6.1(a). We call this the *nexus* of versions of each original node.

The weights of the added edges are:

- weight(blue edge from green to red) = weight(green out)

- weight(blue edge from red to green) = weight(red out)

- weight(green dashed edge) = weight(total in) + weight(total out) = weight(green in) + 2 × weight(green out) + weight(red out)

- weight(red dashed edge) = weight(total in) + weight(total out) = weight(red in) + 2 × weight(red out) + weight(green out)

More formally, let $A_1, ..., A_c$ be the c $n \times n$ adjacency matrices of each of the typed subgraphs, and $D_1, ..., D_c$ be the diagonal matrices of the outgoing degrees of each. The embedding happens in three steps:

1. Bind together the versions of each node in the different colored layers to build a $cn \times cn$ adjacency matrix as:

$$
W = \begin{pmatrix}
A_1 & \cdots & \frac{1}{c-1}D_1 & \cdots & \frac{1}{c-1}D_1 \\
\vdots & \ddots & \vdots & \ddots & \vdots \\
\frac{1}{c-1}D_i & \cdots & A_i & \cdots & \frac{1}{c-1}D_i \\
\vdots & \ddots & \vdots & \ddots & \vdots \\
\frac{1}{c-1}D_c & \cdots & \frac{1}{c-1}D_c & \cdots & A_c
\end{pmatrix},
$$

2. Split each node in every version into *in* and *out* copies as:

$$
M = \begin{pmatrix}
0 & W + D^W_{in} + D^W_{out} \\
W' + D^W_{in} + D^W_{out} & 0
\end{pmatrix},
$$

where D^W_{in} and D^W_{out} are the diagonal *in* and *out* degree matrices of adjacency matrix W.

3. Convert M to a Laplacian matrix and use an eigendecomposition to embed it.

As before, all of the work involves connecting node versions by the appropriate edges, and defining weights for the new edges that were not present in the original graph. Once this is done, the resulting matrix is apparently larger, but does not contain more than a linear number of extra non-zero entries. The (sparse) eigendecomposition required to do the actual embedding is straightforward.

6.3   Applying directed typed embeddings

We will continue to use the Florentine families dataset, in its full richness with edges typed by social and financial connections, and directed by power.

In the embedding of networks that are both directed and have typed edges, there are *four* versions of each node, and it becomes increasingly difficult to interpret visualization of the figures. However, if a particular small set of nodes are of interest, and an interactive environment is available, it is still possible to learn much from the renderings themselves.

It is also useful to compute the distances between the embedded points and consider these distances as markers for interesting properties of nodes. Here we use the *normalized edge length* of the edges (mentioned earlier) for further comparison.

6.3.1   Florentine families

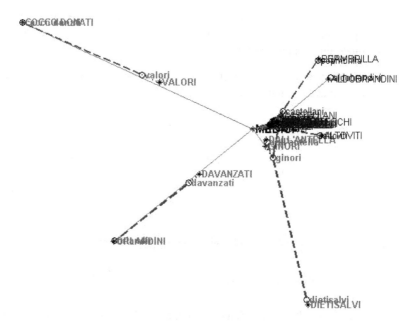

Figure 6.2: Embedding of the typed Florentine families network using the Chung directed embedding

The social network with typed edges and using Chung's approach for the directed edges is shown in Figure 6.2. This embedding structure is similar to Chung's directed embedding in Figure 5.5(a) but with the differentiation of the edge types. Edges connecting the two roles of each individual node are drawn as dotted. As in the undirected typed embedding in Figure 5.5(a), this embedding has misleading folded-back arms for poorly connected groups such as Valori.

The normalized length of the vertical edges can be interpreted as an indication

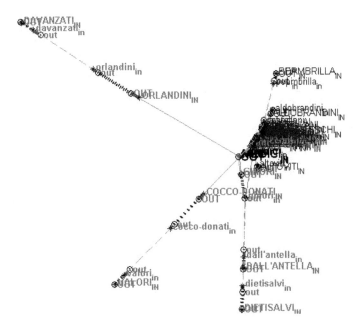

Figure 6.3: Embedding of the typed Florentine families network using our directed embedding

of how different the social (lowercase) and business (uppercase) roles of each family is in this context. Most families play similar roles in both the financial and personal domains, and their financial and personal points are close to one another. This is not surprising, given the close-knit nature of the Florentine community and the fact that these families would not have considered the finance and personal domains as distinct in the way that a modern social system might. However, the difference between the two roles of Medici is large; the personal placement of Medici is close to the oligarch families but the financial placement is close to the Medici-aligned families.

Figure 6.3 shows the embedding of the construction combining our directed approach with typed edges. Figure 6.4 is the zoomed-in version of Figure 6.3, and shows the relations among the four roles of the Medici family. The embedding is similar to previous ones, but shows more detailed structure. The pairwise normalized edge lengths and the average neighborhood edge lengths are given in Table 6.1.

The financial *out* to personal *in* of Medici has the highest normalized value of all normalized added edges. Medici is the key broker between the two blocs in the embedding and the direction indicates who influences whom. We can interpret this as evidence that the Medici family used its financial resources to influence personal relationships with the oligarch families.

There are also some other interesting nodes. For example, Guasconi has a high financial vertical edge, but low average neighborhood edge length, Castellani has a high personal vertical edge, and Castellani and Albizzi have relative high personal

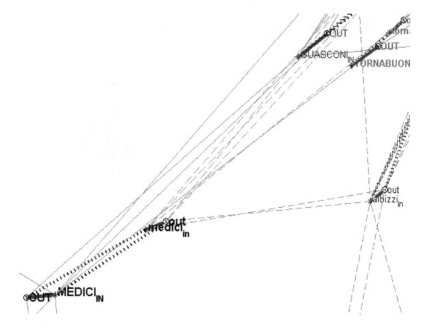

Figure 6.4: Zoom-in typed directed embedding of the Medici nodes

out to financial *in* edges but low average neighborhood edge lengths. The nodes
in the middle of the arms tend to have high edge lengths, for example Orlandini,
Cocco-Donati and Dall'antella.

6.3.2   Criminal groups

Two datasets describing real criminal organizations will also be used as examples.
The structure of both criminal networks were derived from judicial documents from
investigations of two 'Ndrangheta groups involved in drug trafficking in Italy. The
'Ndrangheta is a mafia organization that originated in Calabria, but has spread north
in Italy and now exists in several other countries as well. The organization is divided
into groups whose members tend to come from a localized geographical region and
share a strong internal culture [11, 12, 75, 76].

The data results from two investigations: Operation Chalonero, which targeted
a group bringing cocaine from South America to Italy via Spain, and Operation Stupor Mundi, which targeted a group bringing cocaine from South America to Italy via
Spain and The Netherlands. For convenience, we refer to the target groups by the
names of the associated investigation.

The cultural and purposive similarity of these two groups would suggest that
they would have similar social networks. Earlier work on techniques for identifying
the core subgroup that should be targeted by law enforcement [86] suggested that
this is not the case — the two groups are, surprisingly, structured in substantially

Names	FF	PP	FP	PF	Avg	Din	Dout
BISCHERI	2	20	10	12	20	5	4
GUADAGNI	16	47	57	94	49	6	6
FIORAVANTI	14	9	9	13	25	1	1
DALL'ANTELLA	29	254	108	166	453	0	1
DIETSALVI	27	**348**	209	157	765	1	0
DAVANZATI	28	245	102	158	440	0	1
ORLANDINI	387	241	314	338	622	2	0
COCCO-DONATI	509	330	427	444	**832**	3	0
VALORI	40	346	146	224	620	0	1
GUICCIARDINI	45	4	72	91	106	4	5
GINORI	98	42	213	**460**	462	6	3
TORNABUONI	64	33	10	20	55	4	3
MEDICI	302	191	**470**	264	283	6	19
ARDINGHELLI	1	3	19	10	20	1	2
DA-UZZANO	0	1	32	32	30	2	2
ALTOVITI	5	59	36	27	131	1	0
SOLOSMEI	3	1	7	4	22	2	2
RONDINELLI	88	69	69	19	79	5	4
GUASCONI	179	25	64	68	97	9	8
ALBIZZI	26	107	56	304	150	12	7
DELLA-CASA	4	66	15	15	39	3	3
PEPI	10	133	80	60	294	1	0
CASTELLANI	31	241	156	230	100	7	8
PERUZZI	42	32	43	60	68	6	9
SCAMBRILLA	10	133	80	60	294	1	0
BENIZZI	31	8	4	7	30	2	2
STROZZI	7	44	8	41	55	6	8
PANCIATICHI	8	108	6	16	64	2	1
ALDOBRANDINI	62	5	28	37	136	1	0
RUCELLAI	1	11	20	19	41	2	1
LAMBERTESCHI	7	18	39	11	30	5	6
BARONCELLI	5	3	17	8	22	3	2
VELLUTI	6	4	20	8	40	3	3
Means	63.3	96.4	89.3	105.3	196.2	3.4	3.4
Std	116.8	112.0	116.9	129.8	234.9	2.8	3.9

Table 6.1: Table of normalized edge lengths for Florentine families ($\times 10000$) and degree, where FF= financial in to out (red dash), PP= personal in to out (green dash), FP= financial out to personal in (blue), PF= personal out to financial in (blue), Avg= average neighborhood tension.

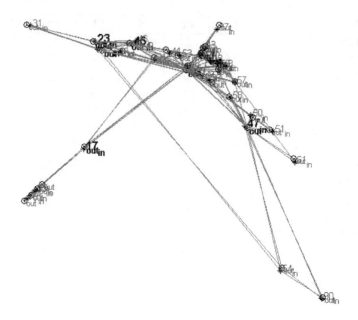

Figure 6.5: Our directed embedding of the Chalonero social network (untyped edges)

different ways.

Law enforcement targeted members of the group by intercepting telephone calls and by observing meetings. They had access to the content of telephone calls, and so were able eventually to determine with precision the functions of members of the group, and who its leadership were. We consider the social network as containing two different edge types: directed edges representing phone calls, and undirected edges representing participation in meetings. Thus, a meeting among three people is represented as a 3-clique (triangle) of undirected edges, a meeting among 4 people as an undirected 4-clique, and so on.

Chalonero organization

For both criminal networks we use only the individuals with at least two contacts and who participate in at least five communications. In the embeddings, we label the key nodes (known from the content of interceptions in the law enforcement investigation) with numbers in a larger font size.

In Chalonero, the general structures in the three embeddings of Figures 6.5, 6.6 and 6.7 are similar. N2 was one of the most active traffickers and the son of the group leader, N1. N2 is placed centrally in the embeddings. Furthermore, N2's four added edges are long, as showed in Table 6.2. The meeting edge lengths are significantly smaller than the others, because these edges are undirected.

N1 was a fugitive during the investigation, and he was unable to manage the group's activities directly. He never spoke on the telephone, preferring to issue orders

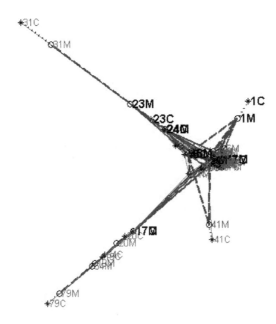

Figure 6.6: Embedding of the typed Chalonero social network using the Chung directed embedding (C = call version, M = meeting version)

through meetings with a few trusted contacts, including his son, N2. In Figure 6.6, N1 is placed far away from his son, N2, while the other two embeddings more accurately place him close to N2.

Table 6.2 shows that the normalized embedded lengths for the important group members are all well above average, and they could have been identified by this alone. Other members with large normalized edge lengths are explicable from their roles in the embedded network: N19 plays a role in the connection between the central group and the subgroup in the lower left; N31 and N79 are peripheral; but N54 has interestingly varying roles that are only made visible by the combined embedding in Figure 6.7.

Stupor Mundi organization

Figure 6.8 shows the embedding of the Stupor Mundi network using our directed typed approach. All the key individuals are placed close to each other. In this network, N46 was the boss; N35 was another high-status trafficker; and two brothers N27 and N28 were "assigned", respectively, to support them. Although N35 is out-ranked by N46, his large normalized edge lengths indicate his importance in communication both by telephone and in meetings. The two brothers, N27 and N28, the assistants, have significantly different normalized edge lengths. The small values for N27 indicate that his roles are consistent with each other, and he has low net flow influence also; but the large values of N28 indicate his importance in the network.

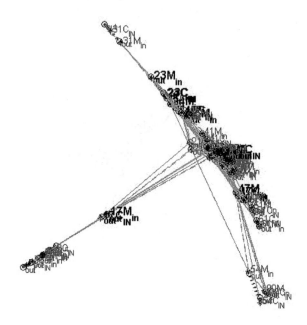

Figure 6.7: Embedding of the typed Chalonero social network using our directed embedding

This is partly the result of the complex role of his boss; but it is also known that N28 was, on one occasion, reproached by N46 for his conduct (he was trying to collect money to pay for a drug smuggling operation organized by N35, but opposed by N46). Some of the other large entries in Table 6.3 point to individuals who are peripheral but with interesting role differences (N120), and to "brokers" (N10 who embeds at the right-hand side of the left cluster).

6.4 Summary

Real-world social networks do not have edges with just one extra property; they are likely to have edges of many different kinds. We have shown how to extend the layer construction to handle edges of two different kinds — typed and directed — by composing the layer construction. These compositions now create many versions of each node, so the housekeeping to keep all of the connections straight requires some care, but the constructions themselves are straightforward. The same arguments that were used to justify the weights added to the newly created edges can be applied to the compositions.

The results now become increasingly difficult to understand by visualization, although in practice an analyst could rotate and zoom into the renderings to gain greater insight. Measures that capture the local distortions implicit in the embedding become increasingly useful as ways to highlight nodes that are playing some kind of

ID	CC	MM	CM	MC	Avg	Din	Dout
1	106	163	39	333	95	12	12
2	1470	109	1312	1352	383	153	207
17	199	55	79	180	455	36	15
19	597	107	473	182	276	9	23
23	1194	318	1859	773	697	37	41
24	561	18	244	340	332	28	30
31	370	109	83	228	505	8	5
45	232	34	278	316	326	32	37
47	304	55	108	125	228	49	32
54	11	24	107	151	132	3	5
79	94	33	24	64	110	6	5
87	23	2	14	18	27	4	2
Means	175.6	39.4	143.6	144.0	173.0	16.4	16.4

Table 6.2: Table of normalized edge lengths for Chalonero ($\times 10000$) and degree, where CC= call in to out (red dash), MM= Meet in to out (green dash), CM= call out to meet in (blue), MC= meet out to call in (blue), Avg= average neighborhood tension. Known important individuals are in bold; other individuals are those with interesting positions in the embedding.

ID	CC	MM	CM	MC	Avg	Din	Dout
3	339	22	124	136	295	39	37
10	195	189	605	73	493	12	11
15	303	6	68	58	231	10	7
16	740	237	636	299	412	14	22
23	551	104	327	226	392	279	297
24	424	51	349	299	133	210	180
27	10	15	8	30	18	14	12
28	226	24	437	374	159	161	150
34	268	73	16	40	234	17	24
35	857	375	1336	240	181	119	388
38	457	74	299	261	213	632	419
46	255	11	164	176	48	46	63
120	82	42	126	19	156	0	6
Means	137.5	40.8	147.0	92.0	126.1	47.8	47.8

Table 6.3: Table of normalized edge lengths for Stupor Mundi ($\times 10000$) and degree, where CC= call in to out (red dash), MM= Meet in to out (green dash), CM= call out to meet in (blue), MC= meet out to call in (blue), Avg= average neighborhood tension. Known important individuals are in bold; other individuals are those with interesting positions in the embedding.

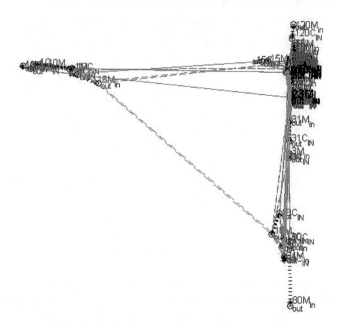

Figure 6.8: Embedding of the typed Stupor Mundi social network using our directed embedding

unusual role in the global structure.

Notes

The approach in this chapter was first presented in Skillicorn and Zheng [88], and the applications to criminal networks appeared in Zheng, Skillicorn, and Calderoni [115].

Chapter 7

Modelling relationships that change over time

So far, all of our social networks have assumed that relationships are static: they either exist or not between any pairs of nodes, and intensities, as described by edge weights, do not change. This is not very realistic. Relationships are created (and sometimes lapse), and the intensity of any particular relationship ebbs and flows over time. It is useful to be able to model the effect of each of these changes on the overall structure of the social network, and so we turn our attention to modelling edges whose intensities change with time. We include in this edges that may come into existence (that is, a change from an intensity of zero to a non-zero value), and that disappear (that is, a change from a non-zero intensity to an intensity of zero).

7.1 Temporal networks

Temporal (dynamic) social network analysis aims to understand the structures in networks as they evolve, building on static analysis techniques but adding a mechanism for variation with time.

The benefits, and drawbacks, of graph representations of relationships is that a single change, for example the addition or deletion of an edge, can change the entire graph structure. When a social network changes from one time to another, reflecting this change completely requires a fresh embedding of the graph into a new space. There is no natural way to compare such embeddings to one another because the shape of the geometric space itself depends on the entire graph. For example, the placement of the origin and axes in one embedding need not have any particular relationship to the origin and axes in others.

This creates a problem when the goal is to understand what has changed in the structure of the graph from one time to another. It is, of course, possible to make qualitative statements ("these two nodes seem to have become less related") but it is hard to make such statements rigorous. It is also impossible to define the *trajectory* of a single node over time since there is no common space within which such a trajectory could exist.

We address these problems by defining a sequence of social networks over time, treating each one as a layer in a way that, by now, should be familiar; binding the layers together; and embedding the whole graph in a single space. The existence of such a space makes it possible to compare, rigorously, the relationships of nodes and edges between time periods. Because the networks at different times are all embedded in the same space, it also becomes possible to define the concept of a trajectory, and therefore to track nodes and relationships across time with a new level of clarity.

A successful embedding makes it possible to ask and answer questions such as: Do two nodes become closer or farther apart over time, and which node drives this process? Are communities or other kinds of subgroups stable over time? If they evolve, how do they change?

As before, we begin by considering the entire social network at each time step as one of a set of layers in the sense of our previous constructions. Thus the network at time $t = 0$ becomes the first layer, the network at $t = 1$ the second layer, and so on. The versions of each node represent that same node of the social network at its different moments of existence. The edges in each layer represent the strengths of the relationship during a particular time period. Edges might appear and disappear from one time to the next; but it is perhaps more common for their weights (the intensities of the relationships) to vary with time. For simplicity, we create placeholder versions of nodes that are not present during any time period but, of course, they will not be connected to the rest of the graph when they are acting as placeholders. Thus each layer contains versions of all nodes that are present in the network at any time.

The obvious approach to binding the subgraphs representing each time snapshot into a single graph would be to connect each node version in one subgraph to its corresponding node version in the subgraph of the next time. Unlike the previous versions of the layer construction, there is a natural ordering for the layers.

However, this does not work — the spectral embedding of a path is a *curve* in two dimensions because the endpoints resemble each other more than they resemble the internal nodes. This effect will happen to some extent to the path connecting each particular node as it appears in subgraphs, creating a geometry where the effects of the structure from the connections across time cannot be cleanly separated from the structure inside each subgraph.

Instead, we connect *all* of the versions of each node together in a c-clique, as we did for typed networks.

We also add a further refinement precisely because there is a natural ordering of the layers. It may be appropriate and useful to allow the embedded structure of the network at previous times to influence the embedded structure in the current period. In other words we may want to force the structure at a particular time step to align more strongly with the structure from earlier times to help with understanding what is changing. This provides a mechanism for putting back one facet of the natural ordering of the layers. Alignment also conceals small-scale changes from layer to layer, making larger changes, or changes that are consistent over time, more easily visible.

The snapshot matrix at time t is combined with the matrices from previous snapshots with a down-weighting given by parameter α. This value can be chosen to vary the relative impact of historical network structure on the analysis of the current snapshot. The aggregate network adjacency matrix A_t is computed as follows: if $t = 1, A_1 = W_1$, else $A_t = W_t + \alpha * A_{t-1}$.

Each of these aggregate adjacency matrices is then converted to a random walk matrix by dividing each row by its row sum to convert entries to probabilities, and producing aggregate random walk matrices R_t.

There is also a low-level technical problem to be addressed. A node may be isolated in one (or more) of the aggregate matrices, either because it genuinely had no relationships during that time, or because it is present in other layers and so was inserted as a placeholder. The row sum of its row in the aggregate random walk matrix will be zero, so we put a 1 in the corresponding diagonal position, representing a self-loop. This ensures that every row sum is 1.

These random walk matrices are then put on the main diagonal of a $cn \times cn$ matrix M_{rw} (for c time periods), and the edges connecting different versions of the same nodes are weighted based on a probability, β. (We could also use the weighting schemes we used previously, basing the "vertical" weights on the connectivity of the nodes in each layer but, in this setting, the node versions we are connecting vertically are the same node at different times, so we do not expect big changes in its connectivity.)

Changing the value of β can be used to bind the structures at different time steps more or less tightly together. For example, if the goal is to understand the behavior of an outlier, a large value of β tends to align the central structure of the network and so make it easier to see changes at the periphery.

The $cn \times cn$ random walk matrix M_{rw} is defined as:

$$
M_{rw} = \begin{pmatrix}
(1-\beta)R_1 & \cdots & \frac{\beta}{c-1}*I & \cdots & \frac{\beta}{c-1}*I \\
\vdots & \ddots & \vdots & \ddots & \vdots \\
\frac{\beta}{c-1}*I & \cdots & (1-\beta)R_t & \cdots & \frac{\beta}{c-1}*I \\
\vdots & \ddots & \vdots & \ddots & \vdots \\
\frac{\beta}{c-1}*I & \cdots & \frac{\beta}{c-1}*I & \cdots & (1-\beta)R_c
\end{pmatrix}
$$

where I is an identity matrix of size n. The entire matrix M_{rw} reflects not only the structure during each time period, but also the evolution of the social network with time.

If the edges of the network are undirected, then the required construction for the embedding is the one we used for typed networks, with each time period corresponding to a color, and with a slightly different weighting for the "vertical" edges.

The choice of α, which is independent of the spectral embedding, reflects the amount of smoothing in the base data. It may be used, for example, to compensate for sampling omissions when data is collected over short time intervals or in settings such as law enforcement where concealment is an issue.

The choice of β determines how much influence the structure of the social network at one time has on its structure at other times, and so is a critical choice for the global model. We prefer to use a larger value of β in order to align the embedding of each node across time. As a result, this will also tend to align the larger structures such as clusters, communities, and cuts.

We have already seen that most realistic social networks have edges that are directed, so we also want to be able to model edges within the original social network that are directed. In this case, the "vertical" edges that connect versions of the same node across time can also be directed. These connections form a directed c-clique.

We have seen that there are two ways to model these directed edges: using Chung's embedding, or using our new directed embedding. With Chung's technique, the algorithm has these 6 steps.

Algorithm: Given temporal adjacency matrices W_t, α, β.

---

1. Compute the aggregate network matrix A_t as:
   If $t = 1, A_1 = W_1$; else, $A_t = W_t + \alpha * A_{t-1}$.

2. Convert each matrix A_t to a random walk matrix R_t.

3. Connect the snapshot random walk matrices R_t together to build a larger random walk matrix M_{rw} with total probability β for random walks to another snapshot.

4. Let Π be the diagonal matrix whose entries are those of the stationary distribution of M_{rw}. Construct the Laplacian matrix:

$$L = I - \frac{\Pi^{1/2} M_{rw} \Pi^{-1/2} + \Pi^{-1/2} M'_{rw} \Pi^{1/2}}{2}.$$

5. Compute the eigenvalues λ_i and corresponding eigenvectors g_i of L.

6. Modify the embedding vectors $f_i = \Pi^{-1/2} g_i$ and embed the graph into k dimensions by using the k vectors f_i corresponding to the k smallest non-zero eigenvalues.

For the composition of the temporal approach with the new directed approach, the algorithm is much simpler.

Algorithm: Given temporal adjacency matrices W_t, α, β.

---

1. Compute the aggregate network matrix A_t as above.

2. Apply the new directed approach (Algorithm 5.2.2) to the aggregate matrix A_t.

7.2   Applications of temporal networks

We illustrate the power of these techniques by applying them to a real-world criminal network, for which some of the structures are already known by other means. The Caviar network was a criminal network for hashish and cocaine importation centered in Montréal. Electronic surveillance data was gathered during a 2-year (1994—1996) investigation (known as Project Caviar) conducted by the Montréal Police, the Royal Canadian Mounted Police and law-enforcement agencies from several countries (England, Spain, Italy, Brazil, Paraguay and Colombia) [64]. In this case, the suspects were not arrested until the end of the 2-year period, although there were 11 seizures (four hashish consignments and seven cocaine consignments). This data gives us the chance to observe a real-world criminal network, particularly its evolution over time and its responses to law-enforcement actions.

The data describes electronically monitored telephone conversations among a total of 105 participants in the criminal network. Edge weights are the number of calls in each period. We begin by treating the edges as undirected.

Data was collected over 11 periods, corresponding to 2-month investigative phases for which interception warrants had to be obtained afresh [64]. Each of these 11 periods is treated as a subnetwork, and its data becomes the adjacency matrix describing a snapshot.

Because law enforcement had access to the content of the telephone calls, they were able to identify 5 key participants [63], N1 (the principal coordinator for hashish importation), N12 (the principal coordinator for cocaine importation), N3 (a partner to N1 and an intermediary between N1 and N12), N76 (a key trafficker), and N87 (a key financial investor in various drug consignments). The 5 key participants are the most active in the network. In the figures, these 5 key participants are often highlighted.

Figure 7.1 shows the Laplacian embedding of the network as a whole, that is adding together all of the undirected interactions of all participants over all 11 time periods. Figure 7.2 shows the center area of Figure 7.1 omitting the edges since the pairwise distances represent similarity whether or not an edge exists in the graph. There are three main clusters: a central one containing N1 and N3; one slightly below it containing N87; and one to the upper left containing N12. There are also several extreme arms of individuals with weak connections to the network. Recall that nodes embedded centrally are most significant, and those embedded extremally are least significant.

7.2.1   The undirected network over time

We can also examine the evolution of the structures in the network. In this example, we use these parameters for the model: $\alpha = 0.5$, $\beta = 0.3$. Even though there are 105 participants, on average only 32.5 participants made or received a phone call in each 2-month period, the number varying between 15 and 42. The total edge weight of the active nodes in each time period ranges from 1 to 453.

The global undirected temporal criminal network is shown in Figure 7.3. In

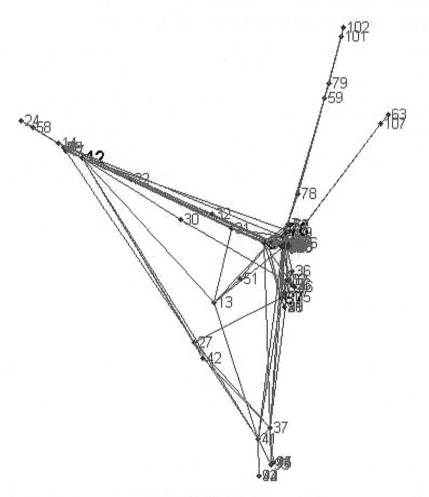

Figure 7.1: Laplacian embedding of the Caviar network with undirected edges with
all time periods merged. Labels are individual identifiers, which range from 1 to 110.

the embedded graph, each participant appears 11 times; the time period follows the
node ID in parentheses. To have a clearer view of the node relationships, we do not
show the edges — in the embedding, distance reflects dissimilarity for all pairs of
nodes, whether they were originally connected or not. There are many participants
who are almost inactive in many time periods and so are clearly peripheral to the
structure of the network — their placement in the embedding is far from the origin,
so we omit them and show only the center part of the embedded graph.

Four important clusters are visible in Figure 7.3. The vertical arm corresponds
to the cocaine importation group with its key figure, N12. There is also a large
cluster that appears centrally, but actually goes back into the plane of the image in
a 3-dimensional representation; this is the hashish importation group with its key

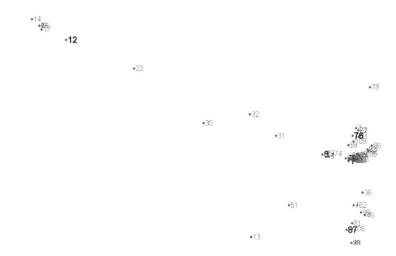

Figure 7.2: Zoomed-in version of the Laplacian embedding of the Caviar network without showing edges.

figures, N1 and N3. The third cluster forms an arm down and to the right. This is the finance group with its key figure, N87. The fourth cluster forms an arm down and to the left, and represents a group including an airport security connection and a foreign supplier with its key figure, N76. From the figure, it is clear that the hashish importation group is the heart of this criminal confederation.

The usefulness of global integration of local pairwise information can be illustrated by considering the phone calls between N1 and N12. Over the 11 time periods the number of calls is [0 2 2 0 2 4 0 0 0 0 0]. Given that N1 made hundreds of phone calls in each period, this data by itself seems to suggest that there is only a weak relationship between them. However, the other members of their groups did telephone each other a lot, and this combined indirect connectivity between N1 and N12 causes them to be embedded quite close together. Their global similarity reflects the sum over many different paths of weak local similarity. This illustrates how spectral techniques discover connections even when those involved might try to conceal them by using intermediaries.

Police records indicated that the two drug groups had known each other and had been cooperating well during the earlier part of the investigation. After consignments began to be seized, the conflicts between them increased. The embedded temporal network allows us to evaluate these changing relationships.

Figure 7.4 shows the change of positions, over time, for the 5 key participants, still treating their communication as undirected. Because the embedding is a global one of the entire set of snapshots, the distances are meaningful, both for any single snapshot and over the entire period. We can estimate the change in the strength of relationships by considering how distances change. During the first 4 time periods, the relative positions of all 5 are stable, but then there is a pattern of accelerating disintegration. The first seizure (estimated at $2.5 million) took place during time

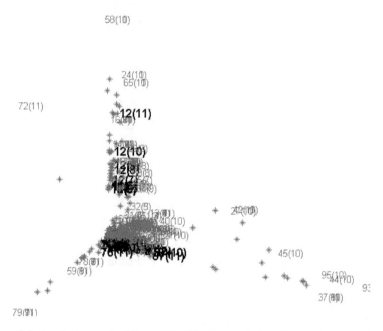

Figure 7.3: Laplacian embedding of the 11-time period undirected temporal network (central region only, with edges omitted)

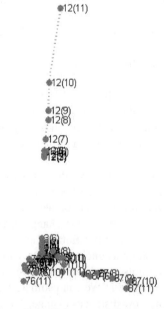

Figure 7.4: The embedding of the 5 key participants over time in the undirected graph

Period	1	2	3	4	5	6	7	8	9	10	11
Pairs	26	35	68	64	49	68	58	73	60	66	71

Table 7.1: Number of pairs in each time period

period 4. The remaining seizures were scattered across the later time periods: one with an estimated cost of $1.3 million during time period 6; $3.5 million during time period 7; $360,000 during time period 8; $4.3 million during time period 9; $18.7 million during time period 10, and $1.3 million during time period 11 [64]. Individuals N76, N12, and N87 all distance themselves from N1, with N12 moving rapidly away especially in the last two time periods. N1 and N3, his primary lieutenant, remain close to each other.

But what about the network as a whole over time? Figure 7.5 shows the structure of the entire network across the 11 time periods. The number of pairs who call each other during each period is shown in Table 7.1. Apart from the first few time periods, where the increase can be attributed to law-enforcement discovery of new members of the network and their addition to the intercept list, the number of pairs that communicate with one another is quite stable. Thus, the expanding radius of the embeddings shown in Figure 7.5 must reflect, at a grassroots level, the same kind of distancing that was visible among the leaders.

This can be made more rigorous by calculating the average size of the network, a concept that is meaningful because each subgraph is embedded in the same space. These subnetwork diameters are shown in Figure 7.6 which plots the average pairwise distances between nodes that appear in at least eight of the time periods. The flat region of this curve suggests that those who are "regular" participants in the network remain at about the same distance until time period 8, but then they also begin to distance themselves from one another.

7.2.2   The directed network over time

Now we turn to the embedding of the *directed* network. The directed representation more accurately reflects the way in which individuals control their position in the network, Chung's directed approach and the new directed approach are both applied.

When an individual A calls another individual B, we consider that A is the more powerful of the two — the call represents some form of command and control, either demanding a response or issuing an instruction. The individual making the call is being proactive and the call reveals that individual's intentionality. However, from the point of view of importance, sources in a directed graph are regarded as less important than sinks. Hence a call from A to B must result in an edge that is directed from B to A. The edge directions of the telephone call graph have to be reversed to create the social network of importance or influence.

The resulting embedding of Chung's directed approach is shown in Figure 7.7. Overall, the network structure is similar, with the same four groups evident. The most significant difference is the placement of N1. In the undirected embedding, he

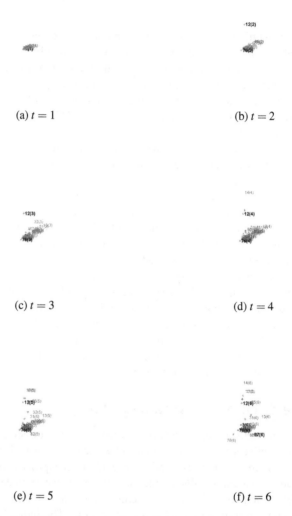

(a) $t = 1$ (b) $t = 2$

(c) $t = 3$ (d) $t = 4$

(e) $t = 5$ (f) $t = 6$

Figure 7.5: Growth of the embedded network over time (on the same scale)

remains central throughout. In Chung's directed embedding, he moves far from the rest of the network in time period 5, drawing N3 and N76 with him. This is the result of a substantial drop in the number of phone calls that he (and his close associates) make to the rest of the network during this time period. While it seems to have taken most members some time to realize that something was wrong after the first seizure,

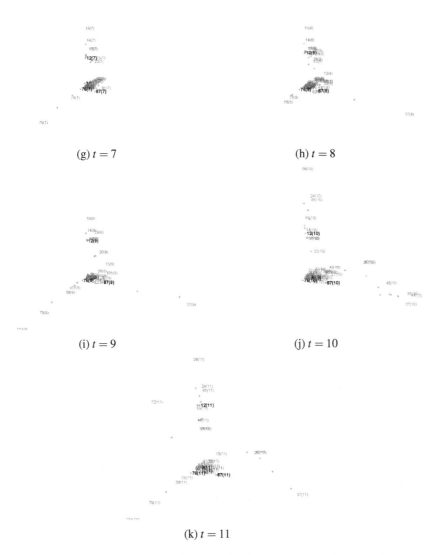

(g) $t = 7$

(h) $t = 8$

(i) $t = 9$

(j) $t = 10$

(k) $t = 11$

Figure 7.5: (continued) Growth of the embedded network over time (on the same scale)

N1 seems to have made a drastic change of habit in the following time period, before moving towards N87 in the later time periods, bringing N3 and N76 with him. The trajectories of the other key players are also more convoluted than they were in the undirected case. It is clear, for example, that N87 moves towards the center of the

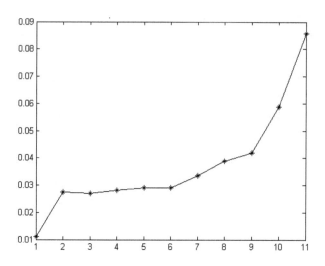

Figure 7.6: Average diameter of the undirected network over time

group in the early time periods, before reversing course quite dramatically after time period 9. In the undirected graph, N12 moves far from the center in time periods 10 and 11; in contrast, in the directed graph he stays at about the same distance from the center in these time periods. This suggests that it is he who is taking steps to remain connected to the center in these late time periods, but the central figures are not doing the same for him. This was confirmed from the intercepted content of the telephone calls.

Figure 7.8 shows the three-dimensional embedding using our new directed approach, where each individual has *in* (triangle) and *out* (circle) versions. Overall, the network structure is similar to the undirected version. The most significant difference is the trajectory of N12. In the undirected embedding, he remains in relatively the same location from time period 2 to time period 6, and then moves far from the center. In our directed embedding, he moves toward the center until time period 6, and then makes a drastic change in the following time periods. Time period 6 is the period that the first seizure of cocaine took place. N12, as the principal coordinator for the cocaine consignments, was panicked and started to have some conflict with N1 and N3 during this time period.

The top 12 nodes of the largest *in-out* edge lengths in each period are shown in Table 7.2. This shows that N1, N3, and N12 have long edges during some early periods and suggests that they are most active moderating communication between the disparate subgroups. However, after time period 8 they start losing these moderator roles. N12 has the longest *in-out* edge in the last time period. This suggests that N12 wanted to take over the whole network as coordinator.

The results of the embedding of the Caviar network are, qualitatively, the kind

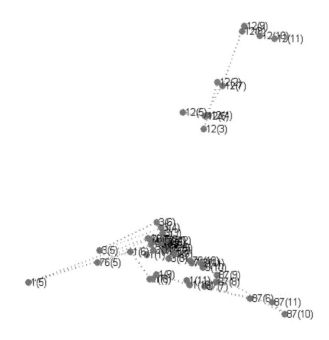

Figure 7.7: Trajectories of the 5 key members from the directed graph — Chung's embedding

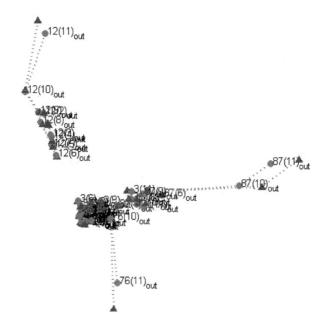

Figure 7.8: Trajectories of the 5 key members from the directed graph — our embedding

Period	1	2	3	4	5	6	7	8	9	10	11
Rank 1	N3	N1	N12	N12	N3	N1	N3	N12	N87	N40	N12
Rank 2	N1	N3	N3	N107	N12	N12	N12	N1	N14	N87	N76
Rank 3	N85	N76	N83	N3	N1	N14	N1	N14	N41	N37	N26
Rank 4	N89	N12	N1	N1	N107	N3	N14	N3	N37	N14	N43
Rank 5	N83	N85	N76	N83	N83	N76	N78	N22	N12	N12	N72
Rank 6	N6	N83	N86	N14	N14	N17	N76	N37	N1	N1	N41
Rank 7	N8	N9	N85	N89	N31	N107	N75	N76	N3	N82	N40
Rank 8	N5	N89	N13	N86	N89	N83	N85	N82	N76	N3	N87
Rank 9	N7	N5	N107	N63	N13	N85	N83	N87	N82	N83	N37
Rank 10	N2	N2	N9	N13	N86	N19	N107	N78	N22	N93	N1
Rank 11	N88	N6	N89	N85	N85	N13	N81	N33	N78	N22	N27
Rank 12	N54	N7	N2	N76	N76	N9	N13	N80	N16	N13	N3

Table 7.2: Individuals with the top 12 largest *in-out* edge lengths in each time period

of information of use to law enforcement: where relationships are strengthening or weakening, and how apparent loyalties are shifting. In this particular dataset, the reaction of the network to law enforcement actions (intercepting shipments) is also detectable. Note especially that this analysis is done using only the *existence* of calls between the members of the group, not the content of these calls. The cost of collecting data on who called whom is orders of magnitude cheaper than collecting content, but we have been able to show that essentially the same kinds of conclusions about group operations and command and control can be drawn from the cheaper data.

The other conclusion from this analysis is that criminal networks do not behave like other kinds of social networks. Criminals do not introduce their friends to one another; so there are many fewer triangles than expected; rather, the network looks like a set of small stars, with occasional overlaps. Although there are detectable clusters, these are not tightly bound as they would be in a more typical social network, but rather are loose aggregations around one or two figures.

7.3 Summary

Social networks change with time, as new members are added, current members leave, and the strength of existing relationships increases or decreases. It is important to be able to model these changes. Our layered approach enables time-varying social networks to be bound into a single structure. Within this structure, comparisons can be made rigorous, and the trajectories of individual nodes can be tracked against the background of other nodes or clusters. When edges are directed, it also becomes possible to draw conclusions about intentions because the individual or group at the source end of a directed edge controls the weight on that edge. Increasing and decreasing weights can therefore be ascribed to the desires or goals of the particular nodes that control them.

Notes

Temporal (dynamic) social network analysis aims to understand the structures in networks as they evolve, building on static analysis techniques but including variation. There are two different ways of framing the problem which have led to two different algorithmic strategies.

The first might be called the "Networks only change slowly" view. Recomputing a spectral embedding after every network change is expensive, especially for large networks. It is more efficient to update the current network structure from the (assumed small) changes that have taken place. For example, Shang et al. [82, 83] keep track of the community structure of temporal networks by using an extended modularity algorithm based on the Newman algorithm. Nguyen et al. [72] update the network structure based on new-Node, remove-Node, new-Edge, remove-Edge primitives. Bouchachia and Prossegger [9] extend the spectral approach with fuzzy c-varieties to cluster incremental data. Aston and Hu [2] update the community structure based on a density-based clustering algorithm. Kas et al. [44] propose an incremental algorithm by updating the affected parts only.

Even a small change in the network can produce a large change in the embedded structure, but these approaches implicitly assume that this does not happen. Finding matching reference points from one embedding to the next is also non-trivial, but again the implicit assumption is that changes have been small enough to enable some level of tracking across time.

The second framing might be called the "Align the independent networks" view. These approaches treat each network at a moment in time independently, but try to get the structures of the network into a consistent form. For example, Qiu and Lin [77] explore the evolution of the organizational structure of a temporal network by comparing the change to the evolving community trees based on random walk and PageRank. Gong et al. [36] propose a novel multi-objective immune algorithm to cluster temporal networks into consistent communities. Yang et al. [109] analyze the community evolution based on a statistical model. However, these approaches only consider the evolution of each network at the level of group structures, and fail to handle changing properties of individual nodes and edges.

The approach in this chapter was described in Skillicorn, Zheng, and Morselli [89, 90].

Chapter 8

Modelling positive and negative relationships

Almost all social networks model relationships as properties that are either non-existent, or have a positive intensity. Now we turn to the situation where the relationship between two nodes might also be a negative one — the two individuals or organizations are in opposition, or have a mutual antipathy.

At one level, this is an easy extension. In social networks so far, adjacency matrix entries are either zero or positive; a negative relationship can be modelled by a negative edge weight. The difficulty arises in trying to model the effects of transitivity. For social networks with positively weighted edges, transitivity has a natural interpretation: if A has a close relationship with B, and B has a close relationship with C, it seems natural that A and C might be considered to be similar, or might be likely to have a positive relationship if they met, because of their mutual connection, B.

However, what is the relationship between A and C, if A and B have a negative relationship and so do B and C? Conventionally, "the enemy of my enemy is my friend" but this cannot be a standard pattern, especially in an environment with a large number of actors [22].

In this chapter, we develop an embedding approach that also enables modelling social networks with negatively weighted edges and, along the way, resolves the issue of how to think about the enemy of my enemy.

8.1 Signed Laplacian

We derive spectral graph embeddings for signed graphs that create embeddings with the obvious desirable properties: nodes connected by positive edges are placed close together, while those connected by negative edges are placed far apart. The difficulty, of course, is how to balance the "pull" of positive edges against the "push" of negative ones to produce appropriate global solutions that approximate optima. We derive an unnormalized and two normalized Laplacian matrices for signed graphs, each in two ways: arguing from Rayleigh quotients as objective functions whose minima represent good node placement, and from cut functions that are the signed analogues of standard cuts. The methods produce, in each case, the same Laplacian matrix representations of a signed graph, increasing confidence that this captures a reasonable model of the balance between positive and negative edges. The difference between them is how they address the issue of what makes a good cut (or, equivalently, good clusters). The resulting Laplacians can be used as embeddings by using some or all of the eigenvectors of an eigendecomposition of such a matrix.

We compare these new embedding techniques with a previously suggested spectral method for signed graphs [48] and show the performance of all of the algorithms on real-world datasets from Epinions, Slashdot, and the Africa Armed Conflict Location & Event Data (ACLED), as well as two small datasets, the Gahuku–Gama alliance network of tribes in New Guinea, and the Sampson monastery network. For the small datasets, we validate our techniques by appealing to visualizations; for the larger datasets we compute measures based on the distances between positively and between negatively connected nodes in the embedding.

8.2   Unnormalized spectral Laplacians of signed graphs

The embedding of a signed network should place nodes that are positively related close together, but must place nodes that are negatively related far from one another, balancing these two different objectives in a globally consistent way that reflects the underlying reality of the social network. We first define an unnormalized Laplacian for signed graphs, and argue for the validity of the resulting construction based on both Rayleigh quotient and graph cut points of views.

There is no reason why there cannot be both a positive and negative relationship between the same two individuals, and this is not necessarily the same as a single relationship whose weight is the difference between the two intensities. In other words, if A has a positive relationship with B with intensity 3, and a negative relationship with intensity -2, this is not necessarily the same as a single relationship of intensity $+1$. In other words, positive and negative relationships are qualitatively different, and do not necessarily cancel out.

Therefore, we begin from two adjacency matrices: W^+ which contains positive values representing the intensity of positive relationships between the pairs of nodes, and W^- which also contains positive values representing the intensity of negative relationships between the pairs of nodes. For the time being, we will consider the edges to be undirected, and so both matrices are symmetric.

Let D^+ be the diagonal degree matrix of W^+, that is $D_{ii}^+ = \sum_{j=1}^n W_{ij}^+$ and D^- be the diagonal degree matrix of W^-, that is $D_{ii}^- = \sum_{j=1}^n W_{ij}^-$. The total degree matrix is therefore: $\overline{D} = D^+ + D^-$.

A method proposed by Kunegis et al. [48] extends the conventional Laplacian approach to signed networks by defining a signed graph Laplacian as:

$$\bar{L} = \bar{D} - W = D^+ + D^- - W^+ + W^-$$

However, there are several difficulties with this definition. We will instead define:

$$L_{sign} = D^+ - D^- - W = (D^+ - W^+) - (D^- - W^-)$$

and show that it leads to a more natural embedding.

8.2.1 Rayleigh quotients of signed unnormalized Laplacians

As usual, the Rayleigh quotient provides some insight into the property that the Laplacian captures. The Rayleigh quotient of the Kunegis Laplacian, $\bar{L}$, is:

$$R_{\bar{L}}(f) = \frac{f'\bar{L}f}{f'f} = \frac{\frac{1}{2}\sum_{i,j=1}^{n}\left(w_{ij}^+(f_i - f_j)^2 + w_{ij}^-(f_i + f_j)^2\right)}{\sum_{i=1}^{n}f_i^2}$$

In the numerator, the first term is the sum of the squared distances between positively connected nodes, the same as for the conventional Laplacian. However, the second term is the square of terms associated with nodes connected by negative edges. As a result, the Rayleigh quotient is made smaller by embedding the negatively connected nodes symmetrically around the origin. There is a certain logic to this, since it certainly tends to place a given pair of negatively connected nodes far apart, but its global effect is hard to determine and, as we will show, turns out not to be appropriate.

Figure 8.1(a) shows the signed Laplacian $\bar{L}$ embedding of a toy graph. In the toy graph, nodes 1, 3, and 5 are positively connected to nodes 2, 4, and 6, respectively, and nodes 2, 4, and 6 are negative connected to each other. Consider the relationship between node 1 and node 4. Although nodes 2 and 4 are antagonistic to one another, it does not seem appropriate that the positive relationship between nodes 1 and 2 should make node 1 *more* hostile to node 4 than node 2 is. Figure 8.1(a) suggests that the $\bar{L}$ embedding does not model transitivity of positive and negative connections as it should.

The natural way to deal with negative edges is to maximize the distances between the pairs of nodes that they connect, regardless of where those nodes want to be embedded given the structure of the rest of the graph. In other words, the problem with the Kunegis approach is that negatively connected nodes are forced to be on opposite sides of the origin, when simply being far apart is enough.

Our definition of an unnormalized Laplacian matrix for signed graphs, L_{sign}, uses this intuition. The corresponding Rayleigh quotient is:

$$R_{L_{sign}}(f) = \frac{f'L_{sign}f}{f'f} = \frac{\frac{1}{2}\sum_{i,j=1}^{n}\left(w_{ij}^+(f_i - f_j)^2 - w_{ij}^-(f_i - f_j)^2\right)}{\sum_{i=1}^{n}f_i^2}.$$

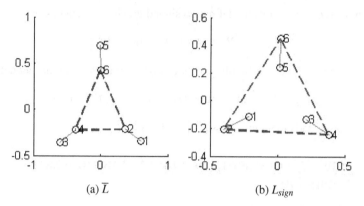

(a) $\overline{L}$ (b) L_{sign}

Figure 8.1: A toy signed graph embedding of unnormalized Laplacians in two dimensions, where edges are weighted ± 1, shown as solid lines $(+1)$ and dashed lines (-1).

A minimum of the Rayleigh quotient $R_{L_{sign}}(f)$ corresponds to an embedding that minimizes the total squared distance between positively connected pairs and maximizes the total squared distance between negatively connected pairs. Thus, embedding using the Laplacian L_{sign} avoids the problem of $\overline{L}$.

Figure 8.1(b) shows that the embedding based on L_{sign} places the nodes in more reasonable positions. For example, node 1 is closer to node 4 than node 2 is.

The matrix L_{sign} has the following properties. First, 0 is an eigenvalue of L_{sign}, and the corresponding eigenvector is the constant one vector $\mathbb{1}$. Exactly as for the conventional Laplacian L, this is a trivial embedding. Second, if f_i and f_j are two different eigenvectors of matrix L_{sign}, then $f_i \perp f_j$. The proofs are similar to those for the conventional Laplacian L.

8.2.2   Graph cuts of signed unnormalized Laplacians

For signed graphs, there is also a direct relationship between spectral embeddings and the cuts used for clustering. In other words, for each Rayleigh quotient of the signed unnormalized Laplacians, there is a corresponding plausible cut function.

When there are negative edges in a graph, balanced minimum cut approaches need to be redefined. For convenience, we represent the basic cut in its positive and negative parts, respectively:

$$cut^+(A_1,...,A_k) = \frac{1}{2}\sum_{i=1}^{k} W^+(A_i,\overline{A}_i),$$

$$cut^-(A_1,...,A_k) = \frac{1}{2}\sum_{i=1}^{k} W^-(A_i,\overline{A}_i).$$

The sum of the positive and negative volumes is the total volume of the nodes in a

group A_i:
$$vol(A_i) = vol^-(A_i) + vol^+(A_i).$$

Kunegis et al. define a signed ratio minimum cut corresponding to their Laplacian definition [48]:

$$\overline{RatioCut}(A,\overline{A}) = scut(A,\overline{A}) \left(\frac{1}{|A|} + \frac{1}{|\overline{A}|} \right),$$

where $scut(A,\overline{A}) = 2cut^+(A,\overline{A}) + W^-(A,A) + W^-(\overline{A},\overline{A})$.

The minimum of the Rayleigh quotient $R_{\overline{L}}$ can be viewed as a relaxation of the minimization of $\overline{RatioCut}$ [48]. This objective function penalizes negative edges within clusters, but it does so without any regard for the size of each cluster. It seems natural that a large cluster ought to be "allowed" to contain relatively more negative edges than a small one, so that a function like this might be more plausible if the weights in $scut$ were fractions of negative edges per cluster rather than simply counts. Furthermore, this definition assumes only 2 clusters and it is problematic to extend it to k clusters [17].

Instead, we define an unnormalized signed cut objective function by:

$$SRcut(A_1,...,A_k) = \sum_{i=1}^{k} \frac{W^+(A_i,\overline{A_i}) - W^-(A_i,\overline{A_i})}{|A_i|}$$
$$= \sum_{i=1}^{k} \frac{cut^+(A_i,\overline{A_i}) - cut^-(A_i,\overline{A_i})}{|A_i|}$$

The minimum of the $SRcut$ function finds a solution with the fewest positive edges and the most negative edges between groups. The value of $SRcut$ could be negative.

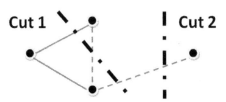

Figure 8.2: Graph cuts of a sample graph

Both unnormalized cuts of signed graphs treat the positive edges in the same way, but treat the negative edges differently. The $\overline{RatioCut}$ emphasizes minimizing the total within-group negative edges. The $SRcut$ maximizes the outgoing negative edges from each group; this tends to create large groups when the sum of the positive edge weights is greater than the sum of the negative edge weights between groups, but small groups otherwise. For example, in Figure 8.2 the minimum cut of the $\overline{RatioCut}$ is "Cut 1", with no negative edge within groups. "Cut 2" is the result of $SRcut$, with the node on the right side alone in a group. The question is which one is the better cut? We argue that it is the second one, because the node on the right side does not have any positive relationship to the nodes on the left.

The minimum of the Rayleigh quotient $R_{L_{sign}}$ can be viewed as a relaxation of the minimization of *SRcut*. The proof follows the same strategy as in von Luxburg [101]. The details of the proof can be found in Appendix C.

8.3   Normalized spectral Laplacians of signed graphs

Using the unnormalized Laplacian has the same issues for signed graphs as it does for unsigned graphs, so it is natural to consider versions of the normalized Laplacians to represent signed graphs.

Kunegis et al. [48] also proposed two versions of signed normalized Laplacians:

$$\overline{L}_{rw} = I - \overline{D}^{-1}W,$$

$$\text{and } \overline{L}_{sym} = I - \overline{D}^{-1/2}W\overline{D}^{-1/2}.$$

However, these two normalized Laplacians have the same issue as the Kunegis unnormalized signed Laplacian.

We restrict ourselves to the case of the random-walk Laplacian and extend it to the signed case in a different way. We derive two normalized Laplacian matrices for signed graphs — the *simple normalized signed graph Laplacian*:

$$L_{sns} = \overline{D}^{-1}(D^+ - D^- - W) = \overline{D}^{-1}\left((D^+ - W^+) - (D^- - W^-)\right),$$

and the *balanced normalized signed graph Laplacian*:

$$L_{bns} = \overline{D}^{-1}(D^+ - W) = \overline{D}^{-1}(D^+ - W^+ + W^-).$$

As before, we justify each in two ways: arguing from Rayleigh quotients as objective functions whose minima represent good node placement, and from cut functions that are the signed analogues of standard cuts.

8.3.1   Rayleigh quotients of signed random-walk Laplacians

The Rayleigh quotient corresponding to Kunegis's $\overline{L}_{rw}$ is:

$$R_{\overline{L}_{rw}}(f) = \frac{f'\overline{L}f}{f'\overline{D}f} = \frac{\frac{1}{2}\sum_{i,j=1}^n \left(w_{ij}^+(f_i - f_j)^2 + w_{ij}^-(f_i + f_j)^2\right)}{\sum_{i=1}^n \overline{d}_i f_i^2}.$$

As before, the numerator can be made smaller by placing nodes connected by negative edges on opposite sides of the origin. Figure 8.3(a) is the normalized version of Figure 8.1(a) and shows that, as before, the $\overline{L}_{rw}$ embedding does not model transitivity of positive and negative connections as it should.

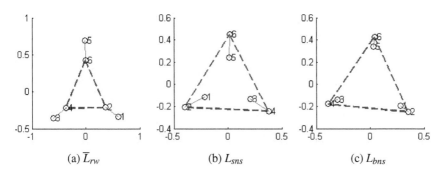

Figure 8.3: A toy signed graph embedding of normalized Laplacians in two dimensions, where edges are weighted ±1, shown as solid lines ($+1$) and as dashed lines (-1).

Our *simple normalized signed* graph Laplacian L_{sns} is motivated by the Rayleigh quotient:

$$R_{L_{sns}}(f) = \frac{f'(D^+ - D^- - W)f}{f'\overline{D}f}$$

$$= \frac{\frac{1}{2}\sum_{i,j=1}^{n} w_{ij}(f_i - f_j)^2}{\sum_{i=1}^{n} \overline{d}_i f_i^2}$$

$$= \frac{\frac{1}{2}\sum_{i,j=1}^{n} \left(w_{ij}^+(f_i - f_j)^2 - w_{ij}^-(f_i - f_j)^2\right)}{\sum_{i=1}^{n} \overline{d}_i f_i^2}.$$

which penalizes long positive edges and short negative edges in the same way as our unnormalized construction.

A minimum of the Rayleigh quotient $R_{L_{sns}}(f)$ corresponds to an embedding that minimizes the total squared distance between positively connected pairs and maximizes the total squared distance between negatively connected pairs, normalized by the total degree $\overline{D}$. Thus, embedding using the Laplacian L_{sns} avoids the problem of $\overline{L}$.

Figure 8.3 shows the embeddings of the three normalized signed Laplacians; the relationships are qualitatively the same as for the unnormalized signed Laplacians.

The matrix L_{sns} has the following properties. First, 0 is an eigenvalue of L_{sns}, and the corresponding eigenvector is the constant one vector $\mathbb{1}$. Exactly as for the conventional Laplacian L_{rw}, this is a trivial embedding. Second, if f_i and f_j are two different eigenvectors of matrix L_{sns}, then $f_i'\overline{D}f_j = 0$. The proof is similar to that for the conventional Laplacian L_{rw}. Third, L_{sns} has n real-valued eigenvalues within range $[-2, 2]$. The proof is based on the Rayleigh quotient. If f is an eigenvector of matrix L_{sns}, the corresponding eigenvalue is equal to the corresponding Rayleigh quotient value.

A small issue remains. There is an asymmetry in the two terms in the numerator of $R_{L_{sns}}(f)$. As two positively connected nodes are moved closer, the change in the magnitude of the contribution to the numerator becomes smaller as desired (but it tends to be in the "flat" part of the quadratic). When two negatively connected nodes are moved farther apart, the change in the magnitude of the contribution to the numerator becomes larger, again as desired (but it also tends to be in the "steep" part of the quadratic). The numerator therefore has a bias towards separating negatively connected pairs rather than placing positively connected pairs closer together — the same relative movement has an asymmetric effect on the numerator. Globally this means that positively connected pairs are embedded farther apart than they "should be".

A better Laplacian, therefore, should slightly reduce the effect of strongly negatively weighted edges. The Rayleigh quotient corresponding to the *balanced normalized signed* graph Laplacian is:

$$
R_{L_{bns}}(f) = \frac{f'(D^+ - W)f}{f'\overline{D}f}
$$

$$
= \frac{\sum_{i,j=1}^{n} \left(\frac{1}{2}w_{ij}(f_i - f_j)^2 + w_{ij}^- f_i^2 \right)}{\sum_{i=1}^{n} \overline{d}_i f_i^2}
$$

$$
= \frac{\sum_{i,j=1}^{n} \left(\frac{1}{2}w_{ij}^+(f_i - f_j)^2 - \frac{1}{2}w_{ij}^-(f_i - f_j)^2 + w_{ij}^- f_i^2 \right)}{\sum_{i=1}^{n} \overline{d}_i f_i^2},
$$

The $w_{ij}^- f_i^2$ term acts to pull nodes with incident negatively weighted edges slightly towards the origin. The effect is shown in Figure 8.3(c), where nodes 1, 3, and 5 are closer to nodes 2, 4, and 6, respectively, than in Figure 8.3(b).

However, the constant one vector $\mathbb{1}$ is no longer guaranteed to be an eigenvector of L_{bns}. In other words, the origin will no longer be the "center" of the embedded graph. L_{bns} has n real-valued eigenvalues which lie between -1 and 2.

8.3.2   Graph cuts of signed random-walk Laplacians

Kunegis et al. also derive a signed normalized minimum cut from their Laplacian [48]:

$$
SignedNcut(A,\overline{A}) = scut(A,\overline{A}) \left(\frac{1}{vol(A)} + \frac{1}{vol(\overline{A})} \right).
$$

As before, *SignedNcut* does not consider the balance of negative edges in each group, which may lead to the same problem as in the positive cut. Their definitions are based on clustering into 2 clusters and it is problematic to extend to general k clusters [17].

We define two normalized signed cuts:

$$SNScut(A_1,...,A_k) = \sum_{i=1}^{k} \frac{W^+(A_i,\overline{A}_i) - W^-(A_i,\overline{A}_i)}{vol(A_i)}$$

$$= \sum_{i=1}^{k} \frac{cut^+(A_i,\overline{A}_i) - cut^-(A_i,\overline{A}_i)}{vol(A_i)}$$

$$BNScut(A_1,...,A_k) = \sum_{i=1}^{k} \frac{W^+(A_i,\overline{A}_i) + W^-(A_i,A_i)}{vol(A_i)}$$

$$= \sum_{i=1}^{k} \frac{W^+(A_i,\overline{A}_i) + W^-(A_i,V) - W^-(A_i,\overline{A}_i)}{vol(A_i)}$$

$$= \sum_{i=1}^{k} \frac{cut^+(A_i,\overline{A}_i) + vol^-(A_i) - cut^-(A_i,\overline{A}_i)}{vol(A_i)}$$

Both objective functions are derived from the normalized cut for signed graphs. The minimum of the SNScut function tries to find a solution with the fewest positive edges and the most negative edges between groups. The solution based on BNScut function tries to minimize the positive edges between groups and the negative edges within each group. These sound equivalent, since the maximum of the negative edges between groups is equal to the minimum of the negative edges within each group, that is $W^-(A_i,A_i) = vol^-(A_i) - cut^-(A_i,\overline{A}_i)$. However, there will be a difference between the mimima when $vol(A_i)$ of each group A_i is considered. The difference between the two normalized signed cut objective functions leads to two different normalized signed Laplacian clusterings.

SNScut corresponds to the Laplacian matrix L_{sns} and *BNScut* corresponds to the Laplacian matrix L_{bns}. We prove this using the same strategy as in von Luxburg [101]. The details of the proofs can be found in Appendix D and Appendix E for L_{sns} and L_{bns}, respectively.

These proofs show that our definitions of Laplacian matrices, derived from a Rayleigh quotient point of view, agree with reasonable definitions of cuts for signed graphs. As usual, the quality of the solution to the relaxed problem is not guaranteed to be optimal, but is almost always good in practice [101].

8.4 Applications of signed networks

Our embedding approach allows the question of how to model the enemy of my enemy to be answered rigorously. Figure 8.4 shows two embeddings of graphs containing only negative edges. In both cases, it is clear that the edges from "me" to my enemy, and from my enemy to his enemy are approximately orthogonal. In other words, the enemy of my enemy is embedded exactly in between complete reflexivity and complete transitivity — the embedding algorithm is agnostic about the behavior of transitivity in the absence of other information (for example, other positive edges).

This intuitive result also answers the question about how many dimensions should be retained in an embedding to get good results from a clustering algorithm.

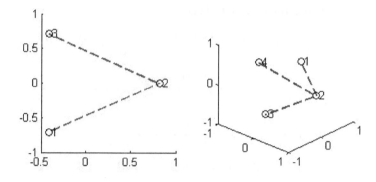

Figure 8.4: Embeddings of the enemy of my enemy

Each group that has a negative relationship with any other group will tend to occupy its own dimension; so choosing the dimensionality equal to the number of antipathetic groups is guaranteed to suffice (but may be too conservative if there are strong positive relationships among some of the groups).

We have shown that our methods are mathematically well behaved and motivated. As applications of our methods to real-world data, we use five signed networks to demonstrate the effectiveness of signed graph spectral embedding. Because normalized Laplacians have better performance than the unnormalized ones [101], we use only the random-walk Laplacians of signed graphs in the experiments. We compare our results with the $\overline{L}_{rw}$ embedding and show how our approach is an improvement for real-world datasets as well.

For small datasets, we validate the results by visualizing the embeddings. To compare the embedding quality for graphs that are too large for straightforward visualization, we define new performance measures. Since the Rayleigh quotients of all three Laplacian matrices $\overline{L}_{rw}$, L_{sns} and L_{bns} are normalized by the total degree of each node, $f'Df$, it is meaningful to compare distances between connected pairs in different embeddings. Since the goal of a signed embedding is to make positively weighted edges short and negatively weighted edges long, we can use the ratio of positive distances to negative distances between connected pairs, and such ratios are also comparable across different embedding algorithms.

We define three ways to compute the ratio. The first is the average edge ratio (AER), which is computed by dividing the average embedded edge length of positively weighted edges by the average embedded edge length of negatively weighted edges:

$$AER = \frac{\left(\sum_{i=1}^{n}\sum_{j=1}^{n} w_{ij}^{+}dis_{ij}\right)/vol^{+}(V)}{\left(\sum_{i=1}^{n}\sum_{j=1}^{n} w_{ij}^{-}dis_{ij}\right)/vol^{-}(V)},$$

where dis_{ij} is the Euclidean distance between node i and node j in the embedding.

The second is the average node ratio (ANR). This measure computes the average embedded lengths of edges from the perspective of each node; in other words, it computes the ratio of the average "pull" on nodes to the average "push" on nodes:

$$ANR = \frac{\left(\sum_{i=1}^{n} \sum_{j=1}^{n} w_{ij}^{+} dis_{ij}/d_{i}^{+} \right) /|V|^{+}}{\left(\sum_{i=1}^{n} \sum_{j=1}^{n} w_{ij}^{-} dis_{ij}/d_{i}^{-} \right) /|V|^{-}},$$

where $|V|^{+}$ and $|V|^{-}$ are the numbers of nodes with positive edges and negative edges, respectively.

The third is the median edge ratio (MER), which is computed by dividing the median embedded edge length of positively weighted edges by the median embedded edge length of negatively weighted edges:

$$MER = \frac{median(dis_{ij} \quad |W_{ij}^{+} > 0)}{median(dis_{ij} \quad |W_{ij}^{-} > 0)}.$$

The three measures are similar, but they emphasize different aspects of an embedding. AER focuses on the total edge lengths. ANR moderates the edge lengths by how they are incident at nodes. MER limits the effects of extreme values, for example a single node embedded far from the rest of the graph.

Gahuku–Gama network

We begin with a small dataset described by Read [78] and used by Hage and Harary [37]. This dataset contains the relations between 16 tribes of the Eastern Central Highlands of New Guinea. Read suggested an alliance structure among three tribal groupings. The dataset is an unweighted signed network, where positive edges are alliance ("rova") relations and negative edges are antagonistic ("hina") relations. The enemy of an enemy is sometimes a friend and sometimes an enemy. The dataset is small enough that we can visualize the embeddings.

The tribe dataset embeddings based on the three signed Laplacian are shown in Figure 8.5. In all three embeddings the positive (solid) edges are short, and the negative (dashed) edges are long. The known alliance structure among three tribal groups is shown clearly in the three embeddings, with only negative edges between groups.

However, there are some important differences among the Laplacian embeddings. First we focus on the tribes in the upper left group. The tribe MASIL not only does not have any enemies, but also plays a key broker role between the upper left and lower left groups. This means that tribe MASIL should be placed close to the center of the embedding. In the embedding of Figure 8.5(a), tribe MASIL is not as close to the right-hand group as it is in the other two embeddings. Furthermore, in the upper-left group, tribes GEHAM, GAHUK and ASARO are most antagonistic

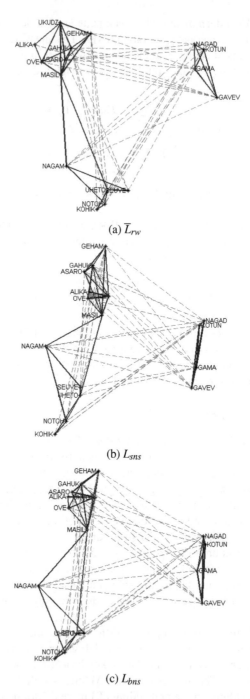

(a) $\overline{L}_{rw}$

(b) L_{sns}

(c) L_{bns}

Figure 8.5: The embeddings of the tribes of the Eastern Central Highlands of New Guinea in two dimensions with alliance relations shown as solid edges and antagonistic relations shown as dashed edges.

towards other groups. In the embedding of Figure 8.5(b) and Figure 8.5(c), they are placed further away from the other groups, which seems appropriate. However, this is not the case in the $\overline{L}_{rw}$ embedding. Other nodes in the $\overline{L}_{rw}$ embedding also show reversed placement of the kind shown in the toy dataset. From both a mathematical and practical point of view, our two proposed signed Laplacian embedding methods are better than the signed Laplacian embedding methods in Kunegis et al. [48].

The embeddings of L_{sns} and L_{bns} are similar to one another. However, if we look at the differences between the two signed Laplacian embeddings, members of each subgroup are closer to one another in the L_{bns} embedding than they are in L_{sns} embedding. The L_{bns} embedding seems to work well rendering this network.

The measures for the Eastern Central Highlands of New Guinea dataset, with distances computed in three dimensions since there are three groupings, are shown in Table 8.1.

	AER	ANR	MER
$\overline{L}_{rw}$	0.42	0.40	0.42
L_{sns}	0.39	0.40	0.40
L_{bns}	0.39	0.40	0.35

Table 8.1: Ratios for the Eastern Central Highlands of New Guinea embeddings —smaller values are better

The ANR values for the three embeddings are similar. The L_{bns} embedding arguably produces the best embedding overall, especially for the MER score which ignores extreme values.

Sampson monastery network

We use another small dataset derived from Sampson's 1969 unpublished doctoral thesis (the data available from the UCINET repository). The data comes from 18 trainee monks who were asked for opinions about their relationships over a period of time in which the group they formed was disintegrating. The monks were asked about who influenced them positively and negatively, whom they esteemed or despised, and whom they praised or blamed, but almost all of the analysis has focused on the like/dislike ratings. Almost any technique applied to the matrix produces four clusters that agree with those that Sampson originally postulated (for example, [29]). The network is directed so we add the transpose to produce an undirected network, ignoring the possibility that A likes B but B dislikes A. For simplicity, we also ignore the difference of the like/dislike ratings.

The Sampson monastery dataset embeddings based on the three signed Laplacians are shown in Figure 8.6. In all three embeddings the positive (solid) edges are short, and the negative (dashed) edges are long. The negative edges are not only between groups, but also within groups. Figure 8.6 shows that the known group structure is clearly visible in all three embeddings.

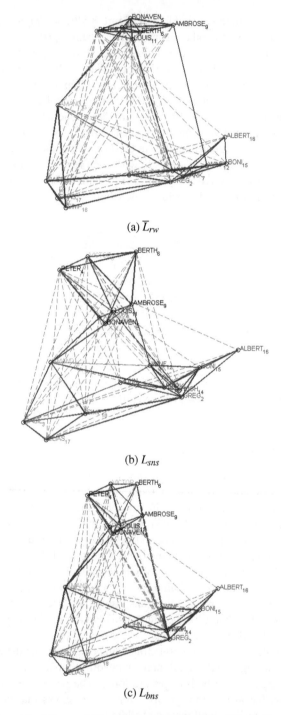

(a) $\overline{L}_{rw}$

(b) L_{sns}

(c) L_{bns}

Figure 8.6: The embeddings of the relations between the 18 monks in two dimensions with like relations shown as solid edges and dislike relations shown as dashed edges.

However, as before, there are some differences among the Laplacian embeddings. For example, Node $WINF_{12}$ (Winifrid), a leader of the "Young Turks" group, does not have any incident negative edges and should be placed close to the center in the embedding. In the embedding of Figure 8.6(a), $WINF_{12}$ is the extremal node in the upper group. In Figures 8.6(b) and Figure 8.6(c), $WINF_{12}$ is placed much closer to other groups, as it should be. $BONAVEN_5$ is a loyalist with no negative incident edges, so ir should be placed close to the center of the network. This is what happens using L_{bns} and L_{sns} but not using L_{rw}. The measures for the Sampson monastery dataset, computed in three dimensions, are shown in Table 8.2.

	AER	ANR	MER
$\overline{L}_{rw}$	0.49	0.47	0.53
L_{sns}	0.46	0.50	0.48
L_{bns}	0.45	0.46	0.50

Table 8.2: Ratios for the Sampson monastery network embeddings — smaller values are better

L_{sns} and L_{bns} have better performance overall, except that the ANR values of the L_{sns} is slightly worse than the ANR values of the $\overline{L}_{rw}$. But this time L_{sns} has a lower value than L_{bns} for the MER score. Based on the embeddings of the two small datasets, our two proposed signed Laplacian embedding methods are better than the signed Laplacian embedding methods in Kunegis et al. [48]. However, it is hard to decide which one of the two is the best.

ACLED violent groups network

The ACLED (Armed Conflict Location & Event Data Project — acleddata.com), is a dataset of political violence events in Africa from 1997 to the present. Subsets of this dataset were converted to directed signed social networks as follows: each record describes an attack by group A on group B, possibly with A assisted by some other group C and group B assisted by some other group D. This record results in a negative directed edge from A to B, and positive directed edges from C to A and/or from D to B. Multiple attacks or collaborations increase the edge weights accordingly. There can be (and are!) both positive and negative edges between the same pair of actors.

We select records involving 21 countries in North and West Africa and the incidents involving violent groups. We use the largest connected component of groups: 173 groups. (As expected, there are small sets of groups that interact only with one another, and we ignore these.) Most edges in this network are negative: 62 groups have only negative edges and some have only one negative edge. The subset has previously been examined from a geographical perspective [106].

Figure 8.7 shows the embeddings in three dimensions. The $\overline{L}_{rw}$ embedding shows a strong bipartite structure, while the other two show a more complex structure.

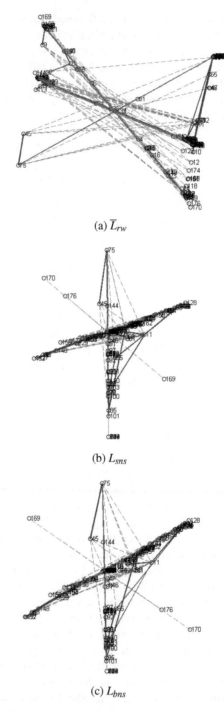

(a) $\overline{L}_{rw}$

(b) L_{sns}

(c) L_{bns}

Figure 8.7: The embeddings of the relationships between violent groups in Northern and Western Africa, plotted in two dimensions with like relations shown as solid edges and dislike relations shown as dashed edges.

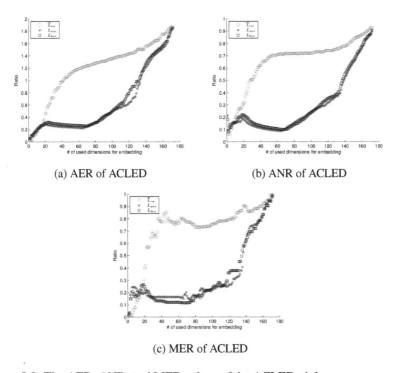

(a) AER of ACLED   (b) ANR of ACLED

(c) MER of ACLED

Figure 8.8: The AER, ANR, and MER values of the ACLED violent groups network as a function of different numbers of dimensions (lower values are better)

Because of the large number of negative relationships in this data, it is not clear how many dimensions are appropriate to reveal the structure in this data. Figure 8.8 shows the three measures computed using increasing numbers of dimensions. All three measures for $\overline{L}_{rw}$ are slightly lower than those of L_{sns} and L_{bns} when only a few dimensions are used. However, when more dimensions are used, L_{sns} and L_{bns} are better than $\overline{L}_{rw}$.

Epinions network

To further compare the quality of the different signed Laplacian embeddings, we use a larger real-world dataset, *Epinions*. The *Epinions* dataset is a who-trusts-whom online social network from a general consumer review site (Epinions.com) [51]. The network is directed so we add the transpose to produce an undirected network.

The network has about 130,000 nodes and hundreds of thousands of edges. We sample different subgraphs from the real-world dataset using two standard sampling techniques for large graphs: random-walk sampling and forest-fire sampling [50]. The two sampling methods have two different goals: creating a sample that is a scaled-down version of the whole graph (random walk), or creating a version of the graph as it would have been at some previous time in its growth (forest fire).

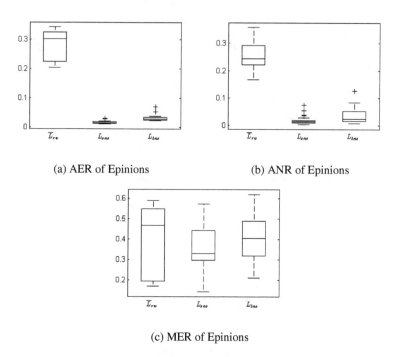

(a) AER of Epinions   (b) ANR of Epinions

(c) MER of Epinions

Figure 8.9: The AER, ANR, and MER values for 30 randomly chosen subsets of 10,000 nodes from the Epinions dataset using the forest-fire sampling method (lower values are better)

We generate 30 sampled subgraphs of a given size, since 30 is large enough for the central limit theorem to apply, giving us dependable scores. For the forest-fire sampling method, to ensure that the sampled graph is connected we restart from a uniformly randomly chosen burned node if the fire dies. (For the random-walk sampling method, the sampled subgraph is necessarily connected; we pick a restart node from the visited list.) We ignore the sign of edges when we use the sampling methods. We use Laplacian embedding in three dimensions to compute the measures. The ratio of positive to negative edges in the samples is larger than for the graph as a whole suggesting that negative edges are relatively rare in the sparser parts of both networks. This seems plausible — those less well connected socially may be more reluctant to become visibly negative, and there is little point to being part of this kind of social network via only negative connections.

Figure 8.9 shows plots of the three measures for sampled 10,000-node subgraphs using the forest-fire sampling method. Here we compute the measures in only three dimensions, since there are not really expected to be clusters in this kind of data. The AER and ANR values of L_{sns} and L_{bns} for this dataset are significantly lower than the values of $\overline{L}_{rw}$. This indicates that L_{sns} and L_{bns} embeddings are better than the $\overline{L}_{rw}$ embedding. The AER and ANR values of L_{sns} and L_{bns} in these exam-

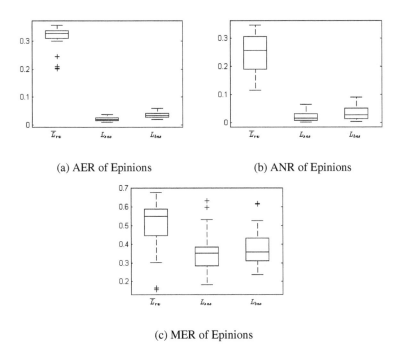

(a) AER of Epinions   (b) ANR of Epinions

(c) MER of Epinions

Figure 8.10: The AER, ANR, and MER values for 30 randomly chosen subsets of 10,000 nodes from the Epinions dataset using the random-walk sampling method (lower values are better)

ples are similar, but the L_{sns} result is always slightly better. Figure 8.9(c) shows that the MER values are similar for all three techniques, so the differences between them must be associated with how they deal with more extremal nodes (and longer edges). Smaller subgraphs, with 100 and 1000 nodes, have measure values similar to those in Figure 8.9.

Figure 8.10 shows plots of the three measures for the sampled 10,000-node subgraphs using the random-walk sampling method. The results are similar to the results using the forest-fire sampling method, with AER and ANR values for L_{sns} and L_{bns} significantly lower than the values for $\overline{L}_{rw}$, but with similar MER values for all. The two sampling methods have different goals, but the embeddings perform similarly for all of the samples.

Slashdot network

We also use another larger real-world signed network, *Slashdot*. *Slashdot* is a technology-related news website. Users are allowed to tag each other as friends or foes. A signed link may also indicate that one user likes or dislikes the comments of another [51]. The network is directed so, as before, we add the transpose to produce an undirected network.

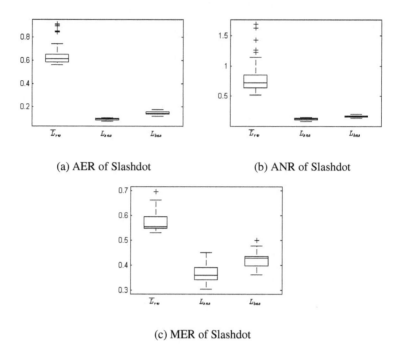

(a) AER of Slashdot   (b) ANR of Slashdot

(c) MER of Slashdot

Figure 8.11: The AER, ANR, and MER values for 30 randomly chosen subsets of 10,000 nodes from the Slashdot dataset using the forest-fire sampling method (lower values are better)

The *Slashdot* network has close to 80,000 nodes and hundreds of thousands of edges. As before, we sample subgraphs using forest-fire and random-walk sampling.

We generate 30 sampled subgraphs of a given size and use a Laplacian embedding in three dimensions to compute the measures. Once again, the ratio of positive to negative edges in the samples is higher for subsets than for the graph as a whole.

Figure 8.11 shows plots of the three measures for 10,000-node subgraphs using forest-fire sampling. Just as for the *Epinions* dataset, the AER and ANR values of L_{sns} and L_{bns} are significantly lower than the values of $\overline{L}_{rw}$. Figure 8.11(c) shows that the $\overline{L}_{rw}$ embedding works poorly on the Slashdot dataset, presumably because its balancing strategy works poorly when negative edges become more common. Furthermore, some values of $\overline{L}_{rw}$ in Figures 8.11(a) and 8.11(b) are greater than 1, which is clearly undesirable for a non-pathological subgraph. The L_{sns} and L_{bns} embeddings seem better than the $\overline{L}_{rw}$ embedding.

Figure 8.12 shows three embeddings of a 100-node subgraph, small enough to be visualized, sampled using forest-fire sampling. In Figure 8.12(a) the negative edges are concentrated at the lower left near the origin, but the long arms are positive edges. Embeddings similar to this show why the AER and ANR values can be greater than 1 for the $\overline{L}_{rw}$ measures. Figures 8.12(b) and 8.12(c) show that the L_{sns} and L_{bns}

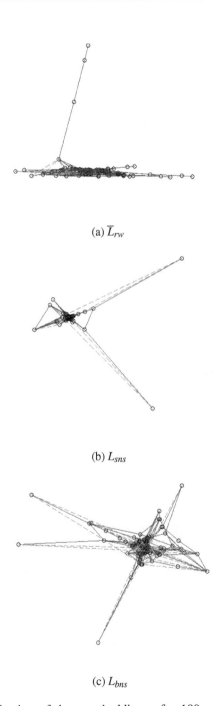

(a) $\overline{L}_{rw}$

(b) L_{sns}

(c) L_{bns}

Figure 8.12: Visualization of three embeddings of a 100-node forest-fire sample subgraph from Slashdot, using the three different Laplacians

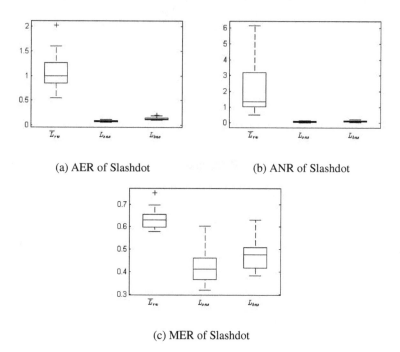

(a) AER of Slashdot   (b) ANR of Slashdot

(c) MER of Slashdot

Figure 8.13: The AER, ANR, and MER values for 30 randomly chosen subsets of 10,000 nodes from the Slashdot dataset using the random-walk sampling method (lower values are better)

embeddings are more plausible but do not necessarily resemble one another.

Figure 8.13 shows the three ratio measures for the sampled 10,000 node subgraphs using random-walk sampling. The results are similar to those of the forest-fire subgraphs — the two measures for L_{sns} and L_{bns} are significantly lower than those for $\overline{L}_{rw}$.

The similarity of results with different sized subgraphs, different sampling methods and different datasets shows the usefulness of the three measures. The AER and ANR measures indicate that the L_{sns} and L_{bns} embeddings have better performance than the $\overline{L}_{rw}$ embedding. The L_{sns} embedding is slightly better than the L_{bns} embedding. The MER measure does not distinguish the different embeddings as much, suggesting that the differences are mainly in the way that the non-core nodes are embedded.

8.5 Summary

It is obviously implausible that the relationships in social networks, even when typed and directed, are always positive. It is useful to be able to include situations where a relationship is negative. However, this is not easy because of transitivity — positive relationships tend to be transitive in a natural way (the friend of my friend might well become my friend), but negative relationships are more complex. The enemy of my enemy could form an alliance with me against out mutual enemy but, on the other hand, I might dislike them even more than my immediate enemy. We have developed a way to balance the similarity implicit in positive relationships with the dissimilarity implicit in negative relationships. Using it as the basis of embeddings produces plausible results, looked at from several different perspectives.

Notes

The spectral method for signed graphs proposed by Kunegis et al. [48] can be used to embed signed networks and do further analysis, such as clustering. However, their signed graph embedding has an obvious weakness, and is also problematic to extend from 2-way signed ratio cut and 2-way normalized cut to the k-way clustering problem [17].

A weighted kernel k-means clustering objective is mathematically equivalent to a general spectral clustering objective [24] and can outperform spectral methods in terms of quality, speed, and memory usage. Chiang et al. [17] modified weighted kernel k-means clustering to apply it to signed graphs. Their signed kernel is similar to one of our methods, but is a different way to solve this problem. Furthermore, an embedding map is more meaningful than a simple index of partitions. For example, the embedding allows us to visualize a graph, and tells us the global quantifiable similarity between unconnected nodes which a simple clustering cannot do.

There are also other signed graph clustering methods. For example, Yang et al. [108] proposed an agent-based approach to partition signed networks; Traag and Bruggeman [98] presented a graph clustering method based on modularity using the Potts model representation; Anchuri and Magdon-Ismail [1] extended an existing modularity-based graph-partitioning technique [70] to signed networks. However, an embedding map is more meaningful than a simple index of partitions.

The approach described in this chapter was first presented in Zheng and Skillicorn [112].

Chapter 9

Signed graph-based semi-supervised learning

We now turn to using the signed graph embedding construction of the last chapter as a new way to frame and solve the problems of semi-supervised prediction, especially for classes of different sizes.

Consider a social network where only a few nodes have been labelled with the value of a particular property. The task is to label all of the other nodes in the way that best respects the known labels *and* the connection structure of the social network. Of course, this will only work well if the property of interest is associated with *homophily* — similar nodes from the social-network perspective are likely to be similar with respect to the property. Examples include political affiliation (friends tend to have similar political views), age (friends tend to be in a similar age cohort), and length of arrest record (criminals tend to have criminal friends).

The intuition for graph-based semi-supervised prediction is that an unlabelled record should be assigned the label of its "closest" labelled neighbor — but "closest" is a subtle relationship because it may depend not only on the *shortest* path from the unlabelled node to the labelled node, but also on the *number* of such paths. In other words, an unlabelled node connected to a class *A* node by a single short path, but to a class *B* node by several slightly longer paths, may still be reasonably classified as class *B*. Graph-based semi-supervised prediction is appropriate when the properties of a node are best understood within some larger context — for example, the decision to buy a product may depend not only on an individual's preferences, but also on those of their neighbors in the social network, either because of social pressure, or because they get trusted recommendations from their neighbors. Graph-based Semi-Supervised Learning (SSL) algorithms tend to have a better performance than non-graph-based SSL approaches [92] and have been successfully used in many areas [93].

The labels of the labelled subset of the nodes could be thought of as a kind of influence that flows along the edges of a graph, flowing most easily along edges with heavy weights and gradually diminishing in intensity, but also flowing in parallel

121

along multiple edges. The label given to an unlabelled node becomes either that of the leading edge of the flow from one of the labelled nodes, or the greatest intensity of flow that reached it from any labelled node. Most existing algorithms use some variant of this "spreading activation" intuition.

When the sizes of the classes are different, or the number of labelled nodes is not proportional to the size of the class that they represent, the performance of these algorithms degrades. It is easy to see why. The flow from the labelled nodes of a small class can quickly reach all of the nodes of the cluster of unlabelled nodes that belong to that class, and then begins to infiltrate the nodes of other clusters, even though these other clusters are only weakly connected to it. If there are few labelled nodes for one of the classes, then the flow from them does not necessarily reach all of the nodes in the appropriate cluster before the flow from nodes with other labels reaches them. These performance degradations can be demonstrated in both synthetic and real-world datasets.

Embedding the social network in a geometric space simplifies the spreading process because it becomes a wavefront moving directly in that space. Or, to put it another way, the label of an unlabelled node can be determined by computing the distance between it and the labelled nodes in the geometry. Using the signed network embedding technique introduced in the previous chapter enables a semi-supervised prediction algorithm that performs at about the same level as other graph-based SSL approaches when the classes, or the labelled class representatives, are balanced. However, when either, or both, are not balanced this approach performs substantially better. Since there is no reason to suppose that real-world datasets will necessarily be doubly balanced, as these other algorithms require, our approach is more general.

We compare our SSL method with existing spectral kernel SSL methods: *LGC* [118], *LapSVMp* [59] and *TACO* [73] by applying them to several synthetic and two real-world datasets: the USPS handwritten digits and ISOLET Spoken Letter datasets.

9.1 Approach

We avoid the problems associated with spreading activation strategies and leverage the ability to embed signed graphs. Consider first the two-class case. The high-level algorithm uses these steps:

1. Add two new nodes ("stations") that act as class representatives;

2. Connect the labelled nodes of each class to their class representative by positively weighted edges;

3. Force the class representatives apart by adding a negative edge between them (which tends to pull the labelled nodes of each class further from one another which, in turn, tends to pull the unlabelled nodes of each class further apart);

4. Embed the graph in a Euclidean space using the spectral signed network embedding algorithm;

5. Allocate each unlabelled node to a class based on the sign of the corresponding entry in the principal eigenvector of the eigendecomposition corresponding to the signed graph Laplacian. It would be plausible to use a subset of k of the eigenvectors, and cluster in k-dimensional space, using any standard clustering algorithm, but this turns out not to be stable.

When there are more than two classes, a one-versus-the-rest strategy is used, in the style of support vector machines. The effect of this strategy is shown in Figure 9.1(a).

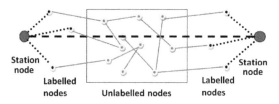

(a) Adding edges between station nodes

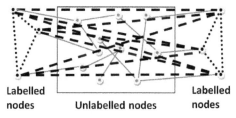

(b) Adding edges between all labelled nodes

Figure 9.1: Two possible ways to add negative edges. The solid edges are positive and the dashed edges are negative.

It would also be possible to add positive nodes between labelled nodes with the same label, and negative edges between nodes with different labels. The result is shown in Figure 9.1(b). With this strategy, the number of added edges increases quadratically in the number of labelled nodes, while our strategy requires extra edges only linear in the number of labelled nodes. As the figures show, even for this small graph the difference is non-trivial.

A technical problem remains which requires an extension to the previous signed spectral embedding technique. Node degree matters and the labelled nodes have all had their degree increased by one by the addition of a new edge to the class representative node. The total degree of the graph has also increased. To avoid the distortions that this might create, we modify the total degree term in L_{sns} so that the total degree of original nodes are computed based on the original graph edges, and the total degree of stations are computed based on the total degree in the new graph.

Let A be the original $n \times n$ graph adjacency matrix, and apw and anw be the added positive and negative edge weights. Assume we have two classes with a $n \times 2$ label indication matrix F, where $F_i = [1,0]$ (the ith row vector of F) if node x_i is labelled as the first class, $F_i = [0,1]$ if node x_i is labelled as the second class, and $F_i = [0,0]$ if node x_i is not labelled. Then the $(n+2) \times (n+2)$ adjacency matrix W of the new graph with extra nodes is defined as:

$$W = \begin{pmatrix} A & apw * F \\ & 0 & -anw \\ apw * F' & -anw & 0 \end{pmatrix}. \tag{9.1}$$

The modified total degree $\hat{D}$ of the new graph is a $(n+2) \times (n+2)$ diagonal matrix with diagonal value:

$$\hat{D}_{ii} = \sum_{j=1}^{n} |A_{ij}|, \qquad \forall i \in [1,n],$$

$$\hat{D}_{ii} = anw + apw * \sum_{j=1}^{n} F_{i-n,j}, \quad \forall i \in [n+1, n+2]. \tag{9.2}$$

Let RS be the row sum diagonal matrix of W, that is, $RS_{ii} = \sum_{j=1}^{n+2} W_{ij}$. Then the modified signed Laplacian becomes:

$$\hat{L}_{sns} = \hat{D}^{-1}(RS - W)$$

where $RS - W = (D^+ - W^+) - (D^- - W^-)$.

Thus, the positive part W^+ of the new graph with extra nodes, a $(n+2) \times (n+2)$ matrix, is defined as:

$$W^+ = \begin{pmatrix} A & apw * F \\ apw * F' & 0 \end{pmatrix}.$$

The negative part, the $(n+2) \times (n+2)$ matrix W^-, is defined as:

$$W^- = \begin{pmatrix} 0 & \cdots & 0 & 0 & 0 \\ \vdots & \ddots & \vdots & \vdots & \vdots \\ 0 & \cdots & 0 & 0 & 0 \\ 0 & \cdots & 0 & 0 & anw \\ 0 & \cdots & 0 & anw & 0 \end{pmatrix}.$$

The modified total degree $\hat{D}$ of the new graph is a $(n+2) \times (n+2)$ diagonal matrix with diagonal value:

$$\hat{D}_{ii} = \sum_{j=1}^{n} A_{ij}, \quad \forall i \in [1,n]$$

$$\hat{D}_{n+i,n+i} = anw + apw * \sum_{j=1}^{n} F_{ij}, \quad \forall i \in [1,2]$$

The modified signed Laplacian becomes:

$$\hat{L}_{sns} = \hat{D}^{-1} \left((D^+ - W^+) - (D^- - W^-) \right)$$

The corresponding Rayleigh quotient is:

$$R_{\hat{L}_{sns}}(f) = \frac{\frac{1}{2}\sum_{i,j=1}^{n+2}\left(w_{ij}^+(f_i-f_j)^2 - w_{ij}^-(f_i-f_j)^2\right)}{\sum_{i=1}^{n+2}\hat{d}_i f_i^2}$$

$$= \frac{\frac{1}{2}\sum_{i,j=1}^{n}A_{ij}(f_i-f_j)^2}{\sum_{i=1}^{n+2}\hat{d}_i f_i^2}$$

$$+ \frac{\sum_{i=1}^{n} apw * F_{i,1}(f_i-f_{n+1})^2}{\sum_{i=1}^{n+2}\hat{d}_i f_i^2}$$

$$+ \frac{\sum_{i=1}^{n} apw * F_{i,2}(f_i-f_{n+2})^2}{\sum_{i=1}^{n+2}\hat{d}_i f_i^2}$$

$$- \frac{anw(f_{n+1}-f_{n+2})^2}{\sum_{i=1}^{n+2}\hat{d}_i f_i^2}.$$

A minimum of the Rayleigh quotient $R_{\hat{L}_{sns}}(f)$ corresponds to an embedding that minimizes the total squared distance between connected nodes in the original graphs, plus the distances of the labelled nodes to the corresponding class-representative nodes, and maximizes the total squared distance between the two stations, normalized by the modified total degree $\hat{D}$.

We use the Rayleigh quotient $R_{\hat{L}_{sns}}(f)$ as a relaxed version of our objective function for our graph-based SSL method. Finding the embedding to minimize the Rayleigh quotient $R_{\hat{L}_{sns}}(f)$ is equivalent to finding the eigenvector corresponding to the smallest eigenvalue of $\hat{L}_{sns}$. Thus we can use eigendecomposition to find the optimal solution of our objective function. Two-class classification is based on the eigenvector associated with the smallest non-trivial eigenvalue — the nodes are divided into two groups based on the sign of their corresponding entries in this eigenvector, and these two groups are predicted to be members of the two classes.

There is also a random-walk interpretation of our approach. For the part of the graph connected by positive edges, the matrix $\hat{L}_{sns}$ without the class-representative nodes has the same eigenvectors as the conventional random walk normalized Laplacian matrix $L_{rw} = I - D^{-1}W$ [84]. A random walk starting from any node wanders around the graph until it reaches a labelled node, but is then likely to go to the class-representative node since the edge to it has high weight. From this perspective, the random walk measures how likely an unlabelled node is to reach the "nearest" class representative. In contrast, a random-walk interpretation of activation spreading approaches begins from the labelled nodes. Unlabelled nodes are labelled by the first random walker that reaches them. When one cluster is small, a random walker from its labelled node(s) can reach unlabelled nodes in other clusters before the random walker from their own labelled nodes.

The modified Laplacian matrix $\hat{L}_{sns}$ has most the properties of L_{sns} except for the range of its eigenvalues. The lower boundary is still -2, but the upper boundary can exceed 2. The eigendecomposition of $\hat{L}_{sns}$ can be calculated using instead the symmetric matrix $\hat{D}^{-1/2}(RS-W)\hat{D}^{-1/2}$. This calculation is fast because the matrix is symmetric. Since we only need one eigenvector, the complexity of the calculation is quadratic in n if the matrix is dense, and linear if the matrix is sparse. As we have already discussed, social network graphs are likely to be sparse (although this algorithm could be applied to graphs generated in other ways, where this might not be true.)

To summarize, the Binary Class Graph Embedding (BCGE) for graph data with a limited class label set can be computed in 6 steps.

Method (BCGE) Input: An undirected adjacency matrix A, an $n \times 2$ label indication matrix F, and apw and anw the added positive and negative edge weights.
Output: One-dimensional embedding vector v.

---

1. Compute the new adjacency matrix W with two added nodes as in equation (9.1).

2. Compute the diagonal matrices $\hat{D}$ as in equation (9.2).

3. Compute the row sum diagonal matrix RS of W.

4. Compute the symmetric Laplacian matrix $\hat{L}_{sym} = \hat{D}^{-1/2}(RS - W)\hat{D}^{-1/2}$.

5. Compute the smallest non-trivial eigenvector u of $\hat{L}_{sym}$.

6. Use 0 as a threshold to allocate objects corresponding to each entry of the eigenvector to one class or the other.

The general process for our graph-based eigenvector SSL algorithm, **GBE**, is:

Input: An undirected adjacency matrix A, an $n \times c$ label indication matrix F, where f_i is the ith column vector of F, and apw and anw the added positive and negative edge weights.
Output: Label prediction vector y^*.

If $c = 2$,   run $v = BCGE(A, F, apw, anw)$;
             $y_i^* = 1$ if $v_i > 0$, else $y_i^* = 2$.
If $c > 2$,   for each $i \in [1, c]$
                $F^* = [f_i, \sum_{j \neq i} f_j]$;
                $V_i = BCGE(A, F^*, apw, anw)$;
             $y_i^* = \arg\max_j V_{ij}$

Each eigenvector f of $\hat{L}_{sns}$ can be computed by $f = \hat{D}^{-1/2}v$, where v is the eigenvector of the $\hat{L}_{sym}$. But this step is unnecessary because the modified total degrees of the nodes do not change for different class labels. When we deal with the multiple class problem, for each node i, the V_{ij} are on the same scale. As a side effect, in the multiple class problem, the major part of $\hat{L}_{sym}$ for each label is the same; only the last two columns and rows need to be changed. Furthermore, because we know the trivial eigenvalue of the symmetric Laplacian is 0 with corresponding eigenvector $\hat{D}^{1/2} * \mathbb{1}$, we can directly compute the smallest non-trivial eigenvector.

This means we only need to compute a single specific eigenvector of the symmetric matrix for each class.

9.2 Problems of imbalance in graph data

There are two ways in which data can be imbalanced. First, the number of records in one class might be much larger than the number in the other class(es). Second, the number of available labelled records in one class might be larger than the number in other class(es). And of course both might happen simultaneously. These imbalances cause performance difficulties for models based on some form of spreading activation.

We have shown that our methods are mathematically well behaved and motivated. Comparing our results with two existing spectral kernel SSL methods: *LGC* [118] and LapSVMp [59], and a method based on probability: *TACO* [73] which was shown to outperform *LP* [3], *MAD* [94] and *AM* [92], we show the advantages of our approach.

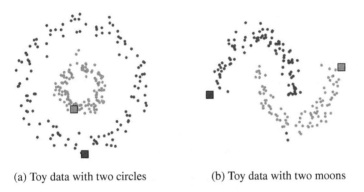

(a) Toy data with two circles   (b) Toy data with two moons

Figure 9.2: Applying GBE to two toy datasets with only one labelled node (square) for each class

First, we start with toy data. The nodes of two toy datasets are generated in two-dimensional space, and adjacency matrices are constructed by connecting each point to its five nearest neighbors. One node of each class is labelled. Figure 9.2 shows that the results of our *GBE* approach work as well as the algorithms of [5, 118].

If the structure of the original graph is consistent with the class labels, only a small repulsive force is needed to model the graph structure. Hence only a small value for the negative edge weight *anw* is needed. Both of these examples have such consistent structure, so only a small value of *anw* leads to good classification results.

A more substantial synthetic data was created, with 0/1 edge weights. Edges between two nodes in the same class were created with probability 10% and between nodes in different classes with probability 2%. Class sizes of 300 were used for balanced datasets; sizes of 250 and 1000 for two-class datasets; and 250, 500, 750, and 1000 for four-class datasets.

We also apply our approach to two real-world datasets: the USPS handwritten digit and the ISOLET Spoken Letter datasets, which are commonly used for graph-based SSL. The ISOLET Spoken Letter dataset [53] was generated by 150 subjects speaking the name of each English letter of the alphabet twice. Thus there are 300 instances for each letter. We use letters "A" and "B" as a binary classification problem and letters "A", "B", "C", and "D" as a four-class problem in our experiments.

The USPS data consists of handwritten grayscale 8-bit (16×16) images of digits "0" to "9". There are 1100 examples of each class, but we only use the first 300 examples of each class to match the size of the ISOLET data. We use digits "2" and "3" as a binary classification problem and digits "1", "2", "3", and "4" as a four-class problem.

Both datasets are not graph-based. We convert the data to adjacency matrices first, and then apply the graph-based SSL. The adjacency matrices are constructed using the K-Nearest Neighbor approach with an RBF kernel, with K set to 5; and the diagonal elements of the created adjacency matrices are set to 0. We add the transpose to symmetrize the adjacency matrices. The average degree in all the generated adjacency matrices is a little less than 5. The average edge weight is little greater than 0.5.

In all the experiments, we set $apw = 150$ for the added positive edges, creating a strong "pull" of labelled nodes towards their class representatives, and $anw = 5$ for the negative edge weight, around the mean value of the degree. A sensitivity analysis over a range of values for apw and anw is shown in Figure 9.3. It is clear that the quality of the results is relatively insensitive to these choices, as long as they are large enough.

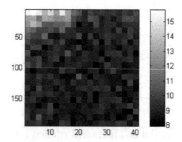

Figure 9.3: Plot of average error over 30 repeated executions for different choices of positive and negative edge weights, apw and anw. These results are for the case of imbalanced group sizes and equal number of labels, but results are similar for all other configurations.

We use $\alpha = 0.8$ in the *LGC* approach; $\gamma_I = 1$, $\gamma_A = 1e - 5$, the normalized Laplacian kernel with early stopping "PCG" in the *LapSVMp* approach; and $\alpha = 1e - 6$, $\beta = 1e - 3$, $\gamma = 1$ in the *TACO* approach. The test errors are averaged over 30 trials of each label pair.

Because there are slight differences between binary classification and c-class classification, we test the performances in both situations.

The balanced case

First, we use SSL for a two-class problem, comparing all four approaches. The number of labelled nodes in each group is varied, increasing gradually. Figure 9.4 shows that the error rates of *LGC* and *TACO* are worse than those of *LapSVMp* and *GBE* for the datasets when the number of labelled nodes is small. However, the difference is negligible when there are 10% or more labelled nodes in each group. Furthermore, the error percentages tend to be stable after more than 10% labels for all three approaches.

The *LapSVMp* approach has a worse performance on the synthetic dataset, but better performances on the real-world datasets. Our *GBE* has good performance on the three datasets.

We also use four equal-sized classes, with the same number of labelled nodes in each group. Figure 9.5 shows that the performance of our approach *GBE* is better than others for the synthetic data, but is similar for the two real-world datasets. Figure 9.5 also shows that the performances of *LapSVMp* and *GBE* are slightly better than *LGC* and *TACO* for the USPS handwritten data, but worse for the ISOLET Spoken Letter data. When the number of labelled nodes in each group reaches 30 (10%) or more, the results of the four approaches tend to be consistent and stable. All of the four approaches perform equally when the class sizes and the numbers of labelled nodes are balanced. The performances for multiple classes are significantly worse than for two classes since the connections among the classes become more complicated.

Imbalance in the number of labelled nodes

Now we consider the case where the class sizes are equal but the number of labelled nodes per class is not. For the two-class classification problem, we set the number of labelled nodes in the second class to be 4 times the number in the first class. Figure 9.6 shows the results of two-class classification in this setting. *GBE* is now substantially better than the others, especially for small numbers of labelled nodes. Its performance remains at the same level as the balanced case.

For the four-class problem, we label the second, third and fourth classes with 2, 3 and 4 times the number of labelled nodes as the first class. Figure 9.7 shows the results. Our *GBE* approach again shows better performances for both datasets.

Figure 9.8 gives the boxplots of the distributions of error percentages in the last column of Figure 9.7. Figure 9.8 shows that the errors of our *GBE* approach are statistically significantly lower than the other two. In this case, we have 30, 60, 90 and 120 labelled instances in the first to fourth classes, respectively, more than 10% of the total instances. From the previous experiments, 10% of nodes labelled is sufficient for a stable result, and this is true for our *GBE* approach in these cases. Error percentages for the *LGC*, *LapSVMp* and *TACO* approaches are far higher than in the previous experiments with the same number of labels.

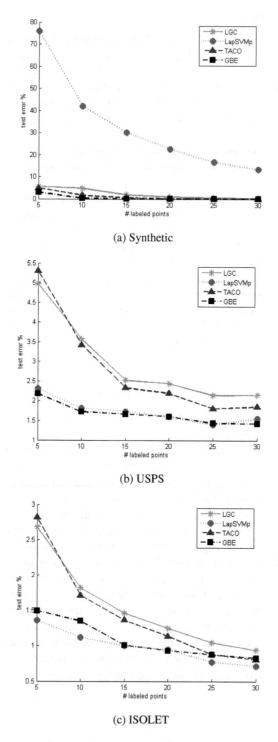

(a) Synthetic

(b) USPS

(c) ISOLET

Figure 9.4: Error rates for two classes, same size classes, same number of labelled nodes in each class (GBE is our technique).

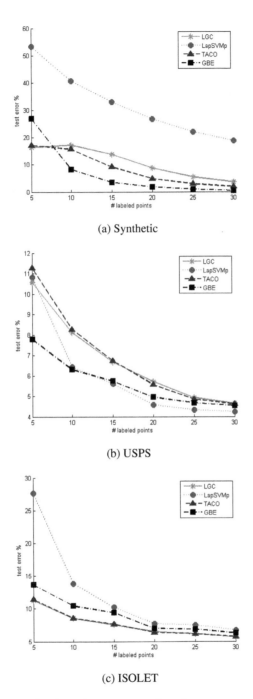

(a) Synthetic

(b) USPS

(c) ISOLET

Figure 9.5: Error rates for four classes, same size classes, same number of labelled nodes in each class (GBE is our technique)

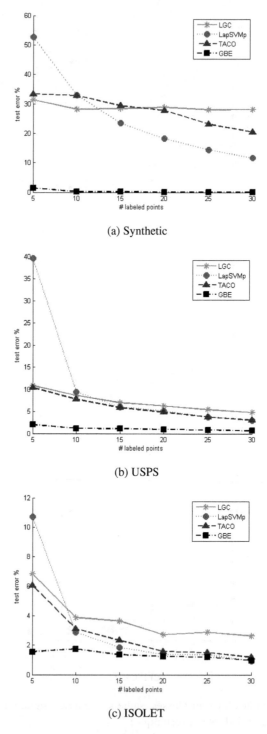

(a) Synthetic

(b) USPS

(c) ISOLET

Figure 9.6: Error rates for two classes, equal class sizes, number of labelled nodes in the second class is 4 times that of the first class.

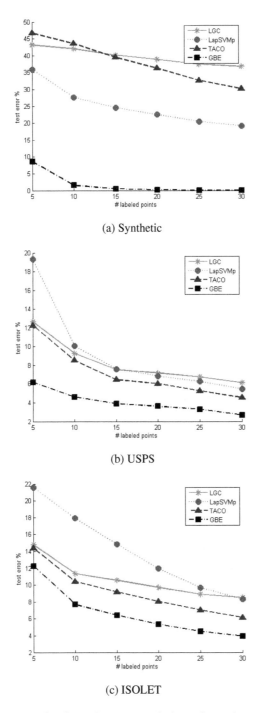

(a) Synthetic

(b) USPS

(c) ISOLET

Figure 9.7: Error rates for four classes, equal class sizes, the number of labelled records in the second, third and fourth classes is 2, 3, and 4 times the number of labelled records in the first class

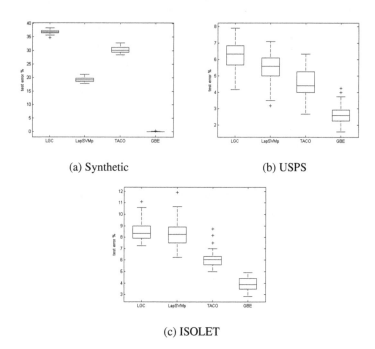

(a) Synthetic   (b) USPS

(c) ISOLET

Figure 9.8: Boxplots of error rates from the last column of the figures in Figure 9.7 (i.e. with 30, 60, 90 and 120 labels in the first to fourth classes, respectively)

When the number of labelled nodes are different in different classes, the threshold of the decision boundaries are different. For simplicity, consider only the two-class case. All four approaches put the labelled nodes at the ends of a structure, and let the rest of nodes "pull" each other according to the edge structure. After the configuration relaxes, the *LGC*, *TACO* and *LapSVMp* place the nodes in the middle. For example, in the *LGC* approach, +1 and −1 are the boundaries of the two labels, and 0 is the threshold for predictions. However, when the number of labelled nodes in one group is much greater than in the other, *all* of the unlabelled nodes tend to be pulled towards the end with more labelled nodes. This discrepancy causes the performance of all of the *LGC*, *TACO* and *LapSVMp* approaches to be poor. This is the same kind of problem that happens in algorithms such as K-means when the obvious clusters are of very different sizes or non-spherical shapes.

On the other hand, our *GBE* approach splits the nodes into two groups based on the constraint $\hat{D}f \perp 1$ and with 0 as threshold. Our approach therefore pulls the nodes out of the middle region of the embedding.

Imbalance in class sizes

We also consider the case where the number of labelled nodes in each class is the same, but the number of instances of each class is different. Figure 9.9 shows the results for the three datasets with four classes. Our approach has better performance

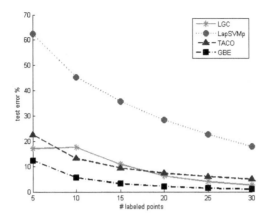

(a) Synthetic — two classes (250, 500, 750, and 1000 nodes).

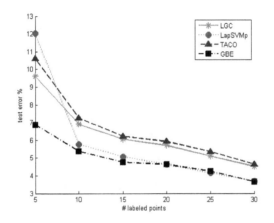

(b) USPS — two classes (250, 500, 750, and 1000 nodes).

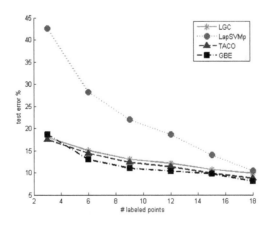

(c) ISOLET — two classes (75, 150, 225, and 300 nodes).

Figure 9.9: Error rates for four classes with the same number of labelled nodes but different numbers of nodes in each class

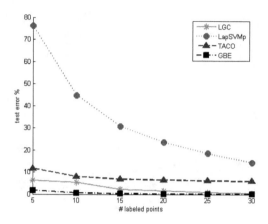

(a) Synthetic — two classes (250 and 1000 nodes).

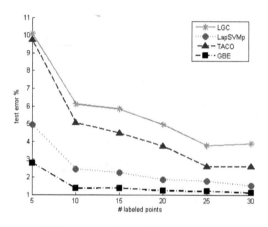

(b) USPS — two classes (250 and 1000 nodes).

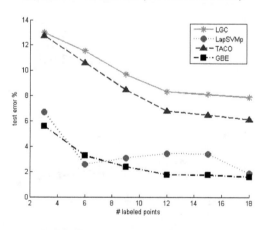

(c) ISOLET — two classes (75 300 nodes).

Figure 9.10: Error rates for two classes with the same number of labelled nodes, but different numbers of nodes in each class

and stabilizes with fewer labelled nodes than *LGC*, *TACO* and *LapSVMp*. The *LGC* and *TACO* approaches have also a stable performance, but *LapSVMp* approach has worse performance on the synthetic dataset and the ISOLET dataset. The results for two classes are similar to the four-class case, but the *LapSVMp* approach has similar performance to ours using the ISOLET data.

Our *GBE* approach shows a lower error rate when the number of labelled nodes in each class is the same, but the number of instances of each class is different. Thus it performs at approximately the same level as the other state-of-the-art algorithms in the balanced cases, but outperforms them in both imbalanced cases: imbalanced class sizes, and imbalanced numbers of labelled points.

9.3 Summary

The attraction of graph-based semi-supervised learning algorithms is that they not only use the class label information, but also exploit the graph structure, in particular the intuition that connected nodes "should", in general, have the same labels. Graph-based SSL approaches tend to have better performance than non-graph-based SSL [92]. We have combined the intuition that graph structure helps class label assignments with our new technique for signed network embedding, The performance of our technique matches that of the comparable approaches when the class sizes are balanced, but exceeds them substantially when classes are imbalanced — which is the typical real-world case. The performance differences illustrate the weakness of these other two methods — their embedding creates the same well-known problem as k-means when the classes are of different sizes and shapes because they place the decision boundary in the "middle" of the class representatives.

Notes

There are two ways of framing the graph-based SSL problem which have led to different algorithmic strategies. One is based on probability. The Information Regularization approach [21, 41] is an example of the early work of this kind. The adsorption approach [3] is another example based on random-walk probability. Two modified versions of the adsorption approach [73, 94] were proposed later. There are also some other similar versions, for example the Quadratic Criteria approach [6] and Measure Propagation [92].

The other way to frame this problem is based on graph cuts and Laplacian kernels. An overview of the properties and interpretation of spectral clustering can be found in [101]. In these approaches, classification is carried out in the embedded graph by classifying each unlabelled point as belonging to the class of its (Euclidean distance) nearest labelled neighbor.

Subsequently, many extensions of spectral graph analysis approaches have been developed, including a signed graph spectral approach based on placing negative pairs on opposite sides of the axis [48], and a signed graph spectral approach based on pushing negative pairs apart [112].

Blum et al. [7, 8] was the first to use graph cut ideas for classification by simple counting the edges between classes. Joachims [42] embeds the graph first, and then learns from the embeddings. Zhu et al. [123] proposed the first approach using a Laplacian kernel in the optimal function and called it the Gaussian Random Fields SSL approach. Zhou et al. [118] proposed a more relaxed version: the Local and Global Consistency (*LGC*) approach, which counts the distances from the labelled nodes to the corresponding labelled node as penalties in the objective function. Belkin et al. [4, 5] proposed two similar versions based on SVM (*LapSVM*) and Regularized Least Squares. Melacci and Belkin [59] later refine the *LapSVM* approach and reduced the computational complexity for training from $O(n^3)$ to $O(kn^2)$.

Subramanya et al. [93] compared various approaches using several common datasets. Based on their experiments, there is no single approach which performs the best for all datasets.

The problem of imbalance has been considered by Li et al. [52] in the context of sentiment prediction. They compare undersampling and oversampling approaches (which assume that labelled examples are relatively plentiful) to dynamic subspaces using attribute selection and show that this latter technique improves prediction performance by 2 to 4 percentage points. However, subspace sampling approaches can only be applied to attributed data, and not to data that is already graphical, for example social networks.

The approach in this chapter was first described in Zheng and Skillicorn [113].

Chapter 10

Combining directed and signed embeddings

We now show how the layer approach and compositions can be used to model networks that have edges that are both signed (with positive and negative weights) and directed. So, for example, we will be able to model the situation where A has a positive relationship with B, but B has a negative relationship with A.

Intelligence, terrorism and law-enforcement applications, in particular, are characterized by asymmetric relationships (command-and-control or flow of information) and by relationships with both allies and foes. Understanding the social dynamics of a group, or the ecosystem of interactions among groups requires social network analysis for networks in which the edges are both signed *and* directed.

In this chapter we take the signed embedding technique, the directed embedding technique, and the composition of layered models technique and show how to use them to embed directed, signed networks. Properties of the network can be understood from visualizations; we also define a measure that highlights nodes with unusual roles.

10.1 Composition of directed and signed layer models

As before, the strategy for embedding based on both sign and direction is to take the information implicit in the network edges (direction and sign) and encode it by introducing multiple versions for each node.

First, multiple versions of each node are created, one connected to the positive edges, and one to the negative edges. Then, each node is replaced by two versions, one coding for its incoming edges and the other for its outgoing edges, as in the new directed network construction. All of the edges connecting versions are undirected, since the directional information is coded in the pattern of connections of these edges. Each node of the original graph is therefore replaced by four versions with these connections: incoming negative edges, outgoing negative edges, incoming positive edges, and outgoing positive edges. The edges of the original graph are connected to these nodes in the obvious way. The four versions of each node are then connected to each other by an undirected four-clique whose edge weights are the sum of (the absolute values of) the incident weight of the original version of the node. Thus both incident positive and negative edges act to make the nexus more closely bound.

Let W^+ be the directed adjacency matrix representing the positive edges; W^- the directed adjacency matrix representing the negative edges (so both matrices containing only non-negative entries); DP_{in} and DN_{in} the indegrees of the two adjacency matrices, and DP_{out} and DN_{out} their outdegrees. The weights on the edges joining the new versions of the ith node will be the sum of the ith entries of these vectors. Let $\overline{D}$ be the matrix with these weights on the diagonal.

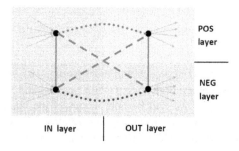

Figure 10.1: Replication of each node first into positive and negative versions and then into in- and out-versions

Define a matrix in which the four versions are connected in a clique as shown in Figure 10.1. First, each node is duplicated and the positive edges connected to one copy and the negative edges to the other. Then each of these nodes is duplicated and the incoming edges connected to one and the outgoing edges to the other. Finally, a clique is added to connect the four versions of each original node.

More formally, define the adjacency matrix for the graph that captures the signed structure of the network by:

$$X = \begin{bmatrix} W^+ + \overline{D} & \overline{D} \\ \overline{D} & -W^- + \overline{D} \end{bmatrix} \tag{10.1}$$

If the network contains n nodes, then X is a $2n \times 2n$ matrix, but as usual the added pieces are only diagonals (so linear in n) and, if W^+ and W^- are sparse, then so is X.

Let $bigD$ be the $2n \times 2n$ matrix:

$$bigD = \begin{bmatrix} 0 & \overline{D} \\ \overline{D} & 0 \end{bmatrix}$$

and then define a $4n \times 4n$ matrix:

$$M = \begin{bmatrix} bigD & X \\ X' & bigD \end{bmatrix} \tag{10.2}$$

Equation 10.1 adds the horizontal (dashed) edges in Figure 10.1 by the entries added to the major diagonal submatrices, and adds the vertical (solid) edges by the submatrices on the minor diagonal. Equation 10.2 adds the diagonal (dotted) edges in Figure 10.1.

Let $\widetilde{DP}$ and $\widetilde{DN}$ be the matrices whose diagonals are the row sums of the absolute values of the positive and negative entries of M, respectively. Let $\widetilde{D}$ be the sum of $\widetilde{DP}$ and $\widetilde{DN}$. Then the desired Laplacian matrix is

$$L_{sns} = \widetilde{D}^{-1}(\widetilde{DP} - \widetilde{DN} - M)$$

Although L_{sns} is much larger than W^+ and W^-, the extra pieces are either diagonals or transposes. The matrix remains sparse if W^+ and W^- are.

If V is the matrix of the eigenvectors of L_{sns}, then the network is embedded in k dimensions by treating the k smallest eigenvectors as coordinates for each point [1].

Because there are now four versions of each node of the original graph, embeddings can become cluttered. Each of the four versions are connected to one another by edges of the same weight. They should therefore be embedded at similar distances from one another, all things being equal.

The effect on added "vertical" edges is not the same for positive and negative edges. When an individual has positive connections *from* one set of participants but positive connections *to* a largely disjoint set of other participants, one edge of the clique will be long because there is a net flow of positivity across the individual.

When an individual has positive connections from many different participants, the corresponding edge of the clique will be short, because the "pull" on its versions comes from many different directions.

When an individual has negative connections from a few nodes that are similar to one another, the embedded negative-negative edge will tend to be longer than expected. This is because negative edges tend to "push" nodes outwards; this push is effectively stronger when most of the outward force is aligned, that is it comes from a set of nodes that are embedded in relatively the same direction.

When an individual has negative connections from many diverse nodes (that is, negativity comes from many different directions), the negative-negative edge will be short, because the "push" will come from many different directions. Thus, an individual whose embedded negative-negative edge is short can be thought of as transmitting negativity among a variety of different subgroups.

Thus the noteworthy distortions within the cliques of versions of the same node are:

- Long positive-positive edges, indicating transmission of positivity from one subset of nodes to a mostly disjoint subset; and

---

[1]One eigenvector with eigenvalue 0 represents the trivial embedding in which each node is placed at the same location and is ignored as usual; however, it can appear at any point in the eigenvalue spectrum since eigenvalues range from -2 to $+2$. Furthermore, it is possible (though unlikely) that another eigenvalue is 0, even for a connected graph, because positive and negative values cancel one another out, so care is needed in this region of the spectrum.

- Long negative-negative edges, indicating focused negativity from a single subset of nodes.

Computing the effective lengths of the edges inside the clique that joins the four versions of each node can therefore provide information about how that node fits into the wider structure of positive and negative connections in the entire network.

10.2   Application to signed directed networks

To illustrate the embedding, we apply it to the Sampson Monastery data (which was used before as an undirected signed network), and another dataset derived from the Armed Conflict Location & Event Data (ACLED) Project (also used earlier).

Figure 10.2: Embedded graph of the Sampson network showing positive-positive edges

Our embedding of the Sampson network produces the same four clusters that we saw earlier; but what we add by using the signs of the edges is the ability to see the *net* like and dislike experienced by each individual. The full embedding contains $4 \times 18 = 72$ points, so the rendering is cluttered. We show the positive-positive edges and the negative-negative edges corresponding to each individual separately, in Figures 10.2 and 10.3.

The positive-positive edges are all short. From this we conclude that there is a strong clique structure, with liking being almost entirely a within-subgroup relationship. The negative edges show more variability. Individuals such as *BONAVEN* or *WINF* appear to be disliked from all directions (short negative-negative edges);

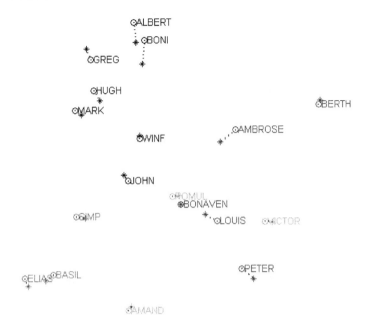

Figure 10.3: Embedded graph of the Sampson network showing negative-negative edges

whereas individuals such as *ALBERT*, *AMBROSE*, and *BONI* are involved in much more focused dislike (longer negative-negative edges).

We also compute the normalized embedded edge lengths for these edges. Table 10.1 shows these edge lengths for each of the monks. PETER stands out with both positive-positive and negative-negative values that are well above the mean. As expected of the leader of the "Young Turks" PETER has discrepancies between those he likes and those who like him (so he mediates the flow of positivity); and he is disliked in a relatively focused way.

We now turn to a more significant real-world dataset: the ACLED (Armed Conflict Location & Event Data Project — acleddata.com), which was used before as an undirected signed network.

10.2.1   North and West Africa conflict

We begin by looking at particular countries with a complex insurgent landscape, both because at the scale of a single country visualizations of the social network are small enough that they can be understood directly, and because there are interesting and practical intelligence benefits to comparing these countries to one another.

We display the positive and negative segments of the embedded social network separately, but with the same orientation and scale so that they can be compared visually. We remove groups that only participate in negative interactions — most

Name	pos-pos	neg-neg
ROMUL	0.848	1.023
BONAVEN	0.247	0.000
AMBROSE	0.899	5.638
BERTH	1.609	1.994
PETER	2.026	10.851
LOUIS	0.747	3.710
VICTOR	1.037	3.372
WINF	0.978	0.696
JOHN	1.731	3.448
GREG	0.523	8.541
HUGH	0.367	3.399
BONI	0.691	5.964
MARK	0.877	2.957
ALBERT	0.544	5.195
AMAND	1.241	1.691
BASIL	0.654	5.921
ELIAS	0.854	3.315
SIMP	1.372	3.283
Means	0.958	3.944
STD	0.478	2.739

Table 10.1: Product of edge length and reciprocal of edge weight; deviations from average indicate nodes with unusual neighborhoods

of these are pairs of groups that attack each other, and so are readily understood by analysts. The embedded position of each node is determined by both the "pull" of the other nodes to which it is connected positively, and the "push" of the other nodes to which it is connected negatively, but both "pull" and "push" are directional, that is asymmetric. The dotted edges represent the embedded positive and negative in-to-out edges, respectively — the longer such an edge, the more net flow involving the node.

Algeria

Figure 10.4 shows the two main axes of the embedding with the four versions of each node. Positive versions tend to be close to the center because the positive versions tend to "pull" each other and the negative versions tend to "push" each other. To show the details of the structure, we show the positive and negative versions in separate figures. Figures 10.5 and 10.6 show the negative and positive relationship ecosystem of groups in that country. The negative edges show clearly the separation of bad actors and good actors: radical groups such as GIA, GSPC, and AQIM on the left,

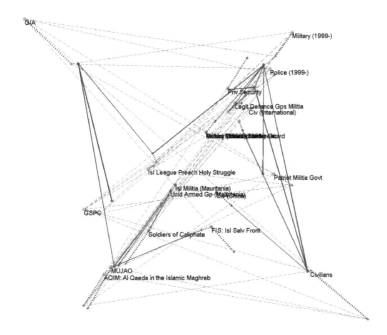

Figure 10.4: Overall relationships among Algerian groups

and police, military, and civilians on the right[2]. Nodes that are not directly connected are embedded close together when they see the same landscape in the rest of the graph; this is often a signal that they are similar, but concealing their similarity. In this case, AQIM and GSPC are unconnected and embedded close together and, in this case, it is because AQIM is a rebranding of GSPC. Differences in strategy are also clearly visible: AQIM, GSPC, and MUJAO tend to target government forces while GIA tends to target civilians. (At the end of the 1990s, the Armed Islamic Group (GIA) lost popular support in Algeria because of its massive atrocities against civilians; the situation was so bad that several GIA commanders decided to create their own, more moderate, Islamist groups, such as GSPC.)

Groups such as, in this figure, the Islamic Salvation Front are folded in towards the middle of the picture because they have a negative relationship with only one other group, GIA. It would be tempting to think of the natural position of such groups as even more peripheral, but their potential relationship to all other groups need not be negative just because of their one known negative relationship, and the more central placement reflects this.

The positive relationships contain a surprise, since they show that GIA has some indirect positive relationships with the government, even though GIA attacks civilians. The good actors have extensive alliances amongst themselves, and the

---

[2]A limitation of the dataset coding is that, while "GIA" is a well-defined group, "civilians" is a placeholder for a number of different groups at different times.

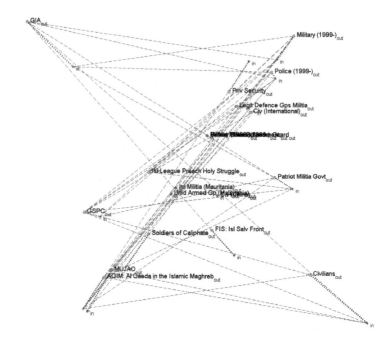

Figure 10.5: Negative relationships among Algerian groups

entire positive social network occupies less space than the negative one (the two figures are to the same scale). There is also a cross-border threat revealed in the relationship between AQIM and MUJAO with Mauritanian groups.

Libya

The relationships in Libya are, as expected, more complex with many combinations of both positive and negative relationships between the same subset of groups. Figure 10.7 shows the two main axes of negative relationships: between Al Qaeda and military special forces, and between Ansar al Sharia (and some related groups) and military and civilians. Figure 10.8 shows this latter axis in greater detail. The positive relationships are shown in Figure 10.9. There are several examples of positive relationships between groups who are, at the same time, closely associated with groups that have negative relationships — a messy ecosystem indeed.

Nigeria

The structure in Nigeria is simpler because it is dominated by Boko Haram, which is opposed to almost every other actor in the country. Figure 10.10 shows this clearly; note the relatively long dashed edge between the in- and out-versions of the Boko Haram node, signalling that negative relationships connect to groups that are similar in their position in the social network. The positive relationships are shown in

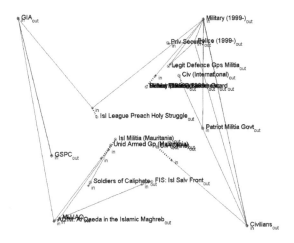

Figure 10.6: Positive relationships among Algerian groups

Figure 10.11. Both of the positive relationships to Boko Haram are of intelligence interest. First, they clearly enjoy some support from civilians; second, they are supported by an Unidentified Armed Group suggesting that they are capable or willing to act under a false flag. Note how far separated the civilian groups are from the police and military post-2010, a situation that did not hold for these groups at an earlier time.

This country-by-country analysis shows that visualizations are able to reveal significant relationships: subsets of groups that are primarily in opposition to one another, subsets that are allies, and groups whose relationships to everyone else are unusual.

The entire North and West Africa ecosystem

We now scale up this analysis to all 21 countries in North and West Africa. This is worthwhile because many groups operate across national borders, and a country-by-country analysis therefore misses significant interactions. We choose incidents coded as violent and in which radical groups participated. For each set of records, we select a large connected component of groups. (As expected, there are small sets of groups that interact only with one another, and we ignore these.) These subsets have previously been examined from a geographical perspective [106].

This much larger set of incidents can still be visualized but it is more challenging, especially as strong negative relationships tend to occupy the more significant

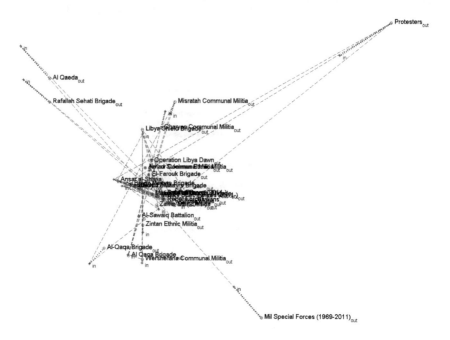

Figure 10.7: Negative relationships among Libyan groups

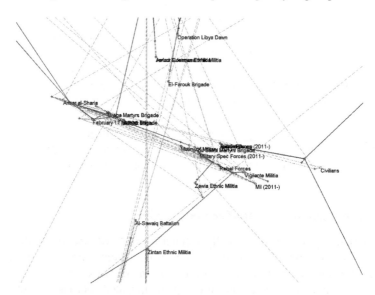

Figure 10.8: Zoomed-in relationships among Libyan groups

dimensions in the embedding.

Figure 10.12(a) shows the interaction structure of the positive edges of a 173-

Figure 10.9: Positive relationships among Libyan groups

node connected component derived from radical incidents; Figure 10.12(b) shows the corresponding negative edges.

The presence of groups with only negative edges to others necessarily produces embeddings in which the first few dimensions capture this oppositional structure, at the expense of showing details of the relationships of other groups, which are all embedded close to the origin. For example, the negative edge weight between node 127 (GIA) and node 49 (Civilians (Algeria)) is 309, while the mean positive edge weight in this entire subgraph is 5.2 and the mean negative edge weight is 12.9.

If we eliminate groups that are only connected to the rest by negative edges, we are left with 111 groups. The embeddings of their positive and negative structure is shown in Figures 10.13 and 10.14. Structures more complex than simply opposition now become visible in both the positive and negative substructure.

Finally, we select a subset of those groups that are connected to at least ten other groups. The relationships among these 16 groups are shown in Figures 10.15 and 10.16. These break into a small number of positively connected components (that is, collaborating groups) that are united into a single structure by their negative edges.

At this granularity, the lengths of the embedded extra edges become visible; for example, node 13 (Ansar al Sharia) has almost no net positive flow (so has mutual positive relationships with the same groups) but a substantial net negative one. The directed social network is important here since Ansar al Sharia has been the

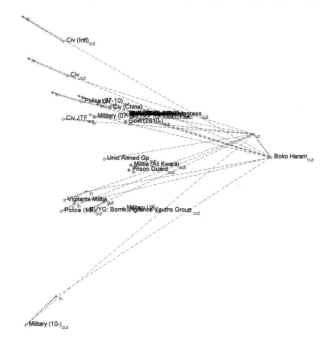

Figure 10.10: Negative relationships among Nigerian groups

aggressor against several different categories of groups including civilians, rebels, the Libyan government, and external groups, including the 2012 attack against the U.S. Consulate in Benghazi, but has also been the target of violence from the Libyan government and external groups. These visualizations give some insights into the complex and shifting alliances and divisions among groups.

The visualizations are useful but become hard to interpret for large numbers of nodes or complex structure. Computing the normalized edge lengths for the extra edges between versions of the same node focuses attention on those that are unusual. This is shown in Table 10.2. First, it is clear that the negative edges are much longer than the positive ones, as expected; there are more negative relationships, and they are quite focused. Second, the nodes that have substantial net flow can be highlighted. For example, node 77 (Civilians (Nigeria)) has unusually high normalized edge lengths in both columns. The figures show why: this node is connected in interesting ways to one set of nodes by positive edges, for example, 11 (Civilians (international)); and to a completely different set of nodes by negative edges (75 Boko Haram, and 85 Military Forces of Nigeria 2010-). Notice that there are both positive and negative edges connecting all three of these groups. The nodes highlighted here are all among the most important actors of the Northern Nigeria conflict, which opposes Boko Haram to both the Nigerian government and to Nigerian civilians. As Walther and Leuprecht show [106], Boko Haram has been successful despite having virtually no allies. (The same can be said of ISIS.)

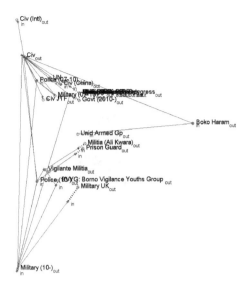

Figure 10.11: Positive relationships among Nigerian groups

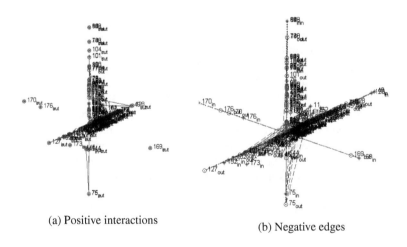

(a) Positive interactions

(b) Negative edges

Figure 10.12: 173 embedded groups involved in incidents with radical groups

The subset of groups associated with violent action contains 1895 members. Since the relationships of weakly connected nodes tend to occupy the more significant dimensions in the embedding, we select the subset of those connected to at least 20 others, resulting in a subset of 65 nodes. The positive and negative embeddings are shown in Figures 10.17 and 10.18. Again, constellations of groups in mutual op-

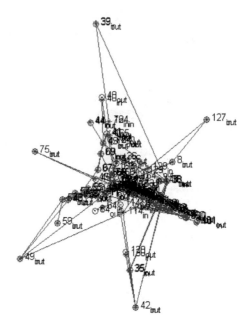

Figure 10.13: 111 embedded groups involved in incidents with radical groups showing positive edges

position are clearly visible, but there are also some interesting (primarily negative) relationships that connect the arms of the clusters. Note especially the strongly focused negativity between groups 195 (Unidentified Armed Group, Nigeria) and 196 (Niger Delta Defence and Security Council).

Table 10.3 shows the normalized edge lengths for some of the groups that either have anomalous values or are visible in the embeddings. The magnitude of the values for Unidentified Armed Group (Nigeria) is a strong red flag, since it signals both that there is a major player in the conflicts in this region, and that it remains unidentified (although the earlier analysis for Nigeria suggested that it is probably Boko Haram acting in ways it does not want to acknowledge).

10.3 Extensions to other compositions

There are some other combination networks that exist in the real world, such as temporal directed networks and temporal signed networks, as well as more complex networks, such as temporal signed directed networks with typed edges. Extending the layered model for those other combinations of connection types requires finding an appropriate construction. Although this is not difficult in principle, an argument about the edge weights in the nexus created by the versions of each node must always be made. Also, a composition of three different properties generates six versions of each node, so visualization becomes more unwieldy and abstract measures must be used instead.

Node	Name	pos-pos	neg-neg
8	GSPC	1.090	5.709
9	Al Qaeda	0.189	0.922
11	Civ (international)	0.143	3.291
13	Ansar al-Sharia	0.285	83.459
24	Mil Forces Libya	0.000	85.975
29	Libya Shield Brigade	0.000	1.443
35	Ansar Dine	3.271	46.533
38	AQIM	1.007	101.464
42	MUJAO	1.871	6.400
43	Mil Forces France	0.567	58.890
48	Police (Algeria, 1999C)	0.042	1.971
53	Mil Forces (Algeria, 1999C)	0.300	102.445
75	Boko Haram	0.543	144.854
77	Civ (Nigeria)	0.803	198.399
85	Mil Forces (Nigeria, 2010C)	0.541	56.623
127	Mil Forces (Algeria, 1994-99)	0.044	4.242
Means		0.668	56.414
STD		0.858	59.733

Table 10.2: Normalized length of embedded edges for the 16 radical groups

Nodes	Name	pos-pos	neg-neg
7	Mil Forces (Algeria, 1999C)	0.523	94.370
10	Police (Algeria, 1999C)	3.223	45.456
13	Rioters (Algeria)	0.708	37.868
18	AQIM	0.281	99.248
27	Civ (international)	0.432	21.145
31	Civ (Mali)	0.336	25.875
46	Unident Armed Group (Libya)	0.084	11.993
56	MUJAO	0.059	11.852
195	Unident Armed Group (Nigeria)	6.945	354.766
196	Niger Delta Def and Sec Council	0.130	211.881
229	Farmers Militia (Cameroon)	0.031	49.918
426	RUF	0.092	14.273
428	RPG (Guinea)	0.422	169.181
440	Union for the New Republic	0.660	117.739
Means		0.570	26.898
STD		1.133	58.828

Table 10.3: Normalized edge lengths for selected nodes in the 65-node violent subset

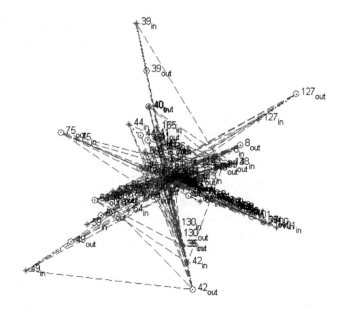

Figure 10.14: 111 embedded groups involved in incidents with radical groups showing negative edges

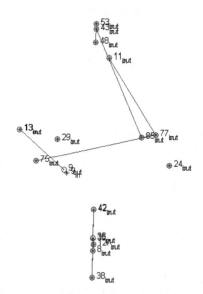

Figure 10.15: 16 embedded groups involved in incidents with radical groups showing positive edges

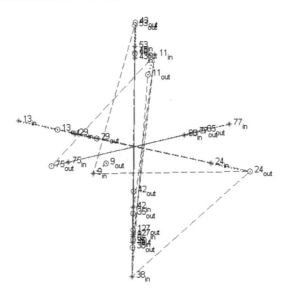

Figure 10.16: 16 embedded groups involved in incidents with radical groups showing negative edges

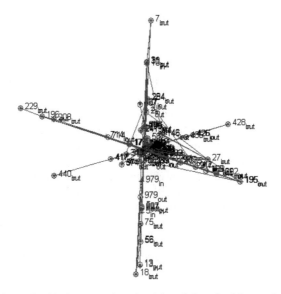

Figure 10.17: 65 embedded groups involved in violent incidents showing positive edges

10.4 Summary

Social networks that contain both positively and negatively weighted relationships often tend also to require the directions of these relationships to be taken into ac-

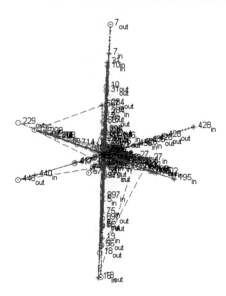

Figure 10.18: 65 embedded groups involved in violent incidents showing negative edges

count. We have seen some practical example, where the edges represent propensity to attack or to join in defence. There are also more mundane examples: influence within a group of friends may have the property that negative influence (for example, poor reviews) flows more easily among some individuals, while positive influence flows more easily among others.

We have shown how to extend the compositional layered approach to create expanded social networks that have layers for positive-negative edges, and layers for outgoing and incoming edges. This expanded graph is, once again, a simple undirected graph, and can be embedded in the usual way.

As with any construction involving two properties, there are now four versions of each node, so that direct interpretation of the visualized embedding becomes difficult (especially in the static views here). However, computing the magnitude of the local distortions that the structures in the original network impose on the edges within the nexus that connects the versions of each node makes it possible to pick out those nodes whose properties are anomalous. Thus we can focus on the parts of the network where interesting and unusual structures are to be found.

Notes

The approach in this chapter was first described in Zheng, Skillicorn, and Walther [116, 117].

Chapter 11

Summary

The way in which the quality of a model depends on the amount of data that it is built from is actually quite subtle. For example, if we want to build a prediction boundary between data of two classes, then having more examples of each class is a good thing, but the accuracy of the boundary does not increase linearly with the number of examples. Rather, it increases quickly and then flattens. The perspective of support vector machines shows why — new records are only useful to improve the boundary when they are support vectors; as the data increases, each new record becomes less and less likely to be a support vector.

If we want to find a clustering, then more data will tend to produce a better clustering, but without some data, it is impossible even to tell whether a few scattered records are a cluster or not. So while a few records from each class can already locate the prediction boundary between the classes quite well, a few records do not enable any conclusions for a clustering. We could say that the clusters are emergent from the data in this weak sense.

When it comes to social networks, the requirement for lots of data becomes even more important. Knowing a few scattered relationships does not enable any general conclusions. As the number of known relationships increases, brand new properties of the social network begin to appear. As the network of relationships becomes connected, we can define the *diameter* of the network. Once the network is more or less complete, we can compute the degrees of the nodes and discover that they tend to follow a power law. We can differentiate those nodes that are somehow *central* and those nodes that are peripheral.

Because social networks are generated by humans, making individual, local decisions about whom to relate to, and what form and intensity that relationship will take, these *emergent* properties are particularly revealing and important, because they provide insights at a more abstract level about why these relationships are formed. From the perspective of each individual, the decision to form a relationship is a local and private one. The emergent structures of social networks show that this cannot quite be true — there are forces arising from the way the human mind works, and from the ways human society works that influence each individual decision. By looking at the structure of the social network, we can infer these higher-level forces, deepening our understanding of psychology and sociology, as well as more operational properties such as influence, advertising, power, and emotional bonding. Understanding the backdrop of normality in social connections also enables us to detect anomalies that may represent criminality or concealment.

All of these properties can, in principle, be computed directly from a representation of the social network as a graph. However, many of these computations have complexities that are cubic in the number of nodes in the graph, so that computing them directly does not scale well to large graphs. This is particularly true if the graph is changing since such properties are brittle in the sense that a change in a single edge, or adding or deleting a single node, can result in changes throughout the graph. Spectral embedding has become the standard way to avoid these difficulties. Once a graph has been embedded in a geometry in such a way that distance accurately reflects dissimilarity, many of the useful emergent properties can be calculated directly in the geometry. If the geometry is low-dimensional, visualizations make it possible for analysts to see and understand emergent properties directly.

However, most social network analysis has been limited to modelling settings where relationships are of a single type, usually with an associated (positive) intensity. We have argued that this is limiting; real-world relationships are multifaceted, including at least: being of multiple, qualitatively different types; asymmetric; negative, as well as positive; and varying with time. There have been attempts to model each of these possibilities individually, with varying amounts of success.

We have introduced a single, comprehensive approach — the layered model — that allows many different edge properties to be modelled in essentially the same way. Instead of trying to represent edge properties directly, the key idea is to replicate each node into multiple versions, each of which can carry the semantics of different edge properties; and then connect simple untyped edges to the appropriate versions of these nodes to preserve their semantics.

The result is a nominally larger graph, but one which includes only a linear number of extra edges, so that if the original graph was sparse (and, in practice, it usually is), the resulting graph is also sparse. This means that the eigendecomposition at the heart of spectral embedding remains inexpensive to compute.

When this layered subgraph process is followed, the layers have to be bound together by edges that connect the versions of the same node to one another. There are strong reasons to use a clique as the basic connection pattern. Choosing the weights requires some skill, perhaps some understanding of the domain from which the social networks are taken, and perhaps some experimentation. We have made some arguments for principled ways in which these weights might be chosen.

Because the larger graph has undirected edges, the embedding step is completely standard, and the embedded graph can be visualized in a few dimensions. All of the theory of spectral embedding applies to the larger graph, so most of its properties follow directly.

The embeddings of the edges added between the layers (the "vertical" edges) reveal many subtle properties about the social network being modelled. At their simplest, the length of such an edge in the embedding measures the discrepancies between the individual's role in the network described by each layer. This can be used to detect that an individual acts quite differently in a social setting than in a work setting, or that an individual has suddenly changed his or her role in a group from one time period to the next.

In general, the length of an embedded edge "should" match its weight — edges with large weights should be shorter than edges with small weights. In a perfectly consistent social network, the ratio of embedded length to weight should be constant. Therefore, edges for which this is not true are of special interest — they are being pushed or pulled from their natural location by the nodes in their neighborhood. Computing measures based on discrepancies between expected and actual embedded length provide a way to focus attention on the interesting pieces of large social networks, those for which visualizations are too complex and cluttered for easy direct analysis.

We have also shown that the layered approach can be composed to model edges with more than one kind of semantics at once. This means that the layered approach can be used to build up models of increasing complexity by adding new edge types one at a time. This is not an automatic process — the difficulty is to choose the weights for the added edges in a principled way as the number of possible connections in the nexus of multiple versions of each individual node increases.

Discrepancies between expected and actual embedded length are particularly useful for the extra edges added in the nexus when a composed layered model is used. These edges represent, as before, discrepancies between the roles of the individual associated with that node with respect to all of the edge semantics in play in the layered composition. Especially as the number of versions of each node almost guarantees a cluttered visualization, calculating the discrepancies for all nodes is a way to focus attention on those parts of the social network that are especially interesting.

We have shown how these techniques can be applied to real-world data of varying kinds. Often, the differences between existing techniques and the layered approach make it clear why the layered approach is an improvement.

Appendices

Appendix A

RatioCut consistency with two versions of each node

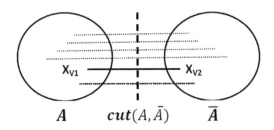

Figure A.1: A cut with the *V1* and *V2* copies of a node *x* in two different clusters

Figure A.1 is a graph cut partition by using our layered model construction, where a pair of nodes x_{V1} and x_{V2} are separated into two different groups of A and $\bar{A}$, and the cut value is $cut(A,\bar{A})$. Let d_{V1x} and d_{V2x} be the degree of nodes x_{V1} and x_{V2} without the added edges (without the edge between x_{V1} and x_{V2} in this case). Thus, the total degrees of nodes x_{V1} and x_{V2} in the layered model matrix M are $2d_{V1x}+d_{V2x}$ and $d_{V1x}+2d_{V2x}$, respectively. Let p be the sum of edge's weight from x_{V1} to nodes in $\bar{A}$ except x_{V2}. Let q be the sum of edge's weight from x_{V2} to nodes in A except x_{V1}. This cut would always be worse than the cut that puts x_{V1} and x_{V2} in the same group based on *RatioCut* and *NCut* theory.

Theorem 1: The two versions of a node will be placed in the same cluster based on RatioCut with two versions of each node, when the added edge weight between two versions of a same node is equal to the sum of the degrees of the two versions.

Proof of RatioCut Consistency with two versions of each node $(c = 2)$: Assume there is a minimum RatioCut which separates at least a pair of nodes x_{V1}

and x_{V2} into two different groups A and $\overline{A}$ as shown in Figure A.1. Thus

$$\min RatioCut = RatioCut(A,\overline{A}) = \frac{cut(A,\overline{A})}{|A|} + \frac{cut(A,\overline{A})}{|\overline{A}|} = \frac{cut(A,\overline{A}) * 2n}{|A||\overline{A}|},$$

where $|A|$ is the number of the nodes in group A.

By moving x_{V2} to A, we get

$$
\begin{aligned}
RatioCut(A + x_{V2}, \overline{A} - x_{V2}) &= \frac{cut(A + x_{V2}, \overline{A} - x_{V2}) * 2n}{|A + x_{V2}||\overline{A} - x_{V2}|} \\
&= \frac{cut(A + x_{V2}, \overline{A} - x_{V2}) * 2n}{(|A| + 1)(|\overline{A}| - 1)} \\
&= \frac{\left(cut(A,\overline{A}) - (d_{V1x} + d_{V2x} + q) + (d_{V2x} - q)\right) * 2n}{(|A| + 1)(|\overline{A}| - 1)} \\
&= \frac{\left(cut(A,\overline{A}) - d_{V1x} - 2q\right) * 2n}{|A||\overline{A}| - |A| + |\overline{A}| - 1}.
\end{aligned}
$$

Similarly by moving x_{V1} to $\overline{A}$, we get

$$
\begin{aligned}
RatioCut(A - x_{V1}, \overline{A} + x_{V1}) &= \frac{cut(A - x_{V1}, \overline{A} + x_{V1}) * 2n}{|A - x_{V1}||\overline{A} + x_{V1}|} \\
&= \frac{\left(cut(A,\overline{A}) - (d_{V1x} + d_{V2x} + p) + (d_{V1x} - p)\right) * 2n}{(|A| - 1)(|\overline{A}| + 1)} \\
&= \frac{\left(cut(A,\overline{A}) - d_{V2x} - 2p\right) * 2n}{|A||\overline{A}| + |A| - |\overline{A}| - 1}.
\end{aligned}
$$

Since the $RatioCut(A,\overline{A})$ is the minimum,

$$RatioCut(A,\overline{A}) \leq RatioCut(A + x_{V2}, \overline{A} - x_{V2})$$

$$\implies \frac{cut(A,\overline{A})}{|A||\overline{A}|} \leq \frac{cut(A,\overline{A}) - d_{V1x} - 2q}{|A||\overline{A}| - |A| + |\overline{A}| - 1} \tag{A.1}$$

and $$RatioCut(A,\overline{A}) \leq RatioCut(A - x_{V1}, \overline{A} + x_{V1})$$

$$\implies \frac{cut(A,\overline{A})}{|A||\overline{A}|} \leq \frac{cut(A,\overline{A}) - d_{V2x} - 2p}{|A||\overline{A}| + |A| - |\overline{A}| - 1}. \tag{A.2}$$

We have an even number of nodes in our layered model graph M, if $|A| > |\overline{A}|$, then $|A| \geq |\overline{A}| + 2$. Thus, $|A||\overline{A}| < |A||\overline{A}| + |A| - |\overline{A}| - 1$. Furthermore, $d_{V2x} \geq 0$ and $p \geq 0$. This implies that (A.2) is not true. Similarly, (A.1) is not true if $|A| < |\overline{A}|$.

If $|A| = |\overline{A}|$, there is at least one other pair of nodes y_{V1} and y_{V2} that is separated into two different groups. By moving x_{V1} and x_{V2} into one group and y_{V1} and y_{V2} into another, the cut value will be reduced, although the number of nodes in each group is the same as before. This implies $RatioCut(A,\overline{A})$ is not the minimum RatioCut if $|A| = |\overline{A}|$.

Thus, by contradiction, the assumption is not true. In other words, there does not exist a minimum RatioCut which separates at least a pair of nodes x_{V1} and x_{V2} into different groups in a RatioCut of two clusters. Similarly, the RatioCut consistency of more than two clusters can be proved, since the Cut variables caused by the unrelated clusters are constant.

Therefore, the RatioCut clustering results would not separate the two versions of any node x_{V1} and x_{V2} into two different groups by using our approach.

Appendix B

NCut consistency with multiple versions of each node

Theorem 2: The versions of a node will be placed in the same cluster based on NCut with multiple versions of each node, when the added edge weight between two versions of a same node is equal to the sum of the degrees of the two versions.

Proof of NCut consistency with two versions of each node ($c = 2$): Following the illustration of Figure A.1, assume there is a minimum NCut which separates at least a pair of nodes x_{V1} and x_{V2} into two different groups A and $\overline{A}$, as shown in Figure A.1. Thus

$$\min NCut = NCut(A,\overline{A}) = \frac{cut(A,\overline{A})}{vol(A)} + \frac{cut(A,\overline{A})}{vol(\overline{A})} = \frac{cut(A,\overline{A}) * vol(V)}{vol(A)vol(\overline{A})},$$

where $vol(A)$ is the degree summation of the nodes in group A, and $vol(V)$ is the degree summation of all the nodes in our double copy structure, means $Vol(V) = \sum_{i=1}^{n}(t_{V1i} + t_{V2i}) = 3\sum_{i=1}^{n}(d_{V1i} + d_{V2i})$. Here $t_{V1i} = 2d_{V1i} + d_{V2i}$ and $t_{V2i} = d_{V1i} + 2d_{V2i}$ are the total degrees of the two versions of node i in the bigger graph M.

By moving x_{V2} to A, we get

$$
\begin{aligned}
NCut(A + x_{V2}, \overline{A} - x_{V2}) &= \frac{cut(A + x_{V2}, \overline{A} - x_{V2}) * vol(V)}{vol(A + x_{V2})vol(\overline{A} - x_{V2})} \\
&= \frac{\left(cut(A,\overline{A}) - (d_{V1x} + d_{V2x} + q) + (d_{V2x} - q)\right) * vol(V)}{(vol(A) + t_{V2x})(vol(\overline{A}) - t_{V2x})} \\
&= \frac{\left(cut(A,\overline{A}) - d_{V1x} - 2q\right) * vol(V)}{(vol(A) + d_{V1x} + 2d_{V2x})(vol(\overline{A}) - d_{V1x} - 2d_{V2x})}.
\end{aligned}
$$

Similarly by moving x_{V1} to $\overline{A}$, we get

$$NCut(A - x_{V1}, \overline{A} + x_{V1}) = \frac{cut(A - x_{V1}, \overline{A} + x_{V1}) * vol(V)}{vol(A - x_{V1})vol(\overline{A} + x_{V1})}$$

$$= \frac{\left(cut(A, \overline{A}) - d_{V2x} - 2p\right) * vol(V)}{(vol(A) - 2d_{V1x} - d_{V2x})(vol(\overline{A}) + 2d_{V1x} + d_{V2x})}.$$

Since the $NCut(A, \overline{A})$ is the minimum,

$$NCut(A, \overline{A}) \leq NCut(A + x_{V2}, \overline{A} - x_{V2})$$

$$\implies \frac{cut(A, \overline{A})}{vol(A)vol(\overline{A})} \leq \frac{cut(A, \overline{A}) - d_{V1x} - 2q}{(vol(A) + d_{V1x} + 2d_{V2x})(vol(\overline{A}) - d_{V1x} - 2d_{V2x})} \tag{B.1}$$

and

$$NCut(A, \overline{A}) \leq NCut(A - x_{V1}, \overline{A} + x_{V1})$$

$$\implies \frac{cut(A, \overline{A})}{vol(A)vol(\overline{A})} \leq \frac{cut(A, \overline{A}) - d_{V2x} - 2p}{(vol(A) - 2d_{V1x} - d_{V2x})(vol(\overline{A}) + 2d_{V1x} + d_{V2x})}. \tag{B.2}$$

Let $cut(B, \overline{B})$ be any cut where every pair of $V1$ and $V2$ copies are in the same group. Thus,

$$cut(B, \overline{B}) \leq \begin{cases} \sum_{i \in B}(d_{V1i} + d_{V2i}) \\ \sum_{i \in \overline{B}}(d_{V1i} + d_{V2i}) \end{cases}$$

$$\text{and} \quad vol(B) = \sum_{i \in B}(t_{V1i} + t_{V2i}) = \sum_{i \in B} 3 * (d_{V1i} + d_{V2i}),$$

$$vol(\overline{B}) = \sum_{i \in \overline{B}}(t_{V1i} + t_{V2i}) = \sum_{i \in \overline{B}} 3 * (d_{V1i} + d_{V2i}).$$

$$\text{Thus,} \quad NCut(B, \overline{B}) = \frac{cut(B, \overline{B})}{vol(B)} + \frac{cut(B, \overline{B})}{vol(\overline{B})} \leq \frac{2}{3}.$$

Since the $NCut(A, \overline{A})$ is the minimum,

$$NCut(A, \overline{A}) = \frac{cut(A, \overline{A}) * vol(V)}{vol(A)vol(\overline{A})} \leq \frac{2}{3},$$

$$vol(V) \geq 6 * (d_{V1x} + d_{V2x}) \tag{B.3}$$

$$\implies 9cut(A, \overline{A})(d_{V1x} + d_{V2x}) \leq vol(A)vol(\overline{A}).$$

(B.1) implies

$$\frac{cut(A, \overline{A})}{vol(A)vol(\overline{A})} \leq \frac{cut(A, \overline{A}) - d_{V1x}}{(vol(A) + d_{V1x} + 2d_{V2x})(vol(\overline{A}) - d_{V1x} - 2d_{V2x})},$$

$$\implies d_{V1x}vol(A)vol(\overline{A})$$

$$\leq cut(A, \overline{A})\left(vol(A)(d_{V1x} + 2d_{V2x}) - vol(\overline{A})(d_{V1x} + 2d_{V2x}) + (d_{V1x} + 2d_{V2x})^2\right).$$

Similarly, (B.2) implies

$$d_{V2x}vol(A)vol(\overline{A})$$
$$\leq cut(A,\overline{A})\left(-vol(A)(2d_{V1x}+d_{V2x})+vol(\overline{A})(2d_{V1x}+d_{V2x})+(2d_{V1x}+d_{V2x})^2\right).$$

By adding the above two equations together, we get

$$(d_{V1x}+d_{V2x})vol(A)vol(\overline{A})$$
$$\leq cut(A,\overline{A})\left(vol(A)(-d_{V1x}+d_{V2x})+vol(\overline{A})(d_{V1x}-d_{V2x})+5d_{V1x}^2+5d_{V2x}^2+8d_{V1x}d_{V2x}\right).$$

Combining with (B.3), we get

$$4d_{V1x}^2+4d_{V2x}^2+10d_{V1x}d_{V2x} \leq (vol(\overline{A})-vol(A))(d_{V1x}-d_{V2x}). \qquad \text{(B.4)}$$

In the inequality (B.1), the left numerator is greater than or equal to the right numerator. Thus, the left denominator has to be greater than or equal to the right denominator:

$$vol(A)vol(\overline{A}) \geq (vol(A)+d_{V1x}+2d_{V2x})(vol(\overline{A})-d_{V1x}-2d_{V2x}).$$

If $vol(A) \leq vol(\overline{A})$, then the above inequality implies

$$\implies vol(\overline{A}) \leq vol(A)+d_{V1x}+2d_{V2x}.$$

When $d_{V1x} < d_{V2x}$, the right side of (B.4) is less than 0.
When $d_{V1x} \geq d_{V2x}$, by applying the above inequality to (B.4), we get

$$4d_{V1x}^2+4d_{V2x}^2+10d_{V1x}d_{V2x}$$
$$\leq vol(A)(-d_{V1x}+d_{V2x})+(vol(A)+d_{V1x}+2d_{V2x})(d_{V1x}-d_{V2x})$$
$$\implies 3d_{V1x}^2+6d_{V2x}^2+9d_{V1x}d_{V2x} \leq 0.$$

Since $d_{V1x} \geq 0$, $d_{V1x} \geq 0$ and $d_{V1x}+d_{V2x} > 0$ for a connected graph, the above inequality is not true. Similarly we can prove that, if $vol(A) \geq vol(\overline{A})$, the inequality (B.4) is not true either. Thus, based on the proof above, the assumption is not true. In other words, there does not exist a minimum NCut which separates at least a pair of nodes x_{V1} and x_{V2} into different groups in a NCut of two clusters. Similarly, the NCut consistency of more than two clusters can be proved, since the cut variables in the unrelated clusters are constant.

Therefore, the NCut clustering results would not separate the two versions of any node x_{V1} and x_{V2} into two different groups by using our approach. $\qquad \square$

Proof of NCut consistency with multiple versions of each node ($c \geq 3$): The property still holds for optimum NCut results when there is more than two roles of each node. The proof is similar to the one for $c = 2$. Again we assume there is a minimum NCut in which there is at least a node whose copies are separated into two different groups A and $\overline{A}$.
Let x_A and $x_{\overline{A}}$ be the copies of x in the two partitions;

$k = |x_A|$ and $\bar{k} = |x_{\bar{A}}|$ be the number of copies of the node x in two partitions, where $k + \bar{k} = c$ and $k \geq 1, \bar{k} \geq 1$;

d_{Ax} and $d_{\bar{A}x}$ be the total degree of nodes x_A and $x_{\bar{A}}$ without the added edges. Thus, the total degrees of all versions of the node x in the bigger matrix M is $(2c-1)(d_{Ax} + d_{\bar{A}x})$ since each version connects to other $c-1$ versions (counting twice) and the total given edges of the node is also counted.

Let p be the sum of edge's weight from x_A to nodes in $\bar{A}$ except $x_{\bar{A}}$. Let q be the sum of edge's weight from $x_{\bar{A}}$ to nodes in A except x_A.

Thus

$$\min NCut = NCut(A, \bar{A}) = \frac{cut(A, \bar{A}) * vol(V)}{vol(A) vol(\bar{A})}.$$

where $Vol(V) = \sum_{i=1}^{n} \sum_{j=1}^{c} (t_{i\_j}) = (2c-1) \sum_{i=1}^{n} (d_{Ai} + d_{\bar{A}i})$.

By moving $x_{\bar{A}}$ to A, we get

$$NCut(A + x_{\bar{A}}, \bar{A} - x_{\bar{A}}) = \frac{cut(A + x_{\bar{A}}, \bar{A} - x_{\bar{A}}) * vol(V)}{vol(A + x_{\bar{A}}) vol(\bar{A} - x_{\bar{A}})}$$

$$= \frac{\left(cut(A, \bar{A}) - (\bar{k}d_{Ax} + kd_{\bar{A}x} + q) + (d_{\bar{A}x} - q)\right) * vol(V)}{(vol(A) + t_{\bar{A}x})(vol(\bar{A}) - t_{\bar{A}x})}$$

$$= \frac{\left(cut(A, \bar{A}) - \bar{k}d_{Ax} - (k-1)d_{\bar{A}x} - 2q\right) * vol(V)}{(vol(A) + \bar{k}d_{Ax} + (c+k-1)d_{\bar{A}x})(vol(\bar{A}) - \bar{k}d_{Ax} - (c+k-1)d_{\bar{A}x})}.$$

Similarly by moving x_A to $\bar{A}$, we get

$$NCut(A - x_A, \bar{A} + x_A) = \frac{cut(A - x_A, \bar{A} + x_A) * vol(V)}{vol(A - x_A) vol(\bar{A} + x_A)}$$

$$= \frac{\left(cut(A, \bar{A}) - kd_{\bar{A}x} - (\bar{k}-1)d_{Ax} - 2p\right) * vol(V)}{(vol(A) - kd_{\bar{A}x} - (c+\bar{k}-1)d_{Ax})(vol(\bar{A}) + kd_{\bar{A}x} + (c+\bar{k}-1)d_{Ax})}.$$

Since the $NCut(A, \bar{A})$ is the minimum,

$$NCut(A, \bar{A}) \leq NCut(A + x_{\bar{A}}, \bar{A} - x_{\bar{A}})$$

$$\implies \frac{cut(A, \bar{A})}{vol(A) vol(\bar{A})} \tag{B.5}$$

$$\leq \frac{cut(A, \bar{A}) - \bar{k}d_{Ax} - (k-1)d_{\bar{A}x} - 2q}{(vol(A) + \bar{k}d_{Ax} + (c+k-1)d_{\bar{A}x})(vol(\bar{A}) - \bar{k}d_{Ax} - (c+k-1)d_{\bar{A}x})}$$

and

$$NCut(A, \bar{A}) \leq NCut(A - x_A, \bar{A} + x_A)$$

$$\implies \frac{cut(A, \bar{A})}{vol(A) vol(\bar{A})} \tag{B.6}$$

$$\leq \frac{cut(A, \bar{A}) - kd_{\bar{A}x} - (\bar{k}-1)d_{Ax} - 2p}{(vol(A) - kd_{\bar{A}x} - (c+\bar{k}-1)d_{Ax})(vol(\bar{A}) + kd_{\bar{A}x} + (c+\bar{k}-1)d_{Ax})}.$$

Let $cut(B,\overline{B})$ be any cut where all version of each node are in the same group. Thus,

$$cut(B,\overline{B}) \leq \begin{cases} \displaystyle\sum_{i\in B}\sum_{j=1}^{c} d_{i\_j} \\[2em] \displaystyle\sum_{i\in \overline{B}}\sum_{j=1}^{c} d_{i\_j} \end{cases}$$

and $\quad vol(B) = \displaystyle\sum_{i\in B}\sum_{j=1}^{c} t_{i\_j} = (2c-1)\sum_{i\in B}\sum_{j=1}^{c} d_{i\_j},$

$$vol(\overline{B}) = \sum_{i\in \overline{B}}\sum_{j=1}^{c} t_{i\_j} = (2c-1)\sum_{i\in \overline{B}}\sum_{j=1}^{c} d_{i\_j}.$$

Thus, $\quad NCut(B,\overline{B}) = \dfrac{cut(B,\overline{B})}{vol(B)} + \dfrac{cut(B,\overline{B})}{vol(\overline{B})} \leq \dfrac{2}{2c-1}.$

Since the $NCut(A,\overline{A})$ is the minimum,

$$NCut(A,\overline{A}) = \frac{cut(A,\overline{A}) * vol(V)}{vol(A)vol(\overline{A})} \leq \frac{2}{2c-1},$$

$$vol(V) \geq 2(2c-1)(d_{Ax}+d_{\overline{A}x})$$

$$\Longrightarrow (2c-1)^2 cut(A,\overline{A})(d_{Ax}+d_{\overline{A}x}) \leq vol(A)vol(\overline{A}). \qquad (B.7)$$

(B.5) implies

$$vol(A)vol(\overline{A})(\overline{k}d_{Ax}+(k-1)d_{\overline{A}x}) \leq cut(A,\overline{A})\left(vol(A)\left(\overline{k}d_{Ax}+(c+k-1)d_{\overline{A}x}\right) \right.$$

$$-vol(\overline{A})\left(\overline{k}d_{Ax}+(c+k-1)d_{\overline{A}x}\right)$$

$$\left. +\left(\overline{k}d_{Ax}+(c+k-1)d_{\overline{A}x}\right)^2 \right).$$

Similarly, (B.6) implies

$$vol(A)vol(\overline{A})(kd_{\overline{A}x}+(\overline{k}-1)d_{Ax}) \leq cut(A,\overline{A})\left(-vol(A)\left(kd_{\overline{A}x}+(c+\overline{k}-1)d_{Ax}\right) \right.$$

$$+vol(\overline{A})\left(kd_{\overline{A}x}+(c+\overline{k}-1)d_{Ax}\right)$$

$$\left. +\left(kd_{\overline{A}x}+(c+\overline{k}-1)d_{Ax}\right)^2 \right).$$

By adding the above two equations together, we get

$$vol(A)vol(\overline{A})((2\overline{k}-1)d_{Ax}+(2k-1)d_{\overline{Ax}})$$

$$\leq cut(A,\overline{A})\left((vol(\overline{A})-vol(A))(c-1)(d_{Ax}-d_{\overline{Ax}}) \right.$$

$$+ \left(\overline{k}d_{Ax}+(c+k-1)d_{\overline{Ax}}\right)^2$$

$$\left. + \left(kd_{\overline{Ax}}+(c+\overline{k}-1)d_{Ax}\right)^2 \right).$$

Combining with (B.7), we get

$$(2c-1)^2(d_{Ax}+d_{\overline{Ax}})\left((2\overline{k}-1)d_{Ax}+(2k-1)d_{\overline{Ax}}\right)$$

$$\leq \left(vol(\overline{A})-vol(A)\right)(c-1)(d_{Ax}-d_{\overline{Ax}}) \qquad\qquad (B.8)$$

$$+ \left(\overline{k}d_{Ax}+(c+k-1)d_{\overline{Ax}}\right)^2 + \left(kd_{\overline{Ax}}+(c+\overline{k}-1)d_{Ax}\right)^2.$$

In the inequality (B.5), the left numerator is greater than or equal to the right numerator. Thus, the left denominator has to be greater than or equal to the right denominator:

$$vol(A)vol(\overline{A}) \geq \left(vol(A)+\overline{k}d_{Ax}+(c+k-1)d_{\overline{Ax}}\right)\left(vol(\overline{A})-\overline{k}d_{Ax}-(c+k-1)d_{\overline{Ax}}\right).$$

If $vol(A) \leq vol(\overline{A})$, then the above inequality implies

$$vol(\overline{A}) \leq vol(A)+\overline{k}d_{Ax}+(c+k-1)d_{\overline{Ax}}.$$

When $d_{Ax} \geq d_{\overline{Ax}}$, by applying it to (B.8), we get

$$(2c-1)^2(d_{Ax}+d_{\overline{Ax}})\left((2\overline{k}-1)d_{Ax}+(2k-1)d_{\overline{Ax}}\right)$$

$$\leq (\overline{k}d_{Ax}+(c+k-1)d_{\overline{Ax}})(c-1)(d_{Ax}-d_{\overline{Ax}})$$

$$+ \left(\overline{k}d_{Ax}+(c+k-1)d_{\overline{Ax}}\right)^2 + \left(kd_{\overline{Ax}}+(c+\overline{k}-1)d_{Ax}\right)^2$$

$$\leq \left(\overline{k}d_{Ax}+(c+k-1)d_{\overline{Ax}}\right)\left((c+\overline{k}-1)d_{Ax}+kd_{\overline{Ax}}\right) + \left(kd_{\overline{Ax}}+(c+\overline{k}-1)d_{Ax}\right)^2$$

$$\leq \left((c+2\overline{k}-1)d_{Ax}+(c+2k-1)d_{\overline{Ax}}\right)\left((c+\overline{k}-1)d_{Ax}+kd_{\overline{Ax}}\right).$$

$$(B.9)$$

Since $c \geq 3$, $c = k+\overline{k}$, $k \geq 1$ and $\overline{k} \geq 1$, so $(2c-1)^2 \geq 3c^2$, $c+2\overline{k}-1 < 3c$ and $c+2k-1 < 3c$. Then (B.9) implies

$$c\left((2\overline{k}-1)d_{Ax}+(2k-1)d_{\overline{Ax}}\right) < \left((c+\overline{k}-1)d_{Ax}+kd_{\overline{Ax}}\right)$$

$$\implies \qquad c(2\overline{k}-1)d_{Ax} < (c+\overline{k}-1)d_{Ax}$$

By using $\bar{k} = 1$ and $\bar{k} \geq 2$, we can show that the above inequality is not true.

If $vol(A) \leq vol(\overline{A})$ and $d_{Ax} < d_{\overline{A}x}$, the inequality (B.6) implies

$$vol(\overline{A}) \geq vol(A) - kd_{\overline{A}x} - (c + \bar{k} - 1)d_{Ax}.$$

By applying it to (B.8), we get

$$(2c - 1)^2(d_{Ax} + d_{\overline{A}x})\left((2\bar{k} - 1)d_{Ax} + (2k - 1)d_{\overline{A}x}\right)$$
$$\leq \left(-kd_{\overline{A}x} - (c + \bar{k} - 1)d_{Ax}\right)(c - 1)(d_{Ax} - d_{\overline{A}x})$$
$$+ \left(\bar{k}d_{Ax} + (c + k - 1)d_{\overline{A}x}\right)^2 + \left(kd_{\overline{A}x} + (c + \bar{k} - 1)d_{Ax}\right)^2$$
$$\leq \left(\bar{k}d_{Ax} + (c + k - 1)d_{\overline{A}x}\right)^2 + \left(kd_{\overline{A}x} + (c + \bar{k} - 1)d_{Ax}\right)\left((c + k - 1)d_{\overline{A}x} + \bar{k}d_{Ax}\right)$$
$$\leq \left((c + 2\bar{k} - 1)d_{Ax} + (c + 2k - 1)d_{\overline{A}x}\right)\left(\bar{k}d_{Ax} + (c + k - 1)d_{\overline{A}x}\right).$$

$$(B.10)$$

Similarly, the above inequality is not true either. Thus, if $vol(A) \leq vol(\overline{A})$, the inequality (B.8) does not hold. Similarly we can prove that, if $vol(A) \geq vol(\overline{A})$, the inequality (B.8) is not true either. Thus, by contradiction, the assumption is not true. In other words, there does not exist a minimum NCut which separates the versions of any node into two different groups.

Similarly, there does not exist a minimum NCut which separates the versions of any node into more than two different groups, since the variables in the unrelated groups are constant. In more detail, considering the case that the versions of a node x are separated into three groups – A_1, A_2 and A_3. The NCut value for group A_3 is unchanged if we move any version of node between groups A_1 and A_2. Based on the above proof, when we move the versions of the node x from A_1 to A_2 or from A_2 to A_1, the NCut value will be reduced. Now the versions of the node x are separated only in groups A_1 and A_3, or A_2 and A_3. Again, the NCut value will be reduced if versions of the node are in a same group.

Therefore, there does not exist a minimum NCut which separates the different versions of any node into different groups.

Appendix C

Signed unnormalized clustering

Let us start with the case of $k = 2$. Our goal is to solve the optimization problem:

$$\min_{A \subset V} SRcut(A, \overline{A}).$$

For a subset $A \subset V$, let u be the vector $(u_1, \ldots, u_n)' \in \mathbb{R}^n$ with entries:

$$u_i = \begin{cases} \sqrt{|\overline{A}|/|A|} & \text{if } v_i \in A \\ -\sqrt{|A|/|\overline{A}|} & \text{if } v_i \in \overline{A} \end{cases}$$

Using the defined vector u, the SRcut objective function can be seen to be equivalent to the unnormalized signed Laplacian L_{sign}:

$$u' L_{sign} u = \frac{1}{2} \sum_{i,j=1}^{n} w_{ij}(u_i - u_j)^2$$

$$= \frac{1}{2} \sum_{i \in A, j \in \overline{A}} w_{ij} \left(\sqrt{\frac{|\overline{A}|}{|A|}} + \sqrt{\frac{|A|}{|\overline{A}|}} \right)^2 + \frac{1}{2} \sum_{i \in \overline{A}, j \in A} w_{ij} \left(-\sqrt{\frac{|A|}{|\overline{A}|}} - \sqrt{\frac{|\overline{A}|}{|A|}} \right)^2$$

$$= \left(cut^+(A, \overline{A}) - cut^-(A, \overline{A}) \right) \left(\sqrt{\frac{|\overline{A}|}{|A|}} + \sqrt{\frac{|A|}{|\overline{A}|}} \right)^2$$

$$= \left(cut^+(A, \overline{A}) - cut^-(A, \overline{A}) \right) \left(\frac{|\overline{A}|}{|A|} + \frac{|A|}{|\overline{A}|} + 2 \right)$$

$$= \left(cut^+(A, \overline{A}) - cut^-(A, \overline{A}) \right) \left(\frac{|\overline{A}| + |A|}{|A|} + \frac{|A| + |\overline{A}|}{|\overline{A}|} \right)$$

$$= |V| * SRcut(A, \overline{A})$$

Additionally, we have

$$\sum_{i=1}^{n} u_i^2 = |A|\frac{|\overline{A}|}{|A|} + |\overline{A}|\frac{|A|}{|\overline{A}|} = n.$$

Furthermore, it is provable that $u \perp \mathbb{1}$.

Thus, $R_{L_{sign}}(u) = SRcut(A,\overline{A})$. In other words, the problem of minimizing $SRcut(A,\overline{A})$ can be equivalently rewritten as: $\min_{A \subset V} R_{L_{sign}}(u)$.

We can relax the problem by taking an arbitrary real value vector f:

$$\min_{f \in \mathbb{R}^n} R_{L_{sign}}(f),$$

$$s.t. \quad f \perp \mathbb{1}; \quad ||f|| = \sqrt{n}.$$

The solution of this problem is the eigenvector corresponding to the smallest eigenvalue of L_{sign}.

The smallest eigenvector is a real-valued solution rather than a discrete indicator vector. The simplest way to partition a graph using such an eigenvector is to use the sign of each entry value. A more sophisticated partition can be obtained by using any standard clustering algorithm — k-means has often been used.

The relaxation of the minimization $SRcut$ in a general case of $k > 2$ follows a similar principle. We define the indicator matrix $H = (h_1, \ldots, h_k) \in \mathbb{R}^{n*k}$, where each column vector h_j with entries

$$h_{i,j} = \begin{cases} 1/\sqrt{|A|} & \text{if } v_i \in A \\ 0 & \text{otherwise} \end{cases} \quad (i = 1, \ldots, n; j = 1, \ldots, k).$$

As before, we see that

$$h_i' L_{sign} h_i = \frac{cut^+(A_i, \overline{A}_i) - cut^-(A_i, \overline{A}_i)}{|A_i|},$$

$$h_i' L_{sign} h_i = (H' L_{sign} H)_{ii},$$

and $h_i' h_i = 1$, $H'H = I$.

Combining those facts, we get

$$SRcut(A_1, \ldots, A_k) = \sum_{i=1}^{k} h_i' L_{sign} h = Tr(H' L_{sign} H),$$

where Tr denotes the trace of a matrix. As before, we relax the problem of minimizing $SRcut(A_1, \ldots, A_k)$ by allowing matrix F to take arbitrary real values $F \in \mathbb{R}^{n*k}$. The relaxed problem becomes:

$$\min_{F \in \mathbb{R}^{n*k}} TR(F' L_{sign} F), \quad s.t. \quad F'F = I.$$

This is the standard form of a trace minimization problem, and it can be solved by choosing F as the k smallest eigenvectors of the Laplacian matrix L_{sign} as columns [100]. Clustering methods can then be applied to (some of) the columns to get a discrete partition as before.

Appendix D

Signed normalized Laplacian L_{sns} clustering

Let us start with the case of SNScut and $k = 2$. Our goal is to solve the optimization problem:

$$\min_{A \subset V} SNScut(A, \overline{A}).$$

For a subset $A \subset V$, let u be the vector $(u_1, \ldots, u_n)' \in \mathbb{R}^n$ with entries:

$$u_i = \begin{cases} \sqrt{vol(\overline{A})/vol(A)} & \text{if } v_i \in A \\ -\sqrt{vol(A)/vol(\overline{A})} & \text{if } v_i \in \overline{A} \end{cases}$$

Using the defined vector u, the SNScut objective function can be seen to be equivalent to the normalized signed Laplacian L_{sns}:

$$u'(D^+ - D^- - W)u = \frac{1}{2} \sum_{i,j=1}^{n} w_{ij}(u_i - u_j)^2$$

$$= \frac{1}{2} \sum_{i \in A, j \in \overline{A}} w_{ij} \left(\sqrt{\frac{vol(\overline{A})}{vol(A)}} + \sqrt{\frac{vol(A)}{vol(\overline{A})}} \right)^2 + \frac{1}{2} \sum_{i \in \overline{A}, j \in A} w_{ij} \left(-\sqrt{\frac{vol(A)}{vol(\overline{A})}} - \sqrt{\frac{vol(\overline{A})}{vol(A)}} \right)^2$$

$$= \left(cut^+(A, \overline{A}) - cut^-(A, \overline{A}) \right) \left(\frac{vol(\overline{A})}{vol(A)} + \frac{vol(A)}{vol(\overline{A})} + 2 \right)$$

$$= \left(cut^+(A, \overline{A}) - cut^-(A, \overline{A}) \right) \left(\frac{vol(\overline{A}) + vol(A)}{vol(A)} + \frac{vol(A) + vol(\overline{A})}{vol(\overline{A})} \right)$$

$$= vol(V) * SNScut(A, \overline{A})$$

Additionally, we have

$$\sum_{i=1}^{n} d_i u_i^2 = vol(A) \frac{vol(\overline{A})}{vol(A)} + vol(\overline{A}) \frac{vol(A)}{vol(\overline{A})} = vol(V).$$

Furthermore, it is provable that $Du \perp \mathbb{1}$.

Thus, $R_{L_{sns}}(u) = SNScut(A,\bar{A})$. In other words, the problem of minimizing $SNScut(A,\bar{A})$ can be equivalently rewritten as: $\min\limits_{A \subset V} R_{L_{sns}}(u)$.

We can relax the problem by taking an arbitrary real-valued vector f:

$$\min_{f \in \mathbb{R}^n} R_{L_{sns}}(f).$$

The solution of this problem is the eigenvector corresponding to the smallest eigenvalue of L_{sns}, or equivalently the generalized eigenvector of $(D^+ - D^- - W)f = \lambda \bar{D} f$.

As before, the smallest eigenvector is a real-valued solution rather than a discrete indicator vector, but standard approaches can be used to turn this into a clustering.

The relaxation of the minimization $SNScut$ in a general case of $k > 2$ follows in a similar way. We define the indicator matrix $H = (h_1,\ldots,h_k) \in \mathbb{R}^{n*k}$, where each column vector h_j with entries

$$h_{i,j} = \begin{cases} 1/\sqrt{vol(A)} & \text{if } v_i \in A \\ 0 & \text{otherwise} \end{cases} \quad (i = 1,\ldots,n; j = 1,\ldots,k).$$

As before, we see that

$$h_i'(D^+ - D^- - W)h_i = \frac{cut^+(A_i,\bar{A}_i) - cut^-(A_i,\bar{A}_i)}{vol(A_i)},$$

$$h_i'(D^+ - D^- - W)h_i = \left(H'(D^+ - D^- - W)H\right)_{ii},$$

and $h_i'Dh_i = 1$, $H'DH = I$.

Combining those facts, we get

$$SNScut(A_1,\ldots,A_k) = \sum_{i=1}^{k} h_i'(D^+ - D^- - W)h_i$$
$$= Tr\left(H_i'(D^+ - D^- - W)H\right),$$

where Tr denotes the trace of a matrix. As before, we relax the problem of minimizing $SNScut(A_1,\ldots,A_k)$ by allowing matrix F to take arbitrary real values $F \in \mathbb{R}^{n*k}$. The relaxed problem becomes:

$$\min_{F \in \mathbb{R}^{n*k}} R_{L_{sns}}(F) \qquad s.t. \quad F'\bar{D}F = I.$$

Substituting $F = \bar{D}^{-1/2}T$, we obtain:

$$\min_{T \in \mathbb{R}^{n*k}} Tr\left(T'\bar{D}^{-1/2}(D^+ - D^- - W)\bar{D}^{-1/2}T\right)$$

$$s.t. \quad T'T = I.$$

This is the standard form of a trace minimization problem, and it can be solved by choosing T as the k smallest eigenvectors of the matrix $T'\overline{D}^{-1/2}(D^+ - D^- - W)\overline{D}^{-1/2}T$ as columns [100]. Resubstituting $F = \overline{D}^{-1/2}T$ and using Proposition 3 in von Luxburg [101], F is the matrix with the k smallest eigenvectors of the Laplacian matrix L_{sns} as columns. Clustering methods can then be applied to (some of) the columns to get a discrete partition as before.

Appendix E

Signed normalized Laplacian L_{bns} clustering

In the case $k = 2$, we use the same defined indicator vector u as in Appendix D:

$$\sum_{i,j=1}^{n} w_{ij}^- u_i^2 = \sum_{i=1}^{n} d_i^- u_i^2$$

$$= \sum_{i \in A} d_i^- \frac{vol(\overline{A})}{vol(A)} + \sum_{i \in \overline{A}} d_i^- \frac{vol(A)}{vol(\overline{A})}$$

$$= \frac{vol^-(A)vol(\overline{A})}{vol(A)} + \frac{vol^-(\overline{A})vol(A)}{vol(\overline{A})}$$

$$= \frac{vol^-(A)vol(V)}{vol(A)} - vol^-(A) + \frac{vol^-(\overline{A})vol(V)}{vol(\overline{A})} - vol^-(\overline{A})$$

$$= \frac{vol^-(A)vol(V)}{vol(A)} + \frac{vol^-(\overline{A})vol(V)}{vol(\overline{A})} - vol^-(V).$$

Then,

$$u'(D^+ - W)u = \sum_{i,j=1}^{n} \left(\frac{1}{2} w_{ij}(u_i - u_j)^2 + w_{ij}^- u_i^2 \right)$$

$$= \left(cut^+(A,\overline{A}) - cut^-(A,\overline{A}) \right) \left(\frac{vol(V)}{vol(A)} + \frac{vol(V)}{vol(\overline{A})} \right)$$

$$+ \frac{vol^-(A)vol(V)}{vol(A)} + \frac{vol^-(\overline{A})vol(V)}{vol(\overline{A})} - vol^-(V)$$

$$= vol(V) * BNScut(A,\overline{A}) - vol^-(V)$$

Thus, $R_{L_{bns}}(u) = BNScut(A,\overline{A}) - vol^-(V)/vol(V)$.

Since $vol^-(V)/vol(V)$ is constant for a graph, the problem of minimizing $BNScut(A,\overline{A})$ can be equivalently rewritten as: $\min_{A \subset V} R_{L_{bns}}(u)$.

Again we can relax the problem by taking an arbitrary real-valued vector f:

$$\min_{f \in \mathbb{R}^n} R_{L_{bns}}(f).$$

The solution of the minimization problem is the eigenvector corresponding to the smallest eigenvalue of L_{bns}, or equivalently the generalized eigenvector of $(D^+ - W)f = \lambda \overline{D} f$.

For the case of finding $k > 2$ clusters, we use the same indicator matrix H defined in Appendix D. We get:

$$h_i'(D^+ - W)h = \frac{cut^+(A_i, \overline{A}_i) - cut^-(A_i, \overline{A}_i) + vol^-(A_i)}{vol(A_i)},$$

$$h_i'(D^+ - W)h = \left(H_i'(D^+ - W)H\right)_{ii},$$

and $h_i'Dh_i = 1$, $H'\overline{D}H = I$.

Combining those facts, we get

$$BNScut(A_1, ..., A_k) = Tr\left(H_i'(D^+ - W)H\right).$$

Again we use an arbitrary real-valued matrix $F \in \mathbb{R}^{n*k}$. Then the relaxed problem becomes:

$$\min_{F \in \mathbb{R}^{n*k}} R_{L_{bns}}(F) \qquad s.t. \quad H\overline{D}'H = I.$$

The minimization problem is solved by choosing F as the first k smallest eigenvectors of the Laplacian matrix L_{bns} as columns.

Appendix F

Example MATLAB functions to implement spectral embeddings

This appendix provides MATLAB library functions that implement the basic spectral embeddings that we have discussed. They each return the appropriate eigenvector matrices that provide the coordinates for embedding each network.

The included functions are:

- Laplacian — implements three of the standard Laplacian embeddings for an undirected network.

- DirLaplacian — implements our directed spectral embedding.

- DirLaplacianChung — implements the directed spectral embedding designed by Fan Chung.

- SignedLaplacian — implements our signed spectral embedding given two positive matrices, representing the strength of positive and negative relationships.

- · TypedDirLaplacian — implements our composition of typed and directed edges; calls DirLaplacian.

- TemporalDirLaplacian — implements our composition of directed edges with temporal changes in intensity; calls TypedDirLaplacian.

- TypedLaplacian — implements spectral embedding of a typed network using Chung's directed embedding; calls DirLaplacianChung.

- TemporalLaplacian — implements spectral embedding of networks with temporal changes in intensity; calls DirLaplacianChung.

- SignedDirLaplacian — implements our composition of signed and directed networks.

The versions of the MATLAB functions below are simplified by omitting the simple, but space-consuming, code that checks input arguments. Full versions are in the Github repository: **https://github.com/PHDZheng/Social-Networks-with-Rich-Edge-Semantics**.

```matlab
function [varargout] = Laplacian(W, type, k)
%   Spectral embedding of an undirected graph
%
% W is the weighted adjacency matrix of a graph.
% type = un and empty: unnormalized graph Laplacian
%        sym: symmetric normalized graph Laplacian
%        rw: random walk normalized graph Laplacian
% k = number of groups to cluster into (default is disabled)
%
% Vector = eigenvector matrix of the embedding
% E = the vector of Laplacian eigenvalues
%
% varargout = cellarray
%                  1: Vector
%                  2: E

[n,m] = size(W);

tempvalue = max(max(W-W'));
if  tempvalue ~= 0
  W = (W + W')/2;
end

D = sparse(1:n,1:n,sum(W,2));
L = D - W;

%unnormalized graph Laplacian

if (nargin < 2) || isempty(type) || strcmp(type,'un')
   || strcmp(type,'Un') ...
   || strcmp(type,'UN')
  display('Unnormalized Laplacian decomposition');
  tempvalue = max(D(:));
  if k == n
    [Vector,eigenvalue] = eig(L);
    e = diag(eigenvalue);
    [e, IXY] = sort(e,1,'ascend');
    Vector = Vector(:,IXY);
  else
    [Vector,eigenvalue] = eigs(2 * tempvalue * eye(n)-L,k);
    e = 2 * tempvalue - diag(eigenvalue);
  end

  varargout{1} = Vector;
  varargout{2} = e;
% symmetric normalized graph-Laplacian
elseif strcmp(type,'sym') || strcmp(type,'Sym') || strcmp(type,'SYM')
  % Normalized spectral clustering according to Ng, Jordan, and Weiss
  % (2002)
  display('Symmetric Laplacian decomposition');
```

```
   D2 = sparse(n,n);
   for i=1:n
     if D(i,i) ~= 0
        D2(i,i)=1/D(i,i)^0.5;
     end
   end
   Lsym = D2 * L * D2;   % L=D^(-0.5)*L*D^(-0.5);
   Lsym= (Lsym + Lsym')/2;
   if k == n
      [Vector,eigenvalue] = eig(Lsym);
      e = diag(eigenvalue);
      [e,IXY] = sort(e,1,'ascend');
      Vector = Vector(:,IXY);
   else
      [Vector,eigenvalue] = eigs(2*eye(n) - Lsym,k);
      e = 2 - diag(eigenvalue);
   end
   varargout{1} = Vector;
   varargout{2} = e;
% random walk normalized graph-Laplacian
elseif strcmp(type,'rw') || strcmp(type,'Rw') || strcmp(type,'RW')
   display('Random walk Laplacian decomposition');
   D2 = sparse(n,n); % D2= D^(-0.5);
   for i=1:n
     if D(i,i) ~= 0
        D2(i,i) = 1/D(i,i)^.5;
     end
   end
   Lsym = D2 * L * D2;   %L=D^(-0.5)*L*D^(-0.5);
   Lsym = (Lsym + Lsym')/2;
   if k == n
      [Vector,eigenvalue] = eig(Lsym);
      e = diag(eigenvalue);
   else
      [Vector,eigenvalue] = eigs(2*eye(n)-Lsym,k);
      e=2-diag(eigenvalue);
   end
   Vector = D2*Vector;
   varargout{1} = Vector;
   varargout{2} = e;
else
    error('Type cannot be identified.');
end
```

```
function [varargout] = DirLaplacian(W, k)
%  Creates spectral embedding from a directed adjacency matrix
%
% The matrix W is the weighted adjacency matrix of a directed graph.
% k = number of eigenvectors.
% Vout = the eigenvector of out versions of nodes
% Vin = the eigenvector of in versions of nodes
% E = the diagonal matrix of Laplacian eigenvalues
% varargout = cell array of results
%                 1: Vout
%                 2: Vin
```

```matlab
%                      3: E

[n,m] = size(W);

din  = sum(W,1)';
dout = sum(W,2);

X = sparse(diag((2*dout+din).^(-0.5))) * (W+diag(din+dout)) * ...
  sparse(diag((dout+2*din).^(-0.5)));

if k == n
  [U, E, V] = svd(X);
else
  [U, E, V] = svds(X, k);
end

e = 1 - diag(E);

Vout = diag((2*dout+din).^(-0.5)) * U;
Vin  = diag((dout+2*din).^(-0.5)) * V;

varargout{1} = Vout;
varargout{2} = Vin;
varargout{3} = e;
```

```matlab
function [varargout] = DirLaplacianChung(W, epsilon, k)
% Spectral embedding of a directed graph using the method of Fan Chung
%
% W is the weighted adjacency matrix of a directed graph.
% epsilon: is a value between 0 and 1, used to avoid the problem
%                  of reducibility of directed graph (default is 0)
% k = number of eigenvectors desired
% Vector = the eigenvector matrix for the embedding
% E = the diagonal matrix of Laplacian eigenvalues
% importance =  importance value of the random walk matrix
% varargout = cell array of results
%                  1: Vector
%                  2: E
%                  3: importance

n = size(W,1);
D = diag(sum(W,2));

RW = sparse(n,n); % RW is the random walk matrix of W

for i = 1:n
  if D(i,i) ~= 0
    RW(i,:) = W(i,:)./D(i,i);
  else
    RW(i,i) = 1;
  end
end

if epsilon > 0
  RW = (1-epsilon) * reshape(RW,n,n)
```

```
       + epsilon/(n-1) * (ones(n,n)-eye(n));
end


% compute principal left eigenvector of RW - the importance in a
%  directed graph

[pie, eigpie] = eigs(RW.',1);
importance = abs(pie);


% build symmetric directed Laplacian

imphalf = diag(sqrt(importance));
impminushalf = sparse(n,n);
for i = 1:n
  if importance(i) > 1e-10;
    impminushalf(i,i) = 1./imphalf(i,i);
  end
end

L = speye(n,n) - (imphalf * RW * impminushalf
    + impminushalf * RW' * imphalf)/2;

if nargin < 3
  [Vector,E] = eig(L);
  [e,IX] = sort(diag(E));
  Vector = Vector(:,IX);
else
  [Vector,E] = eigs(2*speye(n)-L,k);
  e = 2 - diag(E);
end

Vector = impminushalf * Vector;

varargout{1} = Vector;
varargout{2} = e;
varargout{3} = importance;
```

```
function [varargout] = SignedLaplacian(posW, negW, type, k)
%  Spectral embedding of a signed adjacency matrix
%
% The matrices posW and negW are the weighted adjacency matrices of
%   the positive and negative edges of the network
% type= un or empty: unnormalized graph Laplacian
%       SNS: simple normalized signed graph Laplacian
%       BNS: balanced normalized signed graph Laplacian
%
% k = cluster the graph into k groups (default is disabled)
%
% Vector = eigenvector matrix for embedding
% E = the diagonal matrix of the Laplacian eigenvalues
%
% varargout = cell array
%                 1: Vector
%                 2: E
```

```matlab
[n,m] = size(posW);

tempvalue = max(max(posW-posW'));
if  tempvalue ~= 0
  posW = (posW+posW')/2;
end

tempvalue = max(max(negW-negW'));
if tempvalue ~= 0
  negW = (negW+negW')/2;
end

Dpos = sparse(1:n,1:n,sum(posW,2));
Dneg = sparse(1:n,1:n,sum(negW,2));
D = Dpos + Dneg;
D2 = zeros(n,n);
for i=1:n
  if D(i,i) ~= 0
    D2(i,i) = 1/D(i,i)^0.5;
  end
end

pDinv = sparse(n,n);
nDinv = sparse(n,n);
for i=1:n
  if D(i,i) ~= 0
    D2(i,i) = 1/D(i,i)^0.5;
  end
  if Dpos(i,i) > 0;
    pDinv(i,i)=1/Dpos(i,i);
  end
  if Dneg(i,i)>0
    nDinv(i,i) = 1/Dneg(i,i);
  end
end

%unnormalized graph Laplacian
if (nargin < 3) || isempty(type) || strcmp(type,'un')
   || strcmp(type,'Un') ...
   || strcmp(type,'UN')
  display('Unnormalized signed Laplacian decomposition');
  L = Dpos - posW - Dneg + negW;
  tempvalue = max(Dpos(:));
  if k == n
    [Vector,eigenvalue] = eig(L);
    E = diag(eigenvalue);
    [E,IXY] = sort(E,1,'ascend');
    Vector = Vector(:,IXY);
  else
    [Vector,eigenvalue] = eigs(2*tempvalue*eye(n)-L,k);
    E = 2 * tempvalue - diag(eigenvalue);
  end
  varargout{1} = Vector;
  varargout{2} = E;
%simple normalized signed graph Laplacian
elseif strcmp(type,'SNS') || strcmp(type,'Sns') || strcmp(type,'sns')
```

```
display('Simple normalized signed graph Laplacian decomposition');
L = Dpos - posW - Dneg + negW;
D = Dpos + Dneg;
D2 = zeros(n,n);
for i=1:n
  if D(i,i) ~= 0
    D2(i,i) = 1/D(i,i)^0.5;
  end
end
Lsym = D2 * L * D2;   % L=D^(-0.5)*L*D^(-0.5);
if k == n
  [Vector,eigenvalue] = eig(Lsym);
  E = diag(eigenvalue);
  [E,IXY] = sort(E,1,'ascend');
  Vector = Vector(:,IXY);
else
  [Vector,eigenvalue] = eigs(2*eye(n)-Lsym,k);
  E = 2 - diag(eigenvalue);
end
Vector = D2*Vector;
varargout{1} = Vector;
varargout{2} = E;
  % balanced normalized signed graph Laplacian
elseif strcmp(type,'BNS') || strcmp(type,'Bns') || strcmp(type,'bns')
  display('Balanced normalized signed graph Laplacian decomposition');
  L = Dpos - posW + negW;
  D = Dpos + Dneg;
  D2 = zeros(n,n);
  for i=1:n
    if D(i,i) ~= 0
      D2(i,i) = 1/D(i,i)^0.5;
    end
  end
  Lsym = D2 * L * D2;   %L=D^(-0.5)*L*D^(-0.5);
  if k == n
    [Vector,eigenvalue] = eig(Lsym);
    E = diag(eigenvalue);
    [E,IXY] = sort(E,1,'ascend');
        Vector = Vector(:,IXY);
  else
    [Vector,eigenvalue] = eigs(2*eye(n) - Lsym,k);
    E = 2 - diag(eigenvalue);
  end
  Vector = D2 * Vector;
  varargout{1} = Vector;
  varargout{2} = E;
else
  error('Type cannot be identified');
end
```

```
function [varargout] = TypedDirLaplacian(W, k, LazyRate)
% Spectral embedding of a graph with directed typed edges
%
% n is the number of nodes, and c is the number of different edge
% types.
```

```
% W: an n*n*c weighted adjacency matrix of the graph. It can be
%    undirected or directed, or a random walk matrix.
% LazyRate: a value between 0 and 1, the probability of moving
%    to another layer (default is 0.5)
% k: the number of vectors desired, corresponding to the k smallest
%    eigenvalues (default is all)
%
% Vout = the eigenvector matrix of out-roles
% Vin = the eigenvector matrix of in-roles
%    both n*k*c
% E = the diagonal matrix of Laplacian eigenvalues
% bigW = the large constructed matrix
%
% varargout = cell array
%                      1: Vout
%                      2: Vin
%                      3: E
%                      4: bigW

[n,m,c] = size(W);


%%%% Bind together the versions of each node in the different
%%%% layers to build a cn*cn adjacency matrix

bigW = sparse(c*n,c*n);
for i = 1:c
  rowsumd = sum(W(:,:,i),2);
  tempv = sparse(n,1);
  tempv(rowsumd == 0) = 1;
  W(:,:,i) = W(:,:,i) + diag(tempv);
  rowsumd(rowsumd == 0) = 1;
  tempD = diag(rowsumd);
  for j = 1:c
    if i == j
      bigW((i-1)*n+1:i*n, (j-1)*n+1:j*n) = (1-LazyRate)*W(:,:,i);
    else
      bigW((i-1)*n+1:i*n, (j-1)*n+1:j*n) = LazyRate/(c-1)*tempD;
    end
  end
end


%%%% compute our new directed Laplacian

[DirOut,DirIn,e] = DirLaplacian(bigW,k);
Vout = zeros(n,k,c);
Vin = zeros(n,k,c);
for i = 1:c
  Vout(:,:,i) = DirOut((i-1)*n+1:i*n,:);
  Vin(:,:,i) = DirIn((i-1)*n+1:i*n,:);
end

varargout{1}  =  Vout;
varargout{2}  =  Vin;
varargout{3}  =  e;
varargout{4}  =  bigW;
```

```
function [varargout] = TemporalDirLaplacian(W,k,alpha,beta)
%  Spectral embedding of a directed graph changing with time
%
% n is the number of nodes, and c is the number of different time
%   periods
%
% W: is an n*n*c weighted adjacency matrix of the graph. It can be
%    undirected or directed, or a random walk matrix.

% k: the number of eigenvectors corresponding to the k smallest
%    eigenvalues desired (default is all);
% alpha: a value between 0 and 1, down-weighting the contribution of
%    matrices from previous time periods
% beta: a value between 0 and 1, the total probability of a random
%    walk transitioning to one of the other layers in the large
%    constructed graph (default is 0.5)
%
% Vout = the eigenvector matrix of out-roles
% Vin = the eigenvector matrix of in-roles
% E = the diagonal matrix of Laplacian eigenvalue
% bigW =  the large constructed adjacency matrix
%    for rendering purposes

% varargout = cell array
%                1: Vout
%                2: Vin
%                3: E
%                4: bigW

[n,m,c] = size(W);

%%%% incorporate the backwards weighting using alpha
A(:,:,1) = W(:,:,1);

for i = 2:c
    A(:,:,i) = alpha * A(:,:,i-1) + W(:,:,i);
 end

%%%% compute the new typed Directed Laplacian
[Vout, Vin, e, bigW] = TypedDirLaplacian(A, k, beta);

varargout{1} = Vout;
varargout{2} = Vin;
varargout{3} = e;
varargout{4} = bigW;
```

```
function [varargout] = TypedLaplacian(W, k, epsilon, LazyRate)
%  Spectral embedding of a typed directed network
%
% n is the number of nodes, and c is the number of different edge
% types
% W: an n*n*c weighted adjacency matrix. It can be
%    undirected or directed, or a random walk matrix.
% epsilon: a value between 0 and 1, used to avoid the problem
% of reducibility of directed graphs -- the Google trick (default is 0)
```

```matlab
% k: is the number of vectors desired, corresponding to the k smallest
%     eigenvalues (default is all)
% LazyRate: a value between 0 and 1, the transition probability to
%     another layer (default is 0.5)
%
% Vector = the eigenvector matrix
% E = the diagonal matrix of Laplacian eigenvalues
% R =  the large constructed random walk matrix created
%
% varargout = cell array
%                     1: Vector=Eigenvectors
%                     2: E= Eigenvalues
%                     3: R= random walk matrix of the big connected graph

[n,m,c] = size(W);

%%%% convert each layer to a random walk matrix

RW = zeros(n,n,c);

for i = 1:c
  for j = 1:n
    rs = sum(W(j,:,i));
    if rs == 0;
      RW(j,j,i) = 1;
    else
      RW(j,:,i) = W(j,:,i)/rs;
    end
  end
end


%%%%% add epsilon

if epsilon > 0
%     RW = (1-epsilon) * RW+epsilon/n;
  for i = 1:c
    RW(:,:,i) = (1-epsilon) * RW(:,:,i)
       +epsilon/(n-1)*(ones(n,n)-eye(n));
  end
end

%%%% convert entire graph to a random walk matrix R

R = zeros(c*n,c*n);
for i = 1:c
  for j = 1:c
    if i == j
      R((i-1)*n+1:i*n,(j-1)*n+1:j*n) = (1-LazyRate) * RW(:,:,i);
    else
      R((i-1)*n+1:i*n,(j-1)*n+1:j*n) =  LazyRate/(c-1)*eye(n,n);
    end
  end
end

%%%% compute Fan Chung's Directed Laplacian
```

```
[Cvector, e]  =  DirLaplacianChung(R,0,k);

Vector = zeros(n,k,c);
for i = 1:c
  Vector(:,:,i) = Cvector((i-1)*n+1:i*n,:);
end

varargout{1} = Vector;
varargout{2} = e;
varargout{3} = R;
```

```
function [varargout] = TemporalLaplacian(W, k, alpha, beta, epsilon)
% Spectral embedding of a directed graph with changing weights
%    using Fan Chung's directed embedding technique
%
% n is the number of nodes, and c is the number of different time
%   periods
%
% W: an n*n*c weighted adjacency matrix of the graph. It can be
%    undirected or directed, or a random walk matrix.
% epsilon: is a value between 0 and 1, used to avoid the problem
% of reducibility of directed graph -- the Google trick (default is 0)
% k: the number of vectors desired, corresponding to the k smallest
%    eigenvalues (default is all)
% alpha: a value between 0 and 1, the down-weighting value for
%    combining matrices from previous time periods
% beta: a value between 0 and 1, the probability of transitioning out
%    of a layer (default is 0.5)
%
% Vector = the matrix of eigenvectors
% E = the diagonal matrix of Laplacian eigenvalues
% aggregateRW: = the large constructed random walk matrix R
%
% varargout = cell array
%                 1: Vector=Eigenvectors
%                 2: E= Eigenvalues
%                 3: aggregateRW=(cn*cn) matrix

[n,m,c] = size(W);

aggregateRW = sparse(c*n,c*n);

%%% apply the weighting from previous time periods
A = W(:,:,1);
for i = 2:c
  A = alpha * A + W(:,:,i);
end

temprw = sparse(n,n);
%% convert aggregate graph to a random walk matrix
for j = 1:n
  rs = sum(A(j,:));
  if rs == 0;
    temprw(j,j) = 1;
  else
```

```
      temprw(j,:) = A(j,:)/rs;
   end
end

if epsilon > 0
   temprw = (1-epsilon) * temprw + epsilon/(n-1) * (ones(n,n)-eye(n));
end

for j = 1:c    % minimize the disagreement between layers using beta
   if i == j
      aggregateRW((i-1)*n+1:i*n,(j-1)*n+1:j*n) = (1-beta) * temprw;
   else
      aggregateRW((i-1)*n+1:i*n,(j-1)*n+1:j*n) = beta/(c-1)* eye(n,n);
   end
end

%%%% compute Fan Chung's Directed Laplacian
[Cvector, e] = DirLaplacianChung(aggregateRW, 0, k);
Vector = zeros(n, k, c);
for i = 1:c
   Vector(:,:,i) = Cvector((i-1)*n+1:i*n,:);
end

varargout{1} = Vector;
varargout{2} = e;
varargout{3} = aggregateRW;
```

```
function [varargout] = SignedDirLaplacian(posW,negW,type,k)
%   Spectral embedding of a signed directed network
%
% W an n*n*c weighted adjacency matrix
%   with n nodes, and c different edge types
% k is the number of eigenvectors desired, corresponding to the k
% smallest eigenvalues (default is all);
%
% varargout = cell array of output
%                   1: PosOut=Eigenvectors of positive Out role
%                   2: Negout=Eigenvectors of negative Out role
%                   3: PosIn=Eigenvectors of positive in role
%                   4: NegIn=Eigenvectors of negative in role
%                   5: E=Eigenvalues
%                   6: Xpos= the positive adjacency matrix created
%                             by modelling the signed directed graph
%                   6: Xneg= the negative adjacency matrix created
%                             by modelling the signed directed graph

[n,m] = size(posW);

%%%% Bind together the four different versions of each node

Dinpos = sum(posW,1);
Doutpos = sum(posW,2);
Dinneg = sum(negW,1);
Doutneg = sum(negW,2);
crossweights = Dinpos + Doutpos' + Dinneg + Doutneg';
```

```
D = diag(crossweights);
Wp = [posW + D, D; D, D];

bigD = sparse(2*n);
bigD(1:n, n+1:2*n) = D;
bigD(n+1:2*n, 1:n) = D;
Xpos = [ bigD, Wp; Wp', bigD];
Xneg = sparse(4*n);
Xneg(n+1:2*n, 3*n+1:4*n) = negW;
Xneg(3*n+1:4*n, n+1:2*n) = negW';

%%%% compute our signed Laplacian
[Vector,e] = SignedLaplacian(Xpos,Xneg,type,k);
PosOut = Vector(1:n,:);
Negout = Vector(n+1:2*n,:);
PosIn = Vector(2*n+1:3*n,:);
NegIn = Vector(3*n+1:4*n,:);
if nargout == 1
  varargout{1} = Vector;
elseif nargout == 2
  varargout{1} = Vector;
  varargout{2} = e;
else
  varargout{1} = PosOut;
  varargout{2} = Negout;
  varargout{3} = PosIn;
  varargout{4} = NegIn;
  varargout{5} = e;
  varargout{6} = Xpos;
  varargout{7} = Xneg;
end
```

```
function F = BCGE(W,Y,ew)
%  Given a graph with some nodes labelled, build the enhanced
%     signed graph and embed it using out signed spectral embedding
%
%  W: the n*n weighted adjacency matrix of a undirected graph.
%  Y: an n*2 label indication matrix,  with value {0 1};
%     0 rows for unlabelled nodes.
%  ew: [apw,anw] vector for positive and negative added edge weights
%     between labeled points; default value is [1,1].

[n,m] = size(Y);

% build the negative matrix with only one undirected edge.
negW = sparse(n+2,n+2);
negW(n+1,n+2) = ew(2);
negW(n+2,n+1) = ew(2);

% build the positive matrix from the adjacency matrix with
% added positive edges.
posW = sparse(n+2,n+2);
posW(1:n,1:n) = W;
posW(1:n,n+1) = ew(1) * Y(:,1);
posW(n+1,1:n) = ew(1) * Y(:,1)';
```

```matlab
posW(1:n,n+2) = ew(1) * Y(:,2);
posW(n+2,1:n) = ew(1) * Y(:,2)';

% build the modified total degree matrices.
Dpos = diag(sum(posW,2));
Dneg = diag(sum(negW,2));
D = diag(sum(W,2));
D(n+1,n+1) = Dpos(n+1,n+1) + Dneg(n+1,n+1);
D(n+2,n+2) = Dpos(n+2,n+2) + Dneg(n+2,n+2);
D2 = sparse(n+2,n+2);

for i = 1:n+2
  if D(i,i) ~= 0
    D2(i,i) = 1/D(i,i)^0.5;
  end
end

% signed Laplacian embedding
L = (Dpos-posW) - (Dneg-negW);
Lsym = max(sum(abs(D2*L*D2),2)) * speye(n+2) - D2*L*D2;
%- max(sum(abs(D2*L*D2),2))*D3*D3';
Lsym = Lsym + Lsym';
[V,e] = eigs(Lsym,2);

if abs(e(1,1) - 2*max(sum(abs(D2*L*D2),2))) < 1e-10;
  U = V(:,2);
else
  U = V(:,1);
end

% make the output vector consistent with the labels.

if U(n+1,1) > 0
  F = U(1:n,1);
else
  F = -U(1:n,1);
end
```

```matlab
function F = GBE(posW,label,ew)
%   Implements our GBE semi-supervised learning algorithm
%
% posW: is the n*n weighted adjacency matrix of a undirected graph.
% label: is a n*c label indication matrix, with value {-1, 0 1} if
%    label is a vector, {1,0} if label is a matrix; and 0 row for
%    unlabelled nodes.
% ew: is a [apw,anw] vector for positive and negative added edge
%        weight between labeled points; default value is [1,1].

[n,m] = size(label);

if m <= 2 % two classes
  if m==1
    Y(:,1) = label;
    Y(:,2) = -label;
    Y(Y<0) = 0;
```

```matlab
    else
       Y = label;
    end
    F = sign(BCGE(posW,Y,ew));
else % more than two classes
    for i = 1:m
       Y = [label(:,i),sum(label,2)-label(:,i)];
       V(:,i) = BCGE(posW,Y,ew);
    end
    [C,F] = max(V,[],2);
end
```

Bibliography

[1] P. Anchuri and M. Magdon-Ismail. Communities and balance in signed networks: A spectral approach. In *Proceedings of the 2012 International Conference on Advances in Social Networks Analysis and Mining*, pages 235–242. IEEE Computer Society, 2012.

[2] N. Aston and W. Hu. Community detection in dynamic social networks. *Communications and Network*, page 124, 2014.

[3] S. Baluja, R. Seth, D Sivakumar, Y. Jing, J. Yagnik, S. Kumar, D. Ravichandran, and M. Aly. Video suggestion and discovery for YouTube: taking random walks through the view graph. In *Proceedings of the 17th international conference on World Wide Web*, pages 895–904. ACM, 2008.

[4] M. Belkin, I. Matveeva, and P. Niyogi. Regularization and semi-supervised learning on large graphs. *Learning Theory*, pages 624–638, 2004.

[5] M. Belkin, P. Niyogi, and V. Sindhwani. On manifold regularization. In *Proceedings of the Tenth International Workshop on Artificial Intelligence and Statistics*, pages 17–24, 2005.

[6] Y Bengio, O Delalleau, and NL Roux. Label propagation and quadratic criterion. In *Semi-Supervised Learning*. MIT Press, 2007.

[7] A. Blum and S. Chawla. Learning from labeled and unlabeled data using graph mincuts. In *Proceedings of the 18th International Conference on Machine Learning*, ICML '01, pages 19–26, 2001.

[8] A. Blum, J. Lafferty, M.R. Rwebangira, and R. Reddy. Semi-supervised learning using randomized mincuts. In *Proceedings on the 21st international conference on Machine learning*. ACM Press, 2004.

[9] A. Bouchachia and M. Prossegger. Incremental spectral clustering. *Learning in Non-Stationary Environments: Methods and Applications*, page 77, 2012.

[10] T. Bühler and M. Hein. Spectral clustering based on the graph p-Laplacian. In *Proceedings of the 26th Annual International Conference on Machine Learning*, pages 81–88. ACM, 2009.

[11] F. Calderoni. The structure of drug trafficking mafias: the 'Ndrangheta and cocaine. *Crime, Law and Social Change*, 58(3):321–349, 2012.

[12] F. Calderoni. Identifying mafia bosses from meeting attendance. In *Networks and Network Analysis for Defence and Security*, pages 27–48. Springer, 2014.

[13] Y. Chang, D. Pantazis, and R.M. Leahy. Statistically optimal modular partitioning of directed graphs. In *Signals, Systems and Computers (ASILOMAR)*, pages 1075–1079. IEEE, 2010.

[14] Y. Chang, D. Pantazis, and R.M. Leahy. Partitioning directed graphs based on modularity and information flow. In *IEEE International Symposium on Biomedical Imaging: From Nano to Macro*, pages 1105–1108. IEEE, 2011.

[15] T. Chen, Q. Yang, and X. Tang. Directed graph embedding. In *Proceedings of the International Joint Conference on Artificial Intelligence (IJCAI)*, pages 2707–2712, 2007.

[16] Y. Cheng and R. Zhao. Multiview spectral clustering via ensemble. In *IEEE International Conference on Granular Computing*, pages 101–106, Aug. 2009.

[17] K. Chiang, J.J. Whang, and I.S. Dhillon. Scalable clustering of signed networks using balance normalized cut. In *Proceedings of the 21st ACM international conference on Information and knowledge management*, pages 615–624. ACM, 2012.

[18] N.A. Christakis and J.H. Fowler. *Connected: The Surprising Power of Our Social Networks and How They Shape Our Lives – How Your Friends' Friends' Friends Affect Everything You Feel, Think, and Do*. Little Brown, 2009.

[19] N.A. Christakis and J.H. Fowler. Social contagion theory: examining dynamic social networks and human behavior. *Statistics in Medicine*, 32(4):556–577, 2013.

[20] F. Chung. Laplacians and the Cheeger inequality for directed graphs. *Annals of Combinatorics*, 9(1):1–19, 2005.

[21] A. Corduneanu and T. Jaakkola. On information regularization. In *Proceedings of the Nineteenth conference on Uncertainty in Artificial Intelligence*, pages 151–158. Morgan Kaufmann Publishers Inc., 2002.

[22] J.A. Davis. Clustering and structural balance in graphs. *Human Relations*, pages 181–187, 1967.

[23] I.S. Dhillon. Co-clustering documents and words using bipartite spectral graph partitioning. In *Proceedings of the seventh ACM SIGKDD international conference on Knowledge discovery and data mining*, pages 269–274. ACM, 2001.

[24] I.S. Dhillon, Y. Guan, and B. Kulis. Weighted graph cuts without eigenvectors: a multilevel approach. *IEEE Transactions on Pattern Analysis and Machine Intelligence*, 29(11):1944–1957, 2007.

[25] W.E. Donath and A.J. Hoffman. Algorithms for partitioning of graphs and computer logic based on eigenvectors of connection matrices. *IBM Technical Disclosure Bulletin*, 15(3):938–944, 1972.

[26] W.E. Donath and A.J. Hoffman. Lower bounds for the partitioning of graphs. *IBM Journal of Research and Development*, 17(5):420–425, 1973.

[27] X. Dong, P. Frossard, P. Vandergheynst, and N. Nefedov. Clustering with Multi-Layer Graphs: A Spectral Perspective. *IEEE Transactions on Signal Processing*, 60(11):5820–5831, 2012.

[28] X. Dong, P. Frossard, P. Vandergheynst, and N. Nefedov. Clustering on multi-layer graphs via subspace analysis on Grassmann manifolds. *IEEE Transactions on Signal Processing*, 62(4):905–918, 2014.

[29] P. Doreian, V. Batagelj, and A. Ferligoj. *Generalized blockmodeling*, volume 25. Cambridge University Press, 2005.

[30] R.I.M. Dunbar. Neocortex size as a constraint on group size in primates. *Journal of Human Evolution*, 22(6):469–493, 1992.

[31] R.I.M. Dunbar. Coevolution of neocortical size, group size and language in humans. *Behavioral and Brain Sciences*, 16(04):681–694, 1993.

[32] D.J. Felleman and D.C. Van Essen. Distributed hierarchical processing in the primate cerebral cortex. *Cerebral Cortex*, 1(1):1–47, 1991.

[33] P. Felzenszwalb and D. Huttenlocher. Efficient Graph-Based Image Segmentation. *International Journal of Computer Vision*, 59:167–181, 2004. 10.1023/B:VISI.0000022288.19776.77.

[34] M. Fiedler. Algebraic connectivity of graphs. *Czechoslovak Mathematical Journal*, 23(2):298–305, 1973.

[35] F. Fouss, A. Pirotte, and M. Saerens. A novel way of computing similarities between nodes of a graph, with application to collaborative recommendation. In *The 2005 IEEE/WIC/ACM International Conference on Web Intelligence*, pages 550–556. IEEE, 2005.

[36] M.G. Gong, L.J. Zhang, J.J. Ma, and L.C. Jiao. Community detection in dynamic social networks based on multiobjective immune algorithm. *Journal of Computer Science and Technology*, 27(3):455–467, 2012.

[37] P. Hage and F. Harary. *Structural Models in Anthropology*. Cambridge University Press, 1983.

[38] L. Hagen and A.B. Kahng. New spectral methods for ratio cut partitioning and clustering. *IEEE Transactions on Computer-Aided Design of Integrated Circuits and Systems*, 11(9):1074–1085, 1992.

[39] C. Hilgetag, M.A. O'Neill, and M.P. Young. Hierarchical organization of macaque and cat cortical sensory systems explored with a novel network processor. *Philosophical Transactions of the Royal Society B: Biological Sciences*, 355(1393):71–89, 2000.

[40] J. Huang, T. Zhu, and D. Schuurmans. Web communities identification from random walks. In *Knowledge Discovery in Databases: PKDD 2006*, pages 187–198. Springer, 2006.

[41] M.S.T. Jaakkola and M. Szummer. Partially labeled classification with Markov random walks. *Advances in Neural Information Processing Systems (NIPS)*, 14:945–952, 2002.

[42] T. Joachims. Transductive learning via spectral graph partitioning. In *Proceedings of the 20th International Conference on Machine Learning*, volume 3, pages 290–297, 2003.

[43] R. Kannan, S. Vempala, and A. Vetta. On clusterings: Good, bad and spectral. *Journal of the ACM (JACM)*, 51(3):497–515, 2004.

[44] M. Kas, K.M. Carley, and L. R. Carley. Incremental closeness centrality for dynamically changing social networks. In *Advances in Social Networks Analysis and Mining, 2013 IEEE/ACM International Conference on*, pages 1250–1258. IEEE, 2013.

[45] D.J. Klein and M. Randić. Resistance distance. *Journal of Mathematical Chemistry*, 12(1):81–95, 1993.

[46] A. Kumar and H. Daum. Co-training approach for multi-view spectral clustering. *Computer*, 94(5):393–400, 2011.

[47] A. Kumar, P. Rai, and H. Daume. Co-regularized multi-view spectral clustering. In *Advances in Neural Information Processing Systems*, pages 1413–1421, 2011.

[48] J. Kunegis, S. Schmidt, A. Lommatzsch, J. Lerner, E.W. De Luca, and S. Albayrak. Spectral analysis of signed graphs for clustering, prediction and visualization. In *SIAM International Conference on Data Mining*, volume 10, pages 559–559. SIAM, 2010.

[49] E.A. Leicht and M.E. Newman. Community structure in directed networks. *Physical Review Letters*, 100(11):118703, 2008.

[50] J. Leskovec and C. Faloutsos. Sampling from large graphs. In *Proceedings of the 12th ACM SIGKDD International Conference on Knowledge Discovery and Data Mining*, pages 631–636. ACM, 2006.

[51] J. Leskovec, D. Huttenlocher, and J. Kleinberg. Signed networks in social media. In *Proceedings of the SIGCHI Conference on Human Factors in Computing Systems*, pages 1361–1370. ACM, 2010.

[52] L. Li and J. Zhang. Information clustering method in social network. In *Strategic Technology (IFOST), 2011 6th International Forum on*, volume 2, pages 1104–1108, Aug. 2011.

[53] M. Lichman. UCI machine learning repository. http://archive.ics.uci.edu/ml, 2013.

[54] X. Liu, X. Yong, and H. Lin. An improved spectral clustering algorithm based on local neighbors in kernel space. *Computer Science and Information Systems*, 8(4):1143–1157, 2011.

[55] D. Luo, H. Huang, C. Ding, and F. Nie. On the eigenvectors of p-Laplacian. *Machine Learning*, 81(1):37–51, 2010.

[56] F.D. Malliaros and M. Vazirgiannis. Clustering and community detection in directed networks: A survey. *Physics Reports*, 533(4):95–142, 2013.

[57] M. Meila and W. Pentney. Clustering by weighted cuts in directed graphs. In *Proceedings of the 7th SIAM International Conference on Data Mining*, pages 135–144, 2007.

[58] M. Meila and J. Shi. A random walks view of spectral segmentation. In *AI and STATISTICS (AISTATS) 2001*, 2001.

[59] S. Melacci and M. Belkin. Laplacian support vector machines trained in the primal. *Journal of Machine Learning Research*, 12:1149–1184, March 2011.

[60] S. Milgram. The small world problem. *Psychology Today*, 2(1):60–67, 1967.

[61] B. Mohar. The Laplacian spectrum of graphs. *Graph Theory, Combinatorics, and Applications*, 2:871–898, 1991.

[62] B. Mohar. Some applications of Laplace eigenvalues of graphs. *Graph Symmetry: Algebraic Methods and Applications*, 497(22):227, 1997.

[63] C. Morselli, C. Giguère, and K. Petit. The efficiency/security trade-off in criminal networks. *Social Networks*, 29(1):143–153, 2007.

[64] C. Morselli and K. Petit. Law-enforcement disruption of a drug importation network. *Global Crime*, 8(2):109–130, 2007.

[65] L. Muchnik, S. Aral, and S.J. Taylor. Social influence bias: A randomized experiment. *Science*, 341(6146):647–651, 2013.

[66] P. Muthukrishnan, D.R. Radev, and Q. Mei. Edge weight regularization over multiple graphs for similarity learning. In *IEEE 10th International Conference Data Mining*, pages 374–383. IEEE, 2010.

[67] L. Négyessy, T. Nepusz, L. Kocsis, and F. Bazsó. Prediction of the main cortical areas and connections involved in the tactile function of the visual cortex by network analysis. *European Journal of Neuroscience*, 23(7):1919–1930, 2006.

[68] T. Nepusz, A. Petróczi, L. Négyessy, and F. Bazsó. Fuzzy communities and the concept of bridgeness in complex networks. *Physical Review E*, 77(1):016107, 2008.

[69] M.E.J. Newman. Detecting community structure in networks. *The European Physical Journal B-Condensed Matter and Complex Systems*, 38(2):321–330, 2004.

[70] M.E.J. Newman and M. Girvan. Finding and evaluating community structure in networks. *Physical Review E*, 69:026113, Feb. 2004.

[71] A.Y. Ng, M.I. Jordan, and Y. Weiss. On spectral clustering: Analysis and an algorithm. *Advances in Neural Information Processing Systems*, 2:849–856, 2002.

[72] N.P. Nguyen, T.N. Dinh, Y. Xuan, and M.T. Thai. Adaptive algorithms for detecting community structure in dynamic social networks. In *IEEE International Conference on Computer Communications*, pages 2282–2290. IEEE, 2011.

[73] M. Orbach and K. Crammer. Graph-based transduction with confidence. In *Machine Learning and Knowledge Discovery in Databases*, pages 323–338. Springer, 2012.

[74] J.F. Padgett and C.K. Ansell. Robust action and the rise of the Medici, 1400-1434. *American Journal of Sociology*, pages 1259–1319, 1993.

[75] L. Paoli. An Underestimated Criminal Phenomenon: The Calabrian 'Ndrangheta, An. *Eur. J. Crime Crim. L. & Crim Just.*, 2:212, 1994.

[76] L. Paoli. *Mafia Brotherhoods: Organized Crime, Italian Style*. Oxford University Press, 2003.

[77] J. Qiu and Z. Lin. A framework for exploring organizational structure in dynamic social networks. *Decision Support Systems*, 51(4):760–771, 2011.

[78] K.E. Read. Cultures of the central highlands, new guinea. *Southwestern Journal of Anthropology*, pages 1–43, 1954.

[79] V. Satuluri and S. Parthasarathy. Symmetrizations for clustering directed graphs. In *Proceedings of the 14th International Conference on Extending Database Technology*, pages 343–354. ACM, 2011.

[80] A.J. Seary. *MultiNet: An interactive program for analysing and visualizing complex networks*. PhD thesis, Faculty of Applied Science, Simon Fraser University, 2005.

[81] A.J. Seary and W.D. Richards. Spectral methods for analyzing and visualizing networks: an introduction. In R. Breiger, K. Carley, and P. Pattison, editors, *National Research Council, Dynamic Social Network Modeling and Analysis: Workshop Summary and Papers*, pages 209–228. The National Academic Press, 2003.

[82] J. Shang, L. Liu, X. Li, F. Xie, and C. Wu. Targeted revision: A learning-based approach for incremental community detection in dynamic networks. *Physica A: Statistical Mechanics and its Applications*, 2015.

[83] J. Shang, L. Liu, F. Xie, Z. Chen, J. Miao, X. Fang, and C. Wu. A real-time detecting algorithm for tracking community structure of dynamic networks. In *The 6th Workshop on Social Network Mining and Analysis co-held with KDD (SNA-KDD12)*, 2012.

[84] J. Shi and J. Malik. Normalized cuts and image segmentation. *IEEE Transactions on Pattern Analysis and Machine Intelligence*, 22(8):888–905, 2000.

[85] D.B. Skillicorn. *Understanding Complex Datasets: Data Mining with Matrix Decompositions*. CRC Press, 2007.

[86] D.B. Skillicorn, F. Calderoni, and Q. Zheng. Inductive discovery of criminal group structure using spectral embedding. *Information and Security: An International Journal*, 31:49–66, 2015.

[87] D.B. Skillicorn and Q. Zheng. Global similarity in social networks with typed edges. In *2012 IEEE/ACM International Conference on Advances in Social Networks Analysis and Mining (ASONAM)*, pages 79–85, August 2012.

[88] D.B. Skillicorn and Q. Zheng. Global structure in social networks with directed typed edges. In *Social Networks: Analysis and Case Studies*, pages 61–81. Springer, 2014.

[89] D.B. Skillicorn, Q. Zheng, and C. Morselli. Spectral embedding for dynamic social networks. In *Proceedings of the 2013 IEEE/ACM International Conference on Advances in Social Networks Analysis and Mining*, pages 316–323. ACM, 2013.

[90] D.B. Skillicorn, Q. Zheng, and C. Morselli. Modeling dynamic social networks using spectral embedding. *Social Network Analysis and Mining*, 4(1):1–14, 2014.

[91] D.A. Spielman and S.H. Teng. Spectral partitioning works: Planar graphs and finite element meshes. In *Foundations of Computer Science, 1996. Proceedings., 37th Annual Symposium on*, pages 96–105. IEEE, 1996.

[92] A. Subramanya and J. Bilmes. Semi-supervised learning with measure propagation. *The Journal of Machine Learning Research*, 12:3311–3370, 2011.

[93] A. Subramanya and P.P. Talukdar. Graph-based semi-supervised learning. *Synthesis Lectures on Artificial Intelligence and Machine Learning*, 8(4):1–125, 2014.

[94] P.P. Talukdar and K. Crammer. New regularized algorithms for transductive learning. In *Machine Learning and Knowledge Discovery in Databases*, pages 442–457. Springer, 2009.

[95] R. Tamassia. *Handbook of Graph Drawing and Visualization*. CRC Press, 2013.

[96] W. Tang, Z. Lu, and I.S. Dhillon. Clustering with multiple graphs. In *Proceedings of the 9th IEEE International Conference on Data Mining*, pages 1016–1021. IEEE, 2009.

[97] H. Tao, C. Hou, and D. Yi. Multiple-view spectral embedded clustering using a co-training approach. In *Computer Engineering and Networking*, pages 979–987. Springer, 2014.

[98] V.A. Traag and J. Bruggeman. Community detection in networks with positive and negative links. *Physical Review E*, 80(3):036115, 2009.

[99] J. Travers and S. Milgram. An experimental study of the small world problem. *Sociometry*, pages 425–443, 1969.

[100] G. Trenkler. Handbook of Matrices. *Computational Statistics & Data Analysis*, 25(2):243–243, July 1997.

[101] U. Von Luxburg. A tutorial on spectral clustering. *Statistics and Computing*, 17(4):395–416, December 2007.

[102] U. Von Luxburg, M. Belkin, and O. Bousquet. Consistency of spectral clustering. *The Annals of Statistics*, pages 555–586, 2008.

[103] U. Von Luxburg, O. Bousquet, and M. Belkin. On the convergence of spectral clustering on random samples: the normalized case. *Learning Theory*, pages 457–471, 2004.

[104] U. Von Luxburg, O. Bousquet, and M. Belkin. Limits of spectral clustering. *Advances in Neural Information Processing Systems (NIPS)*, 17:857–864, 2005.

[105] D. Wagner and F. Wagner. Between min cut and graph bisection. In *Proceedings of the 18th International Symposium on Mathematical Foundations of Computer Science*, pages 744–750, London, UK, 1993. Springer-Verlag.

[106] O. Walther and C. Leuprecht. Mapping and deterring violent extremist networks in North-West Africa. Working Papers 7, University of Southern Denmark, Department of Border Region Studies, 2015.

[107] T. Xia, D. Tao, T. Mei, and Y. Zhang. Multiview spectral embedding. *IEEE Transactions on Systems, Man, and Cybernetics, Part B*, 40(6):1438–1446, 2010.

[108] B. Yang, W.K. Cheung, and J. Liu. Community mining from signed social networks. *IEEE Transactions on Knowledge and Data Engineering*, 19(10):1333–1348, 2007.

[109] T. Yang, Y. Chi, S. Zhu, Y. Gong, and R. Jin. Detecting communities and their evolutions in dynamic social networks: A Bayesian approach. *Machine Learning*, 82(2):157–189, 2011.

[110] S.X. Yu and J. Shi. Grouping with directed relationships. In *Energy Minimization Methods in Computer Vision and Pattern Recognition*, pages 283–297. Springer, 2001.

[111] Q. Zheng and D.B. Skillicorn. Spectral embedding of directed networks. In *Proceedings of the 2015 IEEE/ACM International Conference on Advances in Social Networks Analysis and Mining (ASONAM)*, pages 432–439, 2015.

[112] Q. Zheng and D.B. Skillicorn. Spectral embedding of signed networks. In *SIAM International Conference on Data Mining*, pages 55–63, 2015.

[113] Q. Zheng and D.B. Skillicorn. Graph based eigenvector semi-supervised learning. In *Foundations of Big Data Analytics, IEEE/ACM ASONAM 2016*, pages 960–967, August 2016.

[114] Q. Zheng and D.B. Skillicorn. Spectral embedding of directed networks. *Social Network Analysis and Mining*, 6:15pp., December 2016.

[115] Q. Zheng, D.B. Skillicorn, and F. Calderoni. Analysis of criminal social networks with typed and directed edges. In *IEEE International Conference on Intelligence and Security Informatics*, 2015.

[116] Q. Zheng, D.B. Skillicorn, and O. Walther. Signed directed social network analysis applied to group conflict. In *IEEE ICDM Workshop on Intelligence and Security Informatics (ISI-ICDM 2015)*, 2015.

[117] Q. Zheng, D.B. Skillicorn, and O. Walther. Signed directed social network analysis applied to group conflict. In *IEEE International Conference on Data Mining, Intelligence and Security Informatics Workshop*, November 2015.

[118] D. Zhou, O. Bousquet, T.N. Lal, J. Weston, and B. Schölkopf. Learning with local and global consistency. *Advances in Neural Information Processing Systems*, 16:321–328, 2004.

[119] D. Zhou and C.J.C. Burges. Spectral clustering and transductive learning with multiple views. In *Proceedings of the 24th International Conference on Machine Learning*, ICML '07, pages 1159–1166, New York, NY, USA, 2007. ACM.

[120] D. Zhou, J. Huang, and B. Schölkopf. Learning from labeled and unlabeled data on a directed graph. In *Proceedings of the 22nd International Conference on Machine Learning*, pages 1036–1043. ACM, 2005.

[121] D. Zhou, B. Schölkopf, and T. Hofmann. Semi-supervised learning on directed graphs. In *The annual Neural Information Processing Systems*, pages 1633–1640. MIT Press, 2005.

[122] W. Zhou, D. Sornette, R.A. Hill, and R.I.M. Dunbar. Discrete hierarchical organization of social group sizes. *Proceedings of the Royal Society of London B: Biological Sciences*, 272(1561):439–444, 2005.

[123] X. Zhu, Z. Ghahramani, and J. Lafferty. Semi-supervised learning using Gaussian fields and harmonic functions. In *Proceedings of the 20th International Conference on Machine Learning*, pages 912–919, 2003.

Index

'Ndrangheta groups, 74

Adjacency matrix, 7, 18
Assortativity, 4
Asymmetric flow, 45
Average edge ratio, 106
Average node ratio, 107

Bipartite graph, 18

Caviar network, 85
Chung's directed embedding, 41
Clique, 18
Combinatorial Laplacian, 10
Communities in social networks, 5
Commute distance, 26
Composing models, 69
Connected graph, 18

Degree, 18
Diameter, 157
Directed adjacency matrix, 7
Directed edge prediction, 45
Directed edges, 41
Directed graph, 17
Dunbar's Number, 3

Edge prediction, 8, 36
    directed, 45
Edge weight prediction, 8
Ego network, 18
Eigendecomposition, 18
    adjacency matrix, 19
    Laplacian, 19
Emergent properties, 1, 157
Enemy of my enemy, 105
Example

'Ndrangheta groups, 74
ACLED dataset, 111, 143
Algeria, 144
Caviar, 85
Epinions, 113
Florentine families, 34, 50, 72
Gahuku–Gama, 107
ISOLET spoken digits, 128
Libya, 146
Macaque brains, 55
Nigeria, 146
North and West Africa, 147
Sampson monastery, 109, 142
Slashdot, 115
UK schools, 50
USPS handwritten digits, 128
Panama Papers, 57

Fiedler vector, 20
Florentine families, 34, 50, 72
Flow in networks, 5

Geodesic distance, 18
Geometric space, 12
Google trick, 43
Graph
    introduction, 7
Graph cut
    min-cut, 25
    normalized cut, 25
    ratio cut, 25
Graph cut clustering, 25
Graph drawing, 7, 9

Homophily, 121

Imbalanced classes, 121

Imbalanced data, 127
In-degree, 18
Influence, 5, 14

Laplacian
    combinatorial, 10
    random walk, 23
    symmetric, 23
    introduction, 7
layer model, 11
Lazy random walk, 15
Link prediction, 8

Median edge ratio, 107
Medicis, 34, 36
Milgram's experiment, 2
Multigraph, 17

Nexus, 71
Normalized edge length, 49, 72

Operation Chalonero, 74, 76
Operation Stupor Mundi, 74, 77
Organizational networks, 2
Out-degree, 18

PageRank, 42
Panama Papers, 57
Path, 18
Power laws, 4

Random walk clustering, 25
Rayleigh quotient, 21, 22

Semi-supervised prediction, 121
Signed graph, 17
Simple graph, 17
Six degrees of separation, 2
Spectral clustering, 24
Spectral embedding, 10
        introduction, 7
Spectral graph embedding, 18
Spreading activation, 122
Strozzis, 36
Symmetric matrix, 7

Temporal social networks, 81

Typed edge prediction, 33

Undirected graph, 17
Unweighted graph, 17

Vertical edges, 32

Weighted adjacency matrix, 7
Weighted graph, 17